Straight
Shooting

Straight Shooting

WHAT'S WRONG WITH AMERICA AND HOW TO FIX IT

John Silber

HARPER & ROW, PUBLISHERS, New York
Grand Rapids, Philadelphia, St. Louis, San Francisco
London, Singapore, Sydney, Tokyo, Toronto

1817

Grateful acknowledgment is made for permission to reprint from John Silber's "Poisoning the Wells of Academe." Copyright © 1974 by *Encounter* Ltd.

FIRST EDITION

Designed by Sidney Feinberg

Library of Congress Cataloging-in-Publication Data

Silber, John R.
  Straight shooting: what's wrong with America and how to fix it / by John Silber.
    p.   cm.
  ISBN 0-06-016184-1
  1. Education—United States. 2. Education—Aims and objectives.
3. Moral education—United States.   I. Title.
LA217.S53   1989
370'.973—dc20   89-45065

---

88 89 90 91 92 93 AT/RRD 10 9 8 7 6 5 4 3 2 1

To Kathryn, who has shared her life with me

For our children

Contents

Acknowledgments

One of the themes of this book is the importance of recognizing that no one can live a fulfilled life, or even survive, without the help of others. This book, like all or nearly all books, is in its small way symbolic of that truth. My thought has been shaped by that splendid procession of great thinkers and writers who created our civilization. Many of them are acknowledged and discussed explicitly in the text; the influence of others will be immediately apparent to the reader. My thought has also been shaped by my parents, Paul and Jewell Silber, to whom my debt is unmeasurable and unrepayable. And I am also pleased to acknowledge the influence upon me, throughout my life, of a host of teachers, friends, and colleagues who have paid me the compliment of instructing me and, sometimes, the even higher compliment of arguing with me. First among these teachers is George Schrader, who introduced me to Socrates. Latest among these is Arthur G. B. Metcalf, who has continued my general education.

In particular, this book would not have been written without the excellent advice, assistance, and criticism of my colleagues Samuel McCracken and Brian Jorgensen. Jon Westling, by assuming duties that would otherwise be mine, has enabled me to find time to complete this book. He has also contributed to it through his vast learning and his astringent but encouraging criticisms. I have also been fortunate in having my prose and my ideas mauled and greatly improved by my friend of many years, William Arrowsmith. Other old friends and colleagues have been generous with their help. I want especially to name and to thank Keith Botsford, Roger Shattuck, and Gerald Gross, and a newer colleague and friend, Joachim Maître. My editor at Harper & Row, Arthur Samuelson, has been a model of editorial discernment; he contributed not only his keen and ruthless eye but also his infectious enthusiasm to this project.

Margaret Rubin of my staff has shepherded the text of this book through its endless revisions with her characteristic good spirits and wry wit. Deborah Baur, for her skillful direction of my office and staff, and my secretaries—Lisa Jones, Karen Klonowski, Christine Carr, and Cyrynda Goody—have my profound thanks.

It is of course conventional for the author to acknowledge his wife's contribution to a book, but here my gratitude extends far beyond conventional limits. Kathryn Silber, always my best critic, helped me to think and rethink this book, and her improvements to it can be found on every page. I am glad to have this opportunity to say how grateful I am for this, as for so much else that she has given me.

I have omitted the conventional exculpatory acknowledgment that all the deficiencies of this book are mine. Of this fact those whom I have mentioned above have already made me acutely aware.

Introduction

Our society is in trouble and we all know it. We know that something is terribly wrong—the way we might know in our own bodies that we are seriously ill. When we have an internal intimation of serious illness it is hard even to talk about the way we feel. We sense that talking about it might make it worse. But we compare the way we feel now with the way we used to feel: "I didn't have this queasiness; it didn't hurt when I bent that way; my coffee doesn't taste right anymore; sometimes life doesn't seem worth the fight, but I don't feel like quitting either."

Most of us know these symptoms. And now it isn't ourselves we worry about so much as our country. We feel for our country. We sense that something is wrong and we don't know what to do about it.

What symptoms tell us our society is ill? The failure of our system of public education is one. Once our common schools, even in unpromising backwoods environments, were capable of producing not only an Abraham Lincoln but a well-educated, literate population fully capable of following the Lincoln-Douglas debates. Now the schools turn out millions of functionally illiterate graduates effectively deprived of *any* cultural heritage. The destructive grip of drugs is another. The hold of drugs on our society is the clearest indication of its sickness. Still another symptom is the breakdown of the family—this is most apparent in the devastated part of our people called the underclass, but also a serious problem among the affluent. Indeed, the very existence of the underclass is another symptom. No society that allows any part of itself to fall into desolating poverty and apathy can call itself healthy.

Our declining ability to compete in world markets is another indication of societal illness. Corporations must be alert to the depredations of corporate raiders heavily armed with junk bonds, who seek out and capture corporations for the very assets that are essential to new product development. These pirates lack even the redeeming productivity of the robber barons, who developed our industrial strength. Computer-driven program trading has converted the stock market, once a forum for raising capital, into an automated casino. Invention and enterprise are further dampened by the cancerous growth of regulation and litigation.

These are alarming symptoms. They reflect widespread, systemic dislocations and failures. I have written this book to explore what is wrong and what we might do about it.

Any reader might fairly ask why I think I am qualified to diagnose and prescribe for our national crises. I am, after all, a university president, an inhabitant of the ivory tower where reality is kept at a distance. Worse still, I am a philosopher, one whose trade is describing the impossible or proving the obvious.

Now, as a matter of fact, university presidents, at least in our time, live about as far from the ivory tower as one can imagine. They confront reality day by day, hour by hour. They raise funds to balance budgets that may exceed half a billion dollars, negotiate with unions, cope with the individualisms of the professoriate and the irrepressible ingenuity of students. Quite apart from their educational responsibilities, the presidents of large universities are the chief executive officers of hotels and restaurants; they arrange the financing and supervise the construction of multimillion-dollar projects; they deal with thousands of federal and state regulations; they operate police departments large enough to meet the needs of small cities. In fact, they attend to the complexities of institutions that are in effect small cities. Moreover, they must cope with national issues—racial, economic, and gender equality, drugs, the draft, economic and foreign policy. University presidents, for example, must promote our national objectives of racial and gender equality without adopting mindless quotas or "reverse discrimination," which morally speaking is no better than just plain discrimination.

In short, their contact with reality is inescapably as immediate as that of any businessman or public official.

Philosophy is sometimes used as a means of escaping reality, but it can also be a means of understanding and shaping reality. That is what, as a philosopher, I have done for most of my life: I have tried to see as clearly as I can what is going on, to think about what to do about it, and, when I have knowledge sufficient to act, to act.

I remember, at the age of eight or so, being exposed to the controversy between creationism and evolution. I thought, "I don't understand the problem. If God is all powerful, why can't He create the universe the way He wants to? Why can't He make it the way the evolutionists say it was made, or in any other way? It would still be God's creation." From that earliest recollection of philosophizing I have felt compelled to make sense of things I have seen and heard and to bring them into coherent order.

In my freshman year of college I took my first course in philosophy; it was taught by a supremely gifted teacher whose respect for his students was such that he assigned only original philosophical texts. And so at 18 I encountered Socrates. And from him I learned lessons that are as valid today as they were in fifth-century Athens: The individual, protected and nurtured by society, has an obligation to it; one must act in the world, and one learns how to act by following sustained thought; and by such thought one can achieve not absolute truth, but the likeliest account of how things are.

I majored in philosophy and continued its study through the Ph.D. Although many of the topics discussed in graduate school were of merely technical interest, my interests were not diverted. Throughout my life I have sought answers to questions that arise in daily life. Although it is fun to join in the philosopher Zeno's speculations on the paradox of how Achilles can overtake the tortoise, I have concerned myself with the paradoxes of want in a land of plenty, of individualism in mass society, of causing war through disarmament and deterring it through military power.

I continue to believe that Socrates was right to philosophize in the marketplace about issues of importance to ordinary people, in fact to everyone.

This last observation seems to me of great political importance. For education—that is, the dissemination of the likeliest or most plausible account of any issue before the public—is surely the best means by which to effect change in a democratic society. If change is to be effected without revolution or an appeal to force, it must come through persuasion. And persuasion, to the extent that it is rational, must be clear and true to the facts.

Rational persuasion is particularly important in a university community. By its very nature the university is dedicated to the solution of conflicts by discussion rather than force. Its student members are at that age when one is least inclined to accept ideas merely because they are stated authoritatively, most inclined to demand careful justification from others. This situation has been described as the generation gap. It is not unbridgeable; moreover, it is not peculiar to our time. The generation gap was noticed early. It was high on the agenda at Mt. Sinai: The practice of honoring fathers and mothers was so deficient as to call forth the Fourth Commandment. Bridging the gap between the generations is an ancient and enduring concern. In generations past, parents were more diligent in passing on their principles and values to their children and were assisted by churches and schools that emphasized religious and moral education. In recent years, in contrast, our society has become increasingly secular, and the curriculum of the public schools has been stripped of almost all ethical content. As a result, universities must confront a student body ignorant of the evidence and arguments that underlie and support many traditional moral principles and practices.

The rediscovery of the foundations of morals awaits many of the younger generation and is a major responsibility of today's educators. The young are neither wicked nor deficient in raising their questions. Their questions have to be asked. The older generation is not wicked in failing to provide the answers it has forgotten or never knew. Although some of our traditional practices may be foolish, harmful, and ultimately grounded on superstition, many more of our traditional beliefs and practices are founded on wisdom, hard-won through thousands of years of human struggle for survival and more abundant living. On many moral and social issues we can observe laws of natural sequence as predictable and as certain as any to be found in the natural sciences.

Many moral laws, no less than laws of physics, are enforced by nature. With regard to lives of specific individuals and with regard to specific nations at specific times, their ends can be foretold at least in the manner of the Hebrew prophets. Occasionally lions do roar and even the deaf can hear. One could foretell that the virulence of the Third Reich would lead to war, as one can foretell the poverty, misery, and despair awaiting a pregnant, unmarried, drug-dependent teenager and the wretched life awaiting her unborn child. In limited situations in which issues are sufficiently specific we can know that many of our moral injunctions were discovered and preserved for the single purpose of reducing human misery and increasing the opportunities for our own well-being.

My greatest regret in being a university president is that I no longer have time to teach a regular class. My need to teach has, however, found another forum in the large number of speeches that a university president is called upon to give. For the past two decades I have been carrying on a continuing dialogue with hundreds of audiences throughout the country. In these lectures I have developed many of the ideas and some of the language that make up this book.

I have attempted here to remind the reader of the often-forgotten foundations that sustain some of our traditional values and practices. Part I, "First Principles," deals with fundamental concepts that give meaning and security to individuals and society. The emptiness of much of modern life results from the loss of these fundamental concepts. In Part II, "Lessons In School," I apply these principles to issues of education in the broadest sense, including, for example, commercial television, its commercials as well as its programs. From earliest childhood, through the primary and secondary schools to our colleges and universities, I show how at all levels our educational institutions have lost their way, frequently failing to do even adequately what they once did superbly. I point out that this decline is not irreversible and offer concrete suggestions for regaining the path. Part III, "Lessons Out of School," also relies on those fundamental principles. In it I consider many of the issues that confront us in domestic and foreign policy, and I show how the loss of philosophical clarity has weakened us internally and in our relations with the rest of the world.

I hope the reader will be stimulated by this book to do something about the problems I have addressed. I also hope the reader will come to share my conviction that much truth and relevance remain in our traditional values provided we take the trouble to discover their true meaning and their underlying rationality.

Throughout I have argued for realism and honesty in facing facts as they are—on independence from doctrinaire, preordained, ideological blinders. I have urged renewed reliance on those aspects of our heritage that after examination we know are sound. And I have advocated thoughtful experimentation in coping with those problems for which precedent solutions are lacking.

The problems we face in our personal lives and in the life of our nation are not to be feared. Fear of problems is not only useless but counterproductive. What we should fear is our failure to think about them and, following thought, to do what we can to solve them. The situation facing our nation is critical. But it is not hopeless.

I

FIRST PRINCIPLES

The Gods of the Copybook Headings

On March 4, 1825, John Quincy Adams came to the presidency of the United States. In his inaugural address he said:

> Since the adoption of [our] social compact, [a generation] has passed away. It is the work of our forefathers. We now receive it as a precious inheritance from those to whom we are indebted for its establishment, doubly bound by examples they have left us and by the blessings which we have enjoyed as the fruits of their labor to transmit the same, unimpaired, to the succeeding generation.

John Quincy Adams was the first president of the United States to speak of the Revolutionaries as belonging to a previous generation. Before him, each president had himself been one of the founders of the nation.

His position had a peculiar poignancy, but it is one in which all responsible individuals find themselves in every generation, and which affects most deeply young people who are completing their education. They look in two directions, behind and ahead.

They look behind to their parents and mentors, to all those teachers who have passed on to them through many generations the legacy that almost two hundred years ago was passed from John and Abigail Adams to John Quincy Adams and by him to his successors and eventually to us.

Young people also look forward. They stand between a generation moving from the scene and a generation yet unborn. It will soon be their responsibility to create another generation and to pass on to it the tradition that was passed on to them. They will be the parents—both physically and spiritually—of the next generation, responsible for passing on an inheritance as good, if possible, as the one they have received.

As I reflect on this process—the handing on of the American inheritance from the founding fathers down to our own sons and daughters, and on to their children—I ask whether the inheritance handed down has been growing or shrinking. In the provision of elementary and secondary education I am not at all sure that my generation has done as well as the generation that preceded it. I received a far better education in the public schools of San Antonio, Texas, than those schools provide their students today. I am convinced that the schools in Boston, where I have lived since 1970, are not equal to the schools in Boston fifty years ago, and certainly not equal to those of a hundred years ago.

It is high time for us to acquaint ourselves with earlier educational standards and expectations, so that we do not diminish the richness of our inheritance, but pass that treasure on to the next generation faithfully and undiminished.

The first objective of early education should be training in the reality principle. It has been argued that the child who grows up with television, finding that the reality of the screen can be altered by changing channels, believes it is just as easy to alter the world itself, a point made brilliantly by Peter Sellers in Hal Ashby's film *Being There*. (Jerzy Kozinski's novel on which the film was based reveals the pathological epistemology of the television medium.) In a world in which the very young are given such misleading intimations of omnipotence, concern for reality is more important than ever.

A hundred years ago, the child's confrontation with reality began with the realization of death, which might come through the death of a sibling, a friend, or a parent, aunt, uncle, or grandparent, any of which was far more likely then than now to be experienced by the young. Today, in contrast, the death of a child is so rare a misfortune as to be thought nearly unbearable, and increases in the life span have significantly postponed the time at which most children experience the death of an elder.

Learning about the fact of death is the most shocking contact with reality. Yet sound education absolutely depends on it because it is the condition on which our full humanity depends. Education should expose us to what is true, to a confrontation with what is real. A true education, therefore, must provide an acquaintance with death and with the conditions by which people can achieve happiness in the awareness of death. It must explain, for example, the essential role of virtue in the attainment of happiness: It must explain that virtue establishes one's worthiness to be happy. These are aspects of reality that must be introduced into the education of a child if the child is to develop fully.

Long before children went to school in nineteenth-century America, or even early twentieth-century America, they learned these things. For several hundred years this confrontation with reality was provided by the *Mother Goose* rhymes. In *Mother Goose* were found moral lessons thought to be far too important to be kept from children until they entered school at age six. The child of three or four learned to repeat: "If wishes were horses then beggars would ride." The child was warned to remember the reality principle and not to be misled by the attractions of wishful thinking.

I recently reviewed some early books used to teach reading and writing—preprimers and primers used in the first grade and even earlier by parents who taught their own children at home. Their authors, capitalizing on the delight that children take in verse, provided rhymed aphorisms for every letter in the alphabet. Here are a few of those aphorisms from the *New England Primer:*

A. Adam and Eve their God did grieve.
B. Life to mend this book attend.
   (This was accompanied by a picture of the Bible.)
C. The cat doth play and later slay.
   (Cats, you see, were not just pets. They tormented, killed, and ate mice, and children were not protected from that grisly fact.)
D. A dog will bite a thief at night.
   (This was an admonition to dogs and thieves alike.)
F. The idle fool is whipped at school.
H. Wrought by hand great works do stand.
J. Job felt the rod yet blessed his God.

Q. Queens and Kings must lie in the dust.
(A child who has not yet gone to school is thus reminded that queens and kings are mortal.)

T. Time cuts down all, the great and small.
(In case the child missed the point earlier or thought it was restricted to kings and queens, the point is generalized: All people must die.)

X. Xerxes the Great shared the common fate.
(Now the child, who has not yet learned to read and write, has been told this fact three times.)

This is the way Americans of earlier generations taught the alphabet. This book addresses the child at a far more dignified level than such contemporary efforts as: "Spot and Jane run and play. Run, Spot, run. Catch, Jane, catch. Dick and Jane are friends." It was written in a period before condescension toward children had been elevated to a dogma.

Reality provides the conditions on which pleasure can or cannot be achieved; it also provides the moral conditions on which pleasure should or should not be achieved. This value-freighted reality reveals the conditions that must be met or avoided if there is to be any gratification at any time. Children learned that wishes were not horses because before they learned to read they were taught through these verses that if wishes were horses beggars would be riding, and every child knew that beggars went on foot. Thus *Mother Goose* taught the child that you do not get something merely by wishing. Unfortunately, few politicians appear to have read *Mother Goose*.

This was the normal education of young children before they went to school. It taught them the alphabet and prepared them to read. It also prepared them for something much more important than reading: It prepared them for life.

Consider, moreover, how children learned to write—a skill on the endangered species list in contemporary America. They did so through the use of copybooks, manuals with beautifully handwritten sentences—copybook headings—printed at the top of each page. The children were expected to imitate the excellent writing of the headings by copying them repeatedly on the lined spaces below until they had learned the headings by heart.

Now, what did these copybook headings say? I quote from

The Art of Penmanship, one of the most widely used copybooks of the period: "Religion conduces to our present as well as our future happiness." This sentence was in the copybook of children so young that they were just beginning to learn to write. And another heading, "Persevere in accomplishing a complete education." The child copied: "Persevere in accomplishing a complete education," "Persevere in accomplishing a complete education," and on and on until the word "persevere" was learned by heart, and the meaning of perseverance was learned by persevering long enough to write it twenty times.

The educators who prepared that copybook knew that children are naturally fascinated and excited by grown-up words. The educators of that period understood the attraction and the power of language. In these copybooks words appear as treasures, language as a treasure-house, and education as the key. Here are a few more of those copybook headings:

Quarrelsome persons are always dangerous companions.
Employment prevents vice.
Great men were good boys.
Praise follows exertion
Trifles alienate friends.
X begins no English word.
(Presumably this was before xylophones and xebecs.)
Build your hopes of fame on virtue.
(A Christian and Kantian thought.)
Death to the good brings joy instead of terror.
(A Christian and Platonic thought.)
Zinc is a white semi-metal useful in galvanism.
(If not edifying, this heading was at least semi-informative.)

One may perhaps understand better why the abolitionist movement began in Boston when one reads the copybook headings that shaped the minds of Boston children: "Justice is a common right." "Magnanimity ennobles." "Overcome all prejudice." "Justice will pursue the vicious." "Zeal for justice is worthy of praise."

If there is to be effective moral education, it must begin in early childhood. Children's education started when they began learning the language. These copybook headings were the efforts of an earlier generation to pass on their moral heritage to their children, to acquaint their children with nature—not merely physical but moral and spiritual. By introducing moral and spiritual reality into the education of the child, they expressed their concern with educating the child in all dimensions of reality, to prepare children, in short, for a true and complete human existence.

It was not enough to teach penmanship merely as beautiful writing. It was important to have something to write *about*, to have content throughout the curriculum, a content that was the distillation of a high culture. It presented as aphorisms the things that thoughtful, understanding people would be expected to know about the nature of the world, about the nature of society, about the nature of the universe, and about themselves. The full meaning and justification of these aphorisms were provided in later stages of the curriculum in the works of Plato, Aristotle, Aquinas, Spinoza, Kant, and many others.

But it never crossed the mind of eighteenth- or nineteenth-century parents or teachers that their principal responsibility was to be a pal to their children or to try to make life easy, comfortable, convenient, or maximally pleasurable for them. Rather, it was their duty to prepare the children, through exposure to reality, for the uncertainty of human life and the ever-present possibility of death. Children were led to the realization that virtue and achievement count, and that since death cannot be avoided, they should prepare for death by living well. It was fine to welcome pleasure when it came, but children had to recognize the folly of basing their lives on mere pleasure-seeking.

If we are to recapture this wisdom, we must go back to the copybooks and primers of the eighteenth and nineteenth centuries. I do not mean that we should literally reintroduce them into the curriculum. But we must reintroduce their subject matter. We must return to reality. And that requires us to look to the past because the past necessarily shapes the future. If our future is to be as strong, as good, as fine, and as just as our past has been, we must reassert what was best in a more distant past out of which that more recent past came to be.

Kipling's 1919 poem "The Gods of the Copybook Headings" is prophetic. The poet speaks as the voice of mankind:

As I pass through my incarnations in every age and race,
I make my proper prostrations to the Gods of the Market-Place.
Peering through reverent fingers I watch them flourish and fall.
And the Gods of the Copybook Headings, I notice, outlast them
  all.

We were living in trees when they met us. They showed us each
  in turn
That Water would certainly wet us, as Fire would certainly
  burn:
But we found them lacking in Uplift, Vision, and Breadth of
  Mind,
So we left them to teach the Gorillas while we followed the
  March of Mankind.

We moved as the Spirit listed. *They* never altered their pace,
Being neither cloud nor wind-borne like the Gods of the Market-
  Place;
But they always caught up with our progress, and presently word
  would come
That a tribe had been wiped off its icefield, or the lights had
  gone out in Rome.

With the Hopes that our World is built on they were utterly out
  of touch,
They denied that Moon was Stilton; they denied she was even
  Dutch.
They denied that Wishes were Horses; they denied that a Pig had
  Wings.
So we worshipped the Gods of the Market Who promised these
  beautiful things.

When the Cambrian measures were forming, they promised
  perpetual peace.
They swore, if we gave them our weapons, that the wars of the
  tribes would cease.
But when we disarmed they sold us and delivered us bound to
  our foe,
And the Gods of the Copybook Headings said: "Stick to the Devil
  you know."

On the first Feminian Sandstones we were promised the Fuller
  Life
(Which started by loving our neighbour and ended by loving his
  wife)

Till our women had no more children and the men lost reason
   and faith,
And the Gods of the Copybook Headings said: "The Wages of Sin
   is Death."

In the Carboniferous Epoch we were promised abundance for all,
By robbing selected Peter to pay for collective Paul;
But, though we had plenty of money, there was nothing our
   money could buy,
And the Gods of the Copybook Headings said: "If you don't work
   you die."

Then the Gods of the Market tumbled, and their smooth-tongued
   wizards withdrew,
And the hearts of the meanest were humbled and began to
   believe it was true
That All is not Gold that Glitters, and Two and Two make
   Four—
And the Gods of the Copybook Headings limped up to explain it
   once more.

As it will be in the future, it was at the birth of Man—
There are only four things certain since Social Progress began—
That the Dog returns to his Vomit and the Sow returns to her
   Mire,
And the burnt Fool's bandaged finger goes wabbling back to the
   Fire;

And that after this is accomplished, and the brave new world
   begins
When all men are paid for existing and no man must pay for his
   sins,
As surely as Water will wet us, as surely as Fire will burn,
The Gods of the Copybook Headings with terror and slaughter
   return.

If we have the courage to face reality, we will know and
proclaim these harrowing truths: that the degenerate society
consumed in pleasure-seeking will not survive ("the wages of sin
is death"), that the society that will not defend its freedom will
lose it ("stick to the Devil you know"), that a society that
consumes more than it produces will go bankrupt ("if you don't
work, you die"). We ill serve ourselves and our children by
preparing ourselves and them for a life of freedom and easy

pleasure that may never come and most certainly will never last. We had better prepare ourselves and them for reality—a reality that is infused with moral laws as surely as it is infused with physical laws; a reality in which there is no consumption without production, no freedom without defense, no self-fulfillment and no self-government without self-disciplined persons who govern themselves, persons who are capable of subordinating their desires long enough to achieve the conditions on which freedom and survival, and even pleasure, depend.

It is often said, mistakenly, that students on graduation finally go out into the "real" world. That is an expression of escapism. It suggests that they were avoiding the real world all the time they were in school. But no world is more real than the world of ideas in which students are, or should be, immersed from kindergarten through college. And educators should ensure that reality is packed into the curriculum so that their students, prior to graduation, will confront reality as presented through the ideas of the copybook headings. Then on graduation they will find themselves in the same world that they learned about in school and in college, and will be guided by ideas and principles that can anchor their lives and can give meaning, direction, and support.

These ideas should prepare young people for the disappointment that is an essential part of the joy of living. All of us must live with disappointment, accept limitations and imperfections. We live in a world of becoming and change. Inevitably we will sometimes be disappointed with friends. We will sometimes be disappointed in marriage, disappointed in institutions, and sometimes disappointed in ourselves. Thus if we are to retain our joy in life, we must find much of that joy in spite of disappointment, for the joy of life consists largely in the joy of savoring the struggle, whether it ends in success or in failure. Our ability to go through life successfully will depend largely upon our traveling with courage and a good sense of humor, for both are conditions of survival. It is for this reason that educators should stress the importance of living with reality and therefore with disappointment.

When I look to the future of our country over the next twenty-five years, I find it difficult to be hopeful in the conventional understanding of that word. But it is easy to be hopeful at a more profound level. The difficult years that lie before us may turn out to be far happier than the twenty-five years through which we have just come, for the ancients knew that happiness is more often achieved in adversity than in luxury and affluence. Juvenal rightly said, "Luxury is more ruthless than war." We now face the disappointments that follow affluence—indeed, that go hand in hand with luxury. As our affluence begins to erode and the struggle for survival increases we may find in adversity greater opportunities for personal achievement, fulfillment, and happiness.

We must quickly come to terms with our unavoidable imperfections and with the unavoidable imperfections of our institutions. We must find it possible to live happily in an imperfect world with self-confidence and joy, for there is stern reality to be faced and much hard work to be done. We must join with one another to build a sounder foundation than pleasure, a foundation of enduring happiness that comes through triumph over one's self in a world not of our making by achieving a disciplined and moral relation to reality. Courage, personal renewal, and, ultimately, happiness may follow from a regained sense of ourselves as a free people joined in common cause on behalf of our free nation, prepared to do, and prepared to do without, whatever is necessary in order to preserve what is best in the American way of life. The phrase may be shopworn, but the reality behind the phrase is still our last, best hope.

Rebuild our defenses, balance our budget, achieve energy independence, rid our cities of crime? Of course! Educate a new generation for reality, for responsible productivity rather than irresponsible consumption? Of course! Regain our sense of direction as a nation, a sense of direction as individuals who seek not pleasure but the lessons of the Copybook Headings and respond creatively and responsibly to those lessons? Again, of course! If we do not, we will succumb to the consequences of ignoring them.

We should heed the words of John Quincy Adams: "Think of your forefathers; think of your posterity." That is to say, we must think of ourselves. And the way we can effectively express our concern for posterity is through the education of our children.

Teachers in a Troubled Society

T HE EDUCATION of our children is a deeply troubled enterprise. The problems confronting American primary and secondary education are desperately serious, ranging from a lack of moral education to a decline in our ability to educate even in the most basic areas. The problems are not insurmountable, nor is it inevitable that the decline continue, but the phenomena are disturbingly real and precisely those by which historians have measured the decline of other nations at other times. Unfortunately we are not observers at a distance: A decline that could become irreversible threatens us here and now. It is by no means too late for us to act. But act we must, and quickly.

The following are a few of the crucial issues that mark our threatening but not yet inevitable decline:

(1) the decline of the family;
(2) loss of respect for teachers;
(3) loss of moral understanding and of moral focus in teaching young people;
(4) the threat to effective education and to our culture posed by misguided programs of bilingual education;
(5) the assumption that money will solve these problems.

1.

Profound changes in the American family affect future generations of students from every level of society and from all parts of our country. These changes are first on the list of things that threaten our society for two reasons: first, because the family is *the* controlling condition of education from the moment children are conceived; second, because education is a fundamental task of any society.

The one-parent family aside, in nearly half the families with two parents, both work outside the home. And with the decline of the extended family, grandparents, aunts, and uncles who might once have provided the nurture and basic education of young children are no longer available. With this decline of the traditional American family, television substitutes for more creative, demanding, and instructive forms of preschool education once provided by books, imaginative play, and—most important—conversation between adults and children. Today, in upper-class, middle-class, and working-class homes, no less than in the homes of the underclass, the television set has become the most pervasive and persuasive educational influence of all. School-age children now spend more time watching television than in any other activity but sleep.

Invaded by television, the home is no longer a sanctuary in which children are protected from exposure to the most sordid elements of human experience. The perverse, the sublime, and the trivial are presented without moral differentiation, and the result is nothing less than a pollution of their sensibilities. Their minds—indeed, if I may use an old-fashioned term, their souls— are being trashed.

2.

As parents and the extended family become less influential in a child's life, the responsibility of teachers increases. But despite their increasingly crucial role as mentors of the young, there is a lamentable lack of respect and dignity associated with the teaching profession today.

Those who believe that the loss of respect can be attributed to the low salaries paid to teachers deceive themselves. Mother Teresa has more than adequately demonstrated that one can be penniless and highly respected.

Teachers *are* underpaid—there is no question about that—

but the lack of professional prestige and public respect are not related to their salary scale. When I was going to school, teachers were highly respected despite their poverty. They were respected because their competence was exemplary; they were respected because their dedication was exemplary; and they were respected because their lives were exemplary. They were, in the literal sense of the word, respectable professionals.

Even today, many such teachers exist—teachers who command respect despite modest incomes. But who would deny that the reputation of teachers as a profession has suffered from the deficiencies of a minority of them?

In making these observations, I am generalizing. I am not making universal statements that apply to each and every member of a class. I am well aware that there are individual exceptions to each generalization, but a sound generalization gives us a clear and accurate account of the total picture.

Surely no one knows better what can be expected of the teaching profession today than the publishers of textbooks. Once upon a time, publishers offered textbooks and teachers' manuals that treated teachers as members of a learned profession. Today, they recognize that they cannot sell their textbooks if they set their standards according to the superbly qualified few or even the reasonably qualified many. Realistically, textbook publishers must accept the fact that the teaching profession has successfully resisted efforts to retrain or remove incompetent teachers. Hence publishers, in preparing their textbooks, reduce their expectations of teachers to meet minimum standards, standards that border on contempt.

Let me prove this. The teacher's manual for a textbook in the recently superseded D. C. Heath American Readers series is written as if the publisher supposes that the course will be taught by someone lacking even the minimal ability to instruct the young. Several pages at the start are devoted to convincing the teacher of how easy teaching will be using the textbook and teacher's manual. "That's right," the teacher is told, in language that seems more appropriate to late-night television ads for cutlery, "you will spend less time preparing and less time organizing because we give you . . . an easy-to-read Teacher's

Edition and a Time Saver binder—just the beginning of reduced preparation time."

When we come to the instructions themselves, we find everything spelled out and spoon-fed in prose very little advanced over that of the primary-grade text. Nothing is left to chance: The operative principle seems to be "tiny steps for baby feet," an astonishingly condescending attitude toward members of a supposedly educated profession.

But let me quote from one of the manual's lessons. It deals with a story about a city girl named Pat who visits her friend Alice on a farm. The dramatic tension of the story is provided by Pat's wish to own a pet pig as Alice does. The story is called "Why Can't I?"

The exercise in spoon-feeding the teacher begins with some questions about literal comprehension, with the answers provided in parentheses:

> What did Pat want to do? *(To stay and play with Alice in a tree.)* What happened when Pat's father called her? *(She and Alice got out of the tree.)* Read the sentence that tells. *(Pat got out of the tree and so did Alice.)*

You will note that the manual does not expect the teacher to be able to answer any of the questions about Pat without help, and it helpfully identifies the sentence telling that the girls got out of a tree. Then the manual moves on to interpretative comprehension.

> How do you think Alice feels about pigs? *(She probably likes pigs, since she lives on a farm. The pig may be her pet.)*

The answer supplied by the manual is a non sequitur; there is no reason to assume that all farm girls like pigs. There is, in fact, substantial contravening evidence on this point. Familiarity with pigs no less than with people can breed contempt.

Next, there are examples of applied comprehension:

> Would you like to have a pig for a pet? Why? *(Answers will vary.)*

This is the only offer of freedom suggested for teacher or student. But the advice to the teacher continues:

> *Some pupils may like how pigs look and think they would make*

*friendly pets. Others may feel that pigs are too messy and too noisy
to have as pets.*

Consider the humiliation of the person who has to write this
manual, forced to assume that teachers cannot anticipate the two
attitudes listed and therefore must be told—otherwise they might
be dumbfounded to discover that some of their pupils can take
pigs and some can leave them.

This level of condescension to teachers is maintained as the
manual moves to more technical questions. The teacher is
instructed as follows:

> Write the words *big, him,* and *did* on the chalkboard. Pronounce
> each word aloud, stressing but not isolating the medial *i* sound. Ask
> the pupils what vowel letter is the same in each word. *(The vowel
> letter i.)*

Note that the teacher is not supposed to be smart enough to figure
out that the vowel letter common to *big, him,* and *did* is "i,"
even though "i" is the only vowel. Or perhaps the writer is in
doubt as to whether teachers can tell vowels from consonants.
The instructions continue:

> Have the pupils pronounce each of the words as you underline the
> vowel letter *i*. Ask the pupils if the sound is the same in each word.

And here, incredibly, the manual again provides the answer:
Yes. The manual is not taking any chance that the teacher hasn't
figured out that "i" is pronounced the same way in each of the
three words.

This Heath teacher's manual clearly assumes that the teacher
did not pass first grade. If what I have just read were not in a
real book but appeared in an issue of *Mad* magazine, it would
be taken as unfair parody. In fact, the text and teacher's manual
do exist, and the tragic joke is on us and on the teachers. Teachers'
unions should take on this issue; they should fight for the dignity
of their members.

It is sobering to compare the string of simpleminded insults
in the 1985 D. C. Heath teacher's manual for first-grade reading
to the preface of the 1903 *First Heath Reader.* D. C. Heath has
been an excellent publisher of textbooks for over a hundred years.
In 1903, their teacher's manual said:

The teacher of elementary reading needs as the basis for her work a series of interesting reading lessons, making use of a practical, well-graded, and properly limited vocabulary. Whatever method may be used for the development of the vocabulary and for the presentation of the elements of reading to the pupils, these materials are essential. It is the purpose of The Heath Readers to supply such lessons, leaving teachers free to use whatever methods their experience and surroundings make most desirable.

Those of us who may be tempted to believe in the inevitability of educational progress should remember that this passage was written in 1903.

There is a ray of hope: In 1989, D. C. Heath scrapped the reading series I have examined here and replaced it with a far more interesting and dignified set of books for children and a greatly improved teacher's manual.

Teachers as professionals should assert their right to choose textbooks that meet standards unadulterated by the lowest common denominator. And if all current textbooks pander to the infantile in both teacher and pupil, teachers should be free to select excellent textbooks from earlier periods. In many fields, questions of currency do not arise. Date of publication has nothing to do with the soundness of textbooks for Latin or reading or writing.

Respect for teachers will follow automatically, at least among textbook publishers, when teachers share the responsibility for selecting texts, and when they are not compelled to teach from texts beneath their dignity. Among other beneficiaries would be textbook writers and, even more important, students.

Full restoration of respect for teachers will require much more, however. If teachers are to regain the respect they once had, they must be prepared to demonstrate their excellence both intellectually and morally. Teachers must once again strive to be and to be known as exemplary individuals.

Teachers and teachers' unions must know that it is in the interest of the profession and the union to insist on the intellectual competence of teachers. It is in the interest of both the profession and the union to accept responsible evaluation and criticism, to stop treating tenure as if it were sinecure, and to retrain or remove teachers who are deficient. There are a number of concrete steps to be taken to achieve these ends.

First, we must break the monopoly of schools of education on teacher certification. For a long time certification standards for teachers have been, in many states, almost entirely in terms of education courses—that is, courses having little to do with education—and this has given education schools their virtual monopoly on the supply of teachers. In doing so, it has also placed almost insurmountable obstacles in the way of highly intelligent students and highly intelligent adults out of school who will simply not accept the intellectual and spiritual indignity of the typical school of education curriculum. The willingness to endure four years in a typical school of education often constitutes an effective negative intelligence test.

Consider that, nationally, the combined 1988 SAT score among students intending to study education is 855, a full 49 points below the national mean of 904 for all college-bound students. Surely teachers should not normally be selected from those who fall below the national mean. Moreover, the quality of prospective teachers will probably decline even further as schools of education, in a desperate effort to sustain their enrollments, lower their standards still further to encourage more admissions.

Boston University's School of Education has successfully resisted this change. We raised our combined SAT average of those preparing for careers in teaching to 1090 by 1988, which is 235 points above the 1988 national mean for students intending to study education. At first this increase in quality required us to accept a substantially smaller student body, but as the reputation of the school became better known, enrollments began to recover and are still rising. Almost everywhere else, Gresham's Law takes its toll.

In our School of Education, those who are preparing for primary education spend two-thirds of their time in the College of Liberal Arts taking substantive courses in science, the humanities, and social sciences on which their professional qualification properly depends. Those preparing for secondary education spend three-fourths of their time taking these courses in the College of Liberal Arts.

Surely some state will have the wisdom and the courage to take the lead in breaking the monopoly of schools of education by passing a ten-year moratorium on certification requirements. During the decade of this moratorium, schools would be free to recruit qualified college graduates with majors in academic subjects whether or not they had any education courses. From a vastly increased pool of talent made up of persons attracted by the ideals of the teaching profession, by its calendar, by the quality of life of teachers, and by intellectual and moral challenge, schools would be able to develop a teacher corps of significantly increased quality.

If such an experiment were tried in one state, that state's educational programs would improve so swiftly and dramatically that parents and taxpayers in each of the other 49 states would demand that the experiment be replicated.

We also need national measures of educational achievement and competence that can be used to evaluate teachers no less than students. That is, we need a national Bureau of Educational Standards, whose criteria would be available, but not compulsory, for all to use.

We need the American equivalent of the British Ordinary and Advanced School–Leaving examinations. The Ordinary-Level exams would be required of all students seeking a high school diploma, and the Advanced-Level exams would be required of those seeking admission to college. At the present moment, I believe very few college graduates could pass the A-Level examinations required in England of students who wish merely to enter the university. The Advanced-Level exams would also provide a very useful test for the minimal certification of the competency of teachers.

Even before such tests are developed on a national scale, local school boards can require their teachers to take the subject-matter tests at the freshman college level. A prospective teacher of mathematics who cannot pass a freshman algebra, geometry, or calculus test with a grade of A is certainly not prepared to teach at the high school level.

Against certifying teachers on the basis of competence, it is frequently argued that no test will demonstrate competence, much less excellence, in teaching. This is true, of course. But this inability to test exhaustively an individual's ability to teach should not obscure the fact that there are many tests on which failure demonstrates the inability to teach. A teacher who cannot handle differential and quadratic equations is certainly not competent to teach mathematics in high school. A person who does not know that England is a democracy despite the fact that it has a monarch is not competent to teach history. While we may not be able to prove competence completely, the sheer absence of knowledge is sufficient to demonstrate incompetence. It is a measure of our decline that such an obvious point has been overlooked: Knowledge of the subject is a *sine qua non* of competence.

Accepting standards and demonstrating competence in meeting those standards is a way for teachers to regain intellectual respect and public support for taxes to finance salary increases. In addition, they must also regain the respect that, as individuals of outstanding moral integrity, they once enjoyed. Most adults can think back to the times when teachers were greatly respected and revered in the community for the quality of their lives. The notion that today's teachers will command respect from the community and from their students without demonstrating similar qualities is unrealistic.

3.

In general, nothing undermines the confidence of parents and the general public in our teachers and schools more than the way in which many of our schools teach children and teenagers about sex. The idea has caught on that we should teach sex early and often, that we should keep on teaching it right through high school, and that we should teach it without reference to moral values or social standards. It is becoming increasingly obvious that the sexual revolution that has swept our society has left us incapable of coping with grave problems that range from the dissolution of the family to AIDS. We have been immobilized by our almost casual rejection of the most elementary and essential wisdom about sex.

We believe that we can treat sexuality like any other product sold on television, in terms of consumer demand. We think of sex as an important but inconsequential pleasure, and think that we can treat different modes of sexual behavior as similar to the difference between apples and oranges. It all depends upon what you prefer, and *only* on what you prefer.

This is evident in one of the splashiest books on the market, used in many high schools: *Changing Bodies, Changing Lives.*[1] Aimed at teenagers, the text reduces all moral norms to what it calls "personal value judgments." This locution, by the way, contains a contradiction in terms evident to any competent philosopher. A value judgment is an objective claim; a personal judgment is merely a preference. Those who espouse "personal value judgments" treat value judgments as if they were Good Housekeeping Seals of Approval that one licks and pastes on any idea, object, or activity that one happens to like. Such preferences are not values.

For each aspect of sex that it considers, *Changing Bodies, Changing Lives* offers reassuring quotations from teenagers who have and have not engaged in it and who think it is or isn't right. The book does not consider sex between teenagers and animals, or between adults and prepubescent children, because, though the authors presumably do not approve of these things, they have not developed or even stated any moral grounds for disapproving; therefore, the only way they can handle these issues is to ignore them. But on the basis of the evidence they do adduce, they presumably would view bestiality as perfectly satisfactory behavior as long as people could be found to testify that it was enjoyable. The ethic of *Changing Bodies, Changing Lives* is that if you like it, or you and someone else like it, you're in good company; and if you don't like it, or somebody else doesn't like it, you and they are OK, too.

The title of this book really tells it all: Whatever your body "is," whatever messages it sends you, these will rule your life. The title of another book by the same authors puts it even more plainly: *Our Bodies, Ourselves.* The implication is clear: You are the sum total of your bodily desires.

There is not a philosopher or moral teacher in the history of mankind who has approved such rubbish. Taken seriously, it offers no basis for human rights or human dignity since, by definition, human existence has been reduced to the level of animals, to stimulus/response. The notion that we are moral beings—that our selfhood comes from disciplining and controlling our bodily urges—is foreign to *Changing Bodies, Changing Lives* and presumably to the classrooms where it is used.

To explain homosexuality, the book offers teenage boys and girls a diagram consisting of a horizontal line. Exclusively homosexual individuals are at one end of the line, high schoolers are told, and exclusively heterosexual individuals are at the other. In an effort to provide underpinning for its relativist moral theory, the book asserts that most people lie somewhere in between, tending toward one or the other of these extremes. The implied question is: Where are you on the line?

Of course, this is an insipid and intellectually insulting nonexplanation. But more important than the intellectual insult is the implied moral teaching: that the normal is found anywhere along the line, and that any point on the line is as morally good as any other. Instead of locating the normal toward one end, and locating the vast majority of persons at that point, the normal—heterosexuality—is misrepresented as an extreme, a counterpart to the opposite extreme—homosexuality—with the largest segment of the line reserved for those of varying degrees of sexual ambivalence. Since anywhere on the line is as good as any other, there is no basis for moral, medical, or any other assessment of sexual practices. It is all merely a matter of "preference."

Many young people, the book goes on to say, can experiment all along the line. All of this is normal, unless you happen to think it isn't. Then it isn't normal—or, more likely, you aren't.

Thus human sexuality, a complexity of enormous creative force to be used or misused, is reduced to a banal horizontal line on which one can "locate" oneself. The idea that any location along this line is equally satisfactory denies all the costly and important things civilized man has learned about sexuality.

A school system that accepts this approach can only forfeit the respect of thoughtful and concerned parents. To treat human sexuality in this way is to invite personal and national tragedy. It is to deny, and thus to fail to develop, what is specifically human about human beings: the capacity for awareness and self-control. The ignorance of moral principles is not merely a symptom but a major cause of our national decline. It is perhaps the most important issue to be addressed. Every citizen, every member of a local school board, should make it plain to their principals, administrators, and teachers that they are unwilling to forgo the moral education of their children, and that anything less than sound moral instruction is unacceptable.

4.

Bilingual education also poses problems. At stake are the futures of hundreds of thousands of children whose native language is not English. Our national cultural heritage is likewise at stake.

The motive behind bilingual education is praiseworthy. We are properly concerned to educate all children no matter what their native language. But our approach has been seriously confused, and one of the casualties of this confusion is the failure to bring all children to a level of competence in English.

School systems spend huge amounts of money—some of it from their own budgets, much of it from the federal budget—on bilingual education. A great deal of this money is wasted in scattered programs that have no common goal and produce unsatisfactory results.

Bilingual education can have only one valid goal: the achievement of genuine competency in reading, writing, hearing, and speaking the English language. Thus it is not, strictly speaking, bilingual education. It is the education of non-English-speaking children in the language of their country.

Parents understand this. Many Chinese and Vietnamese families in particular want no part of today's misdirected bilingual education programs. They put their children into English-speaking classrooms so that they can become fluent in English as quickly as possible and eventually graduate at the top of their class from West Point, or achieve goals equally as distinguished. This is not because they are anxious to leave their cultural heritage behind, or because they are ashamed of their background. They remain very aware of their cultural heritage, more so than many other ethnic groups, but they recognize that their ability to compete and thrive in America will be greatly enhanced by learning English.

Of course, this awareness is not confined to the Chinese and

Vietnamese. Concerned parents from all ethnic groups realize that it is essential for their children to grow up speaking English.

The most succinct and telling statement I have heard on the subject came from Ernesto Ortiz, a foreman on a south Texas ranch, who said: "My children learn Spanish in school so they can grow up to be busboys and waiters. I teach them English at home so they can grow up to be doctors and lawyers."

Wave on wave of immigrant groups followed the example provided by the English-speaking Irish, who learned how to make the American system work for them. Germans, Italians, Jews, and other groups, emulating the success of the Irish, realized that they had to learn the language and enter the political stream. The result was the melting pot.

In recent years it has, unfortunately, become fashionable to question the validity of the melting pot and to encourage groups of what Theodore Roosevelt called "hyphenated Americans," who perpetuate their ethnic particularism at the expense of their integration into American society.

In arguing that all citizens should be Americans, I would not deny ethnic groups their right to preserve their language and heritage. To the contrary, ethnic groups should be encouraged to maintain their languages and customs. We should not deny any ethnic group its identity or its children the opportunity to speak their native language. The perpetuation of linguistic identity by ethnic groups that preserve their native language in newspapers, church services, festivals, and businesses adds strength and vitality to the United States and preserves the pluralism out of which our national unity is forged.

But we must not ignore the need for a common language on which our national unity depends. The citizens of the Roman Empire spoke many diverse tongues, but Latin was the official language, the language of law, commerce, and government. A German or Briton who came to Rome asserted his citizenship by being able to say *civis romanus sum* (I am a Roman citizen). Roman society never considered it necessary or desirable to provide him with German or Celtic legal, educational, or political institutions. And we should not forget that when Greek became the official language of its eastern provinces, the Roman Empire split in two.

Except for Switzerland, no country has ever prospered with more than one official language. And even Switzerland must promulgate its laws in Latin, so that there is a single authoritative text should linguistic push come to linguistic shove. The country is known in its various regions as Suisse, Schweiz, Svizzera, and Svizra, but officially it is named in Latin: Confoederatio Helvetica.

The citizens of India speak diverse tongues, but Hindi and English are, like Latin, official languages. And it is worth noting that Hindi's position in this regard is more theoretical than practical. Pandit Nehru, on whom the successful negotiation of Britain's withdrawal depended, did not learn Hindi until he entered politics; he had grown up speaking only English. India is unified by the language of the conqueror. The Tamils of southeast India, for example, find English acceptable as an official language, while objecting to Hindi. There is, in fact, no realistic foundation for the preservation of India's unity apart from reliance on the English language. The very independence of India depended on English, for the national groups that drove the English from power had no common language but English. And they used English in planning and achieving their liberation. For so vast and diverse a nation, India enjoys a considerable measure of cohesion, but the Indian Empire of Queen Victoria has already split into three nations, and had it entirely lacked a common language, it would almost certainly have fragmented further.

With these examples in mind, no one can contemplate with equanimity the loss of a national language in a democracy spread over half a continent.

The bilingual movement in America, as presently misdirected, would, if successful, establish the United States as a multilingual nation deprived of a national language—a Babel brought up to date. Until fairly recently, the United States was unique in the world as a very large nation covering a great land mass that maintained a single national language with dialects that are easily mutually intelligible. Our comparative peace and our single language are almost certainly related; unlike Canada, Belgium, and other nations with explosive linguistic problems, the United States has been able to sustain, along with freedom, a diverse culture within the context of one official language.

Bilingual ballots strike at this notion of a national language by assuming that it is possible to be a citizen without being able to read the national language as long as one is literate in the language of one's ethnic group. This argument cannot be founded on any theory of right, for if that were the case, each citizen would have the right to have a ballot printed in whatever language he was reared, no matter how obscure it might be, no matter how many ballots had to be printed. If we make no pretense of providing ballots in the more than 100 separate languages of American Indians, how then do persons who came to this country after English was well-established as our national language acquire this right?

In practice, we exempt only one large group of citizens—Hispanic Americans—from a requirement that has hitherto been expected of all citizens: the acquisition of some competence in the national language. This is to reduce the standards of perform-ance expected of a citizen to a derisory level. It is also to patronize Hispanic culture by implying that it, unlike Polish culture, for example, cannot survive in a predominantly English-speaking country.

Special pleading for Spanish also has racist overtones, suggesting that Spanish-speaking American citizens cannot be expected to attain the same level of competence acquired by immigrants from Germany, Italy, Poland, Greece, Russia, and many other countries, and until recently by all Spanish-speaking citizens as well.

A similar question arises with regard to the various dialects of English. Recall, for instance, the movement in the 1960s maintaining that students who grow up speaking black English or other dialectal variants of English should not be required to learn standard English, and that to require them to do so was racist.

Nothing could be further from racism than requiring students from the ghetto to learn standard English. This is to treat them as the equals of the great majority of students.

My own experience is perhaps instructive. Like all native Texans, I had to learn English as a foreign language when I started school. Later, as an instructor at Yale, I insisted on standard English from all my students. I did not exempt recent immigrants to Connecticut from Lithuania, Atlanta, or Pearsall, Texas. They neither spoke nor wrote standard English at the beginning of their freshmen year, but all them ignernt boys done right good by the time they wuz thew. Later, as a professor in Texas, it never occurred to me to exempt *any* student, white, black, or Hispanic, from the requirement of standard English.

The teacher who condones the substitution of ghetto English for standard educated English, expecting less of black students than of whites, is a racist. Such condescension can have good results in neither the short nor the long term. It is especially disturbing to hear a minority student arguing for his exemption from standard English, since by doing so he greatly weakens his ability to oppose racism. He cannot plausibly use his race or ethnicity as a basis for claiming supposed privileges and exemptions from standards without provoking others to use the same basis for denying him genuine rights.

Unfortunately, the United States Congress is deeply confused about the goal of bilingual education; and since Congress provides much of the funding for bilingual programs, the confusion is promulgated and replicated throughout the land. The current law governing bilingual education, as well as Senate and House bills under consideration, all contain the following policy clause: "A primary means by which a child learns is through the use of such child's native language and cultural heritage." This seemingly benevolent statement contains a recipe for disaster, and one of its main ingredients is ignorance of how language acquisition really works. Once we accept that the primary means by which a child in the United States learns is through his native language rather than English, and that a school should try to teach him through his native language rather than English, and that it is the school's responsibility to preserve the child's native cultural heritage in his native language, we have taken on a task that is both practically and financially impossible.

In my home state of Massachusetts there is a perfect test case that demonstrates this impossibility. In Massachusetts, every public school is governed by the Transitional Bilingual Education Law. And because the task set by the law is impossible, and so must be reduced in some way, the Commonwealth has resorted to magic. But rather than use a wand, or investigate the astrological signs of non-English-speaking residents, the Common-wealth uses the much more respected and up-to-date magic of numerology. Massachusetts bilingual numerology is based on the magic number twenty. If fewer than twenty students speak the same foreign language and have limited ability in English, they have no rights; but when twenty such students come forward the school board must provide a program of transitional bilingual education. This means—and the schools have no choice—that all required courses must initially be taught in the students' native language, rather than putting all students into one basic program where they would learn English and go on from there to learn other subjects as quickly as possible.

This Massachusetts law is misnamed. It is called the Transitional Bilingual Education Law, but for a great many children who begin with classes taught in their native language, there is no transition. The Commonwealth ought to indicate more accurately the effect on these children and call the law the Bilingual Dropout Encouragement Law.

To the extent that a child can function by working in his native language, he will, of course, do so; to the extent that he can get along without learning English, he will. And this is why, jeopardizing their futures, many children stay in bilingual programs year after year—up to five or six years—and then, finding that they are unable to cope in English when their bilingual programs come to an end, drop out of school.

In dealing with bilingual education, Congress and state legislatures have also failed to realize that our resources are not infinite. Programs focused on teaching children in their native language, and teaching them about their native cultural heritage, face the problem of the number of languages involved. Chinese provides one example: Bilingual programs in Mandarin Chinese are based on the false assumption that all Chinese-speaking children speak Mandarin. In fact, many speak Cantonese and other quite dissimilar dialects. The native language of a Boston student may be any one of thirty, but the Boston school system offers only twenty different bilingual programs. It does not even attempt to meet the impossible standards put forth by the Commonwealth.

Clearly many school systems are going about the problem

√backwards, trying to feed every branch of the tree when they should be watering the roots. The resources are not available, even if it were deemed desirable to provide instruction in all the necessary languages and cultures. But school systems do have the resources to teach English to children from any linguistic background. Furthermore, as the Irish, Jews, Poles, and so many other ethnic groups in this country have amply demonstrated, we may properly and confidently leave to parents and ethnic groups the responsibility of preserving and transmitting their cultural heritage. If there is not sufficient ethnic identity to sustain the culture, the public schools are incapable of generating it.

But this in no way excuses teachers and students who fail to show respect for children from homes in which a foreign language is spoken. And we must not overlook the educational advantage that will accrue to English-speaking pupils once their foreign-language-speaking classmates have achieved proficiency in English. Those bilingual children will demonstrate to their class-mates that mastery of two languages is well within the reach of the average child. Perhaps this will encourage American-born children and their parents to support vigorous programs of foreign language instruction in the primary grades, when languages can most easily be learned.

The mastery of English should primarily be the responsibility of programs in the preschool and primary grades. From ages three to six, children can achieve mastery of English appropriate to their age levels within a few months. Programs that focus on the first three grades would achieve the maximum results at minimum cost. Such programs would be operating wholesale, whereas now the process is retailed, with each separate group having its own set of programs at a wide variety of levels. Nor should there be any doubt about what sort of programs we should have. The goal must be to make children proficient in English— the national language of the country in which they live—in the shortest possible time.

Without a common language, there is at best a very limited common political, social, and cultural life; and there are severe economic limitations as well. How can anyone be successful in a job interview without knowledge of the language in which it is conducted? Participation in the political life of the nation is equally dependent upon a common language. Without a knowledge of English, how will those who speak only Spanish or Vietnamese choose a president? How will they be able to assess the merits of one candidate or another when all they know of them is derived from unintelligible talking faces on television? And how will individuals participate in our national life if they lack at least some acquaintance with the Constitution, the Bill of Rights, and *The Federalist?*

Perhaps we need to ask ourselves whether we believe that there is such a thing as a United States culture, which is a prominent part of Western culture, and which should be preserved and augmented for future generations. Do we believe future generations should read the formative documents of our political culture? If the answer is yes, we should remember that all of these documents were written in English.

Our nation will be severely crippled if we do not preserve a single national language. Many of the things we hope non-English-speaking members of our society will be able to share—good education, a well-paying job, democratic government—will be denied them if we fail in the task of teaching children proficiency in their nation's language.

Bilingual education is distinct from another important issue, monoglottal Americans. If the United States is to compete effectively in the world economy, and carry on effective diplomatic relations, we need to introduce instruction in the major foreign languages that few Americans speak—in particular, Japanese, Chinese, Russian, Portuguese. This instruction should begin in the elementary grades. An effective program of bilingual education for Hispanics would ensure a large pool of Americans fluent in English and Spanish, but that would be only a start at solving the problem of what Senator Paul Simon has called "the tongue-tied American." But developing America as a multilingual country in no way requires depriving it of a national language; in European countries, the possession of a national language goes hand in hand with a high degree of multilingualism.

5.

It is conventional wisdom that there is one simple solution to all these problems—the decline of the family, loss of respect for the teaching profession, an amoral approach to sexuality, misguided programs in bilingual education. Conventional wisdom holds that the most important element in solving these problems is money.

I disagree. We must dispel the myth that we can improve our educational system simply by spending more money on it. This is a demonstrable falsehood, and yet we subscribe to it over and over again, at great cost to the taxpayer, and at far greater cost to the quality of our children's education.

The relationship between education and money concerns citizens, school boards, school administrators, and parents. Because almost all parents love their children, they are more than willing to meet the considerable expense of sending them to the best schools they can afford. But many parents do not have a great deal of choice in the matter. Their financial situation forces them to send their children to public schools. The only other choice for many of them is to transfer their children to parochial schools—which, subsidized by the Catholic Church, offer an option of relatively inexpensive quality. If the public schools were finally to lose the last vestige of parental confidence, their very existence would be in doubt.

The flight from the public schools, as it occurs in many inner cities, is not a flight primarily grounded on racial issues, but on the refusal of people to subject their children to disastrously inadequate educational programs. Politicians who have supported the laws that leave parents with these limited options frequently send their own children to expensive private schools because they are unwilling to impose on them the disastrous social experiments they impose on the children of the less affluent.

Parents today are acutely aware that their children are very much at the mercy of the school system and that the education of their children is inadequate. And after long experience with increasing school budgets and declining results, they have good reason to doubt that spending more of the taxpayers' money will improve the schools.

Again, unfortunately, the Boston school system provides an excellent case in point. Boston students perform badly on all national examinations in reading and mathematics. Their 1988 median combined SAT score is 764, 140 points below the national average of 904. And I might point out that this figure for the Boston schools includes the examination schools, where SAT scores are from 75 to 175 points higher than in the rest of the school system.

This is not a question of money. The Boston school system spends more than $6000 per student, whereas nearby Lexington, whose combined 1988 SATs of 1047 are 283 points higher, spends $1600 *less* per student. Boston school officials attempt to excuse their poor performance and justify even higher spending because of special problems: high minority enrollments, high bilingual enrollments, and high enrollments of students from impoverished backgrounds.

Their arguments might explain one of two things: why the Boston schools must be more expensive or why they must be inferior. It will not explain why they must be *both* more expensive *and* inferior. Consider the schools of Springfield, Massachusetts, roughly of the same quality and sharing the same problems as those of Boston. With combined SATs of 727 in 1988, and slightly higher scores than Boston in reading and mathematics, the Springfield schools, subject to all the problems suffered by those of Boston, do at least as well. Spending only $2079 per pupil, or less than half of what is spent in Boston, Springfield proves that you can have bad schools for far less money.

In fact, money spent has very little to do with educational achievement. Studies I have made indicate that the correlation between the national decline in SAT scores and the level of teachers' salaries, for instance, is exactly 0. There is no correlation between teachers' salaries and performance on SATs. This is not to argue against an increase in teachers' salaries. It is rather to point out that increases in salaries will not necessarily improve the schools. This is explained in part by the motivation that brings people into teaching. Since the best teachers are motivated less by money than by idealism, they do not turn away from teaching merely because of lower compensation than they could find in another profession.

It is also explained by the fact that teaching is, in and of itself, one of the most desirable of professions, not merely in terms of the self-development characteristic of the life of the teacher, not merely in terms of the quality of his or her work, or the excitement of working with young people. Teaching is also highly desirable because the calendar of the teacher provides more time to be with one's family than is possible in most other professions.

Parents and taxpayers have a right to expect that teachers' self-development will result in increased teaching competence. In several states, taxpayers have been willing to raise teachers' salaries if the teachers will accept testing, but are unwilling to tax themselves further to pay for teachers who refuse to have their competence tested.

In any case, since teachers' salaries are not the cause of declining SAT scores, they are irrelevant to the explanation of that decline; nor, surprisingly, are other ways of spending money very relevant. Total educational funding per pupil can account for only 9 percent of the SAT variance among states. This is a noticeable but not significant factor.

One of the most striking facts to emerge from my investigations is that there is a high negative correlation between dependence on federal funds and SAT scores. For instance, 31 percent of the variance in SAT scores can be predicted from knowing only the level of federal dependency and putting a minus sign in front of it. This does not, of course, prove that federal funds are bad for learning, but it does suggest how ineffective federal spending has been in improving the public schools.

The reason is not hard to find. Local responsibility for quality is attenuated when a large proportion of the funding comes from outside. The vaporous presence of the federal government is no substitute for local taxpayers monitoring the stewardship of local taxes. When the people who pay for the schools are watching the people who spend the money, there is direct accountability, and quality improves. Federal funding shifts responsibility and accountability to Washington, beyond the control of local taxpayers and parents.

It is argued, rightly, that the skills needed to perform well on the SATs are not the whole of education. But no one can seriously argue that the mathematical and linguistic skills measured by the SATs are irrelevant to education. Far from it. They are the very foundation without which education cannot proceed.

New Hampshire students consistently score well above the national average in SATs. In 1987 they were first in the nation at 32 points above the national average. Those who believe there is a direct connection between money and the quality of education would do well to note that New Hampshire is twenty-sixth in the nation in total funding per student, spending an average of $3542 per pupil; the average salary of a New Hampshire teacher ranks forty-second in the nation. More important, New Hampshire is first in the nation in terms of the percentage of funding derived from local taxpayers. There is an obvious reason why schools that are largely locally funded are better. A typical school superintendent in New Hampshire, where the average SAT score is 938, gets 90 percent of his money from his "customers," that is, from the parents of the students in his schools.

A typical school superintendent in Hawaii, by contrast, where the average SAT score is 55 points lower, gets 90 percent of his funds from the state and only 0.1 percent from his local government. The rest comes from the government of the United States. The point is worth repeating: State and federal bureaucrats are not spending their own local tax money on the schools and are consequently less demanding evaluators of the schools than local taxpayers who must pay for them out of their own pockets or parents whose children's success depends upon the quality of those schools.

School superintendents in New Hampshire must fight for their appropriations from selectmen, notorious for their frugality and their demands for results. Taxpayers and parents are not inclined to excuse a school system that fails to teach their children to read and to write effectively; rather, they are outraged by such fiscal and intellectual profligacy. Bureaucrats, by contrast, interpret failure in a school system as merely another occasion—indeed, an opportunity—to request additional funds from state and federal agencies.

There is no easy and simple explanation for which schools

perform well and which do not. There are striking variations depending upon individual school superintendents, individual school principals, individual teachers, and individual school boards. But as a general rule, local control, local funding, and local initiative with regard to curriculum, which mean localized responsibility and accountability, are clearly dominant factors.

If we are to compensate for the decline of the family, if the respect for teachers is to be restored, if we are to awaken young people to the true nature of personal autonomy and moral choice, if we are to have bilingual programs that help rather than retard children in learning English—then we must have the courage to face our problems and cope with them. The crisis of our schools is the crisis of our democracy. It will reach the point of disaster unless parents, educators, politicians, and citizens unite to reverse the trend and provide our children with dedicated teachers and excellent schools. America does not lack concern, intelligence, resources, manpower, tradition, but the nation has not yet shown that it has the resolve without which we will lose the vision of what has made us great.

Of Mermaids and Magnificence

Iᴛ ɪs ᴀ sᴛʀɪᴋɪɴɢ paradox that democracy places the highest value upon the development of the individual, yet is frequently indifferent to heroes and hostile to greatness. Alexis de Tocqueville, observing the American scene in the 1830s and 1840s, devoted a chapter of *Democracy in America* to the extreme scarcity of lofty ambitions among otherwise intensely ambitious Americans. Moreover, among free people in a vigorous democracy there is a natural and admirable skepticism regarding those with heroic ambitions, above all when their ambitions tend toward the dictatorial.

Yet democracies, like all human societies, and indeed like all individuals, need heroes and require a vision of greatness if they are to achieve their potential. The Athenian poet Aristophanes has his chorus praise Athena, the presiding goddess of that democratic city-state: "Thou great aristocrat: Make this people noble. Help us to excel." True excellence, the poet suggests, is accessible to all, not merely to those of noble lineage. It is essential to American democracy, no less than it was to Athenian democracy, to reconcile greatness of soul with liberty and equality.

How can this be done? What does the hero, the extraordinary man, have to do with the *demos*, the people in all their varieties of ordinariness? What effect *does* the hero have on the *demos*, and what effect *ought* he have? Or is the concept of a democratic hero at best a paradox, at worst an oxymoron?

The Greek tragedians were preoccupied with just such questions. The essential tension in all the great plays is between the protagonist and the chorus—that is, between the hero and the *demos*. In the plays of Sophocles, the chorus has the last word, but it is the hero who acts with elevated insight and daring. The chorus is often frightened, confused, or revolted by the heroic action of the play. The hero may turn to them for advice or comfort, or he may chastise them, scorn them, or simply move beyond them. In the end, the hero suffers violence, death, or translation to another world, while the chorus survives. And, as the poet and critic Will Fletcher has observed, in Sophocles above all, the chorus usually speaks better than it knows, since the religious truisms and gnomic pieties with which it begins have, thanks to the hero's actions, been transformed and deepened, enriching our understanding of the human condition.

Shakespeare's *Coriolanus* dramatizes this tension between hero and people. Coriolanus, a general of heroic proportions, is forced to submit to the approval of the Roman mob in order to be elected to office. The electoral process involves his standing in the marketplace, showing his war wounds to the public, and begging for their vote. He finds this ordeal repugnant and disgusting. The mob admires his heroic qualities, for he has saved them from their enemies both recently and on prior occasions. He is so feared by the enemy that the mob believes him to be personally responsible for such peace as the city enjoys. But the mob also fears his contempt and hates his very greatness. In other words, the *demos* is deeply ambivalent toward the hero Coriolanus.

On the other hand, the Roman tribunes—envious, sly, small men whose power will be checked if Coriolanus is elected—are violently jealous of him. He arouses in them *ressentiment*, as Nietzsche and Scheler understood it, and they fear his *virtù*—just as lesser people always fear the genuine. They know that if provoked, his arrogance and pride will cause him to turn on his fellow citizens. By controlling the mob, the tribunes bring about their desired result. Coriolanus, infuriated by the people, speaks truthfully and outrageously, and is finally banished from Rome. Informed of his banishment, he replies with sublime arrogance:

You, . . .
. . . whose loves I prize
As the dead carcasses of unburied men
That do corrupt my air, *I* banish *you!*
And here remain with your uncertainty!
Let every feeble rumor shake your hearts!
Your enemies, with nodding of their plumes,
Fan you into despair! Have the power still
To banish your defenders; till at length
Your ignorance, which finds not till it feels,
. . . deliver you as most
Abated captives to some nation
That won you without blows! Despising,
For you, the city, thus I turn my back.
There is a world elsewhere.

This completes the first great action of Shakespeare's tragedy. But the play goes further: In a sense, once banished from Rome, for Coriolanus there is no "world elsewhere." His reputation as a great general and his status as a man without a city combine with his own willfulness to further darken the tale. Banished from Rome, Coriolanus becomes Rome's greatest enemy. He joins forces with the general Aufidius, once his greatest rival, Rome's most powerful enemy. Together they lead a huge force to the walls of Rome. Coriolanus's heroism and pride have led to betrayal of the city that had fostered in him precisely those qualities. Drawing on the greatness that made him the noblest Roman, he becomes the most treacherous. "A man outside his city," Aristotle observes, "is either a beast or a god." Coriolanus, godlike in his power and sense of his own nobility, becomes bestial in pushing those qualities beyond tolerable human limits.

But there is a final development in the play, which unifies what has gone before. The Romans send Coriolanus's mother to plead with him not to destroy Rome. The mother says much and Coriolanus says very little, but he agrees to spare the city even though he realizes that this will cost him his life.

Not only in *Coriolanus* but in many of Shakespeare's dramas, as in life, there is a point of no return. For instance, until Duncan has been murdered, Macbeth might still have been a "royal" man. By joining with Rome's enemies, Coriolanus passes the point of no return. He commits moral suicide. His virtues, everything that once made him great, are Roman virtues. In turning against Rome, he is destroying the city that has been his spiritual mother. When his natural mother speaks to him as Rome, his civic mother, he regains his integrity, but pays with his life. Morally saved but physically lost, the hero-become-villain is hero once more. His civic crime aborted, he is guilty only of betraying the alien Aufidius, who sets upon his old rival with a large number of men and kills him, trampling him into the ground. Thus the hero is again united with his spiritual motherland—Rome.

In following the movement of a great man from popular hero to villain and back again to a lonelier but perhaps even greater hero, Shakespeare explores the paradoxical status of the democratic hero. The proud, capable man must be both better than the mob and acceptable to the mob if he is to lead them and save them. The outstanding man must transcend and yet be accessible to the ordinary citizens of Rome. The difficulties of this concept must be examined if the democratic hero is to be understood.

In a democracy, a fundamental obstacle to the emergence of political heroes lies in the electoral process itself. If heroes are to lead the people, the people will have to elect them. It is the conventional wisdom that a successful American politician must please a majority of his constituents. But what attracts everyone or even a majority? Goethe provides one answer:

> Baseness attracts everyone; if you see something being done quickly by a number of people, you may at once conclude that it is something base.

Or, as William Blake put it:

> Great things are done when Men & Mountains meet.
> This is not done by Jostling in the Street.

Such considerations may explain the sneering tone of some remarks recorded in Alexis de Tocqueville's diary in 1831:

> When the right of suffrage is universal, and when the deputies are paid by the state, it is singular how low and how far wrong the people can go.

(Tocqueville here looks askance at the American practice of paying legislators so that people without independent means might serve. In Tocqueville's time, neither the French deputies nor the English members of Parliament were paid a salary.) Several days later, traveling on a steamboat, Tocqueville met a man who had left his first wife, gone to live among the Indians, taken an Indian wife, and also on many occasions taken to drink. On hearing that this man was also a former government official who, in Mark Twain's phrase, had lit out for the territory, Tocqueville believed he had found proof that the people can go low and far wrong indeed:

> We are traveling at this moment with an individual named Mr. Houston [Tocqueville writes]. . . . This man was once Governor of Tennessee. . . . I asked what could have recommended him to the choice of the people. His having come from the people, they told me, and risen "by his own exertions." . . . They assured me that in the new western states the people generally made very poor selections. Full of pride and ignorance, the electors want to be represented by people of their own kind. . . . [To get elected,] you have to haunt the taverns and dispute with the populace.

But Tocqueville was soon forced to reappraise the wisdom of the backwoods Jacksonians who had elected Sam Houston governor of Tennessee and would, a few years later, elect him the first president of the Republic of Texas. Fascinated by this man of the people, Tocqueville questioned Houston about his life among the Indians, and before long was taking notes on their religion, their government, their concepts of justice, and the roles of their women.

> Does it seem to you [Tocqueville asked] that the Indians have great natural intelligence?
> Yes [Houston replied], I don't believe they yield to any human race on this point. However, I am also of the opinion that it would be the same for the negroes.

The conversation then turned to an analysis of U.S. government policy toward the Indians, and once again Tocqueville took copious notes. Both men, it turned out, were concerned with protecting the Indians. Summing up his impression of Sam

Houston, Tocqueville no longer sneers but is sympathetic and, finally, deeply impressed by this man of the people:

> The disappointments and labors of all kinds that have accompanied his existence have as yet left only a light trace on his features. Everything in his person [concludes Tocqueville] indicates physical and moral energy.

Sam Houston is one type of the democratic hero: ambitious, large-spirited, driven by a personal code of honor, in touch with the people and with the land, a friend to the indigenous peoples, and yet one of the foremost in promoting the spread of civilization into their territories. As Mark Antony says of Brutus in Shakespeare's *Julius Caesar:*

> His life was gentle and the elements
> So mix'd in him that Nature might stand up
> And say to all the world "This was a man!"

But it is surely worth remembering that Houston, honored as a genuine hero, died an outcast, despised by his fellow Texans for opposing the secession of Texas from the Union. Houston and other heroes have found that doing the right thing is seldom popular and often fails to achieve success in any obvious sense. Indeed, recognizing this fact—braving the unpopularity of opposing the popular—is one of the traits that defines the hero, especially in a democracy.

In September 1960 Dr. Frances Oldham Kelsey, an official of the Food and Drug Administration responsible for the approval of new drugs, received an application for a new sedative called thalidomide. Although the manufacturer pressed again and again for quick approval, Dr. Kelsey withheld it because she found the testing incomplete. This led to accusations that she had libeled the manufacturer. After pressuring Dr. Kelsey for a year, the manufacturer conceded that the drug had been withdrawn from sale in West Germany. Incredibly, however, the company continued to press the application in the United States. Dr. Kelsey held firm. By March 1962 the association of thalidomide with birth abnormalities was clear, and the manufacturer finally withdrew the application. As a result of Dr. Kelsey's heroism, this country was spared the birth of perhaps thousands of seriously deformed infants. Europe, lacking similar heroes in its bureaucracies, was not spared.

Coriolanus raises still another question about the democratic hero. Besides the relationship of the great man to the crowd, with all its vagaries and vulgarities, what is the special role of the military hero or, more generally, the man of force? Two of the greatest speeches produced by democracies are eulogies for those who died in battle: Pericles' funeral oration and Lincoln's Gettysburg Address. And these great orators use a similar argument: that the deeds of dead soldiers are difficult or perhaps impossible to celebrate or memorialize in words. Speaking of the Gettysburg battlefield, Lincoln said, "The brave men, living and dead, who struggled here, have consecrated it far beyond our poor power to add or detract." And two thousand years earlier Pericles, defining what makes a democracy great, observed:

> To me, . . . it would have seemed sufficient, when men have proved themselves brave by valiant acts, by acts only to make manifest the honors we render them. . . . For it is a hard matter to speak in just measure on an occasion [such as this].

Yet Pericles also emphasizes that the essence of democracy is peaceful interaction between man and man. And Thucydides, who reports Pericles' speech, ascribes much of the later tragedy of the Athenian empire to an overemphasis on military adventurism.

The question may be posed in this way: What is the relationship between the peaceful working of a democracy and the man of force? Our own American military heroes have given us presidents that are great, good, and deficient: Andrew Jackson, Dwight Eisenhower, Ulysses Grant.

Still another question raised by *Coriolanus* involves what might be called the shadow of the hero, that is, the shadow cast by the hero—his effects on other men. On the one hand, he exalts and motivates; on the other, he intimidates and demeans. This tension, particularly severe in a democracy, is clearly recognized in Pericles' funeral oration. After speaking of honor, he directly addresses the relatives of those who died defending Athens:

> But for those of you here who are sons and brothers of these men, I see a great conflict awaiting you. For the dead are always praised;

and you, even were you to attain to surpassing virtues, will have a hard time being thought of—not as their equals, but even as men slightly inferior.

This phenomenon has frequently been seen in the history of art and literature, where preeminent artists, by the magnitude of their genius, have intimidated brilliant and gifted successors. Even so great an artist as Goethe suffered from this experience. Reflecting on Shakespeare's works, Goethe observed that, had they been written in German, there would have been nothing left for him to write.

Under the rubric of the heroic shadow, I group several negative effects of greatness. Among these are, above all, resentment—the envy and rancor greatness evokes among the less great; irresponsibility, as ordinary men look to those greater than themselves to shoulder all burdens; discouragement in those who despair of equaling heroes of the past; and, by no means least, harm—since greatness may consist in doing great evil. But perhaps most far-reaching, the hero's shadow is the seedbed of the antihero—not the villain, not the greatly evil man, but precisely the *anti*hero. That the hero should produce a climate repellent to heroism and conducive to its opposite is, though paradoxical, inescapable.

The examination of the hero and the ordinary man, the man of force and the peaceful citizen, and the shadow of the hero are aspects of our central problem. All concern the relationship between the hero and the people for whom he is a hero.

What can, what should be the relationship between the hero and a democratic people? The answer is that democracies, like all human societies, indeed like all individuals, need heroes and require a vision of greatness if they are to achieve their potential.

Our backgrounds inevitably shape our ideas about how greatness and democratic equality are to be reconciled. My own were molded by my Texas origins and by the role of the hero in Texas culture. The story of the fall of the Alamo is part history, part legend, and part myth. Now new light has been shed on it by the actor Peter Ustinov.

Asked by a Texan how he had liked making *Viva Max*, a fantasy on the retaking of the Alamo by the Mexican army,

Ustinov replied that he had not been terribly popular walking the streets of San Antonio dressed as a Mexican general.

But he remembered, he said, a meeting with Governor Preston Smith of Texas. The Governor ritually retold how the leader of the Texans, Colonel Travis, had drawn his sword, cut a line across the dirt floor, and voiced his famous challenge: "All who choose to fight and die for Texas' independence, cross over and stand with me."

"And Governor Smith concluded,"—and at that point Ustinov developed a rich Texas accent—" 'Every Texan crossed over that line with Colonel Travis.' " "But Governor," Ustinov replied, "If all those in the Alamo crossed the line and stayed, and if they all died with Colonel Travis, how is it that we know the story?"

Governor Smith was undaunted: "Mr. Ustinov, that's because a French feller named Rose refused to cross the line; he turned tail and ran. But he weren't no Texan."

"Ah," Ustinov responded, "Would he perhaps be the one who inspired that famous song 'The Yellow Rose of Texas'?"

This yarn did nothing to diminish the glory of our heroes; nor did an incident in 1960, during John F. Kennedy's presidential campaign. After a stunning speech to a large, enthusiastic crowd assembled in front of the Alamo, Kennedy wanted to make a quick exit. Turning to Maury Maverick, Jr., a local politician and a great-great-grandson of Sam Maverick of Boston, who, according to family legend, cradled the dying Crispus Attucks on the scene of the Boston Massacre,[1] Kennedy said: "Maury, let's get out of here. Where's the back door?" "Senator," said Maury, "if there'd been a back door to the Alamo, there wouldn't have been any heroes!"

It is extremely unlikely that we owe our account of the heroism of Davy Crockett, Jim Bowie, Colonel Travis, and the others to the yellow Rose of Texas. Rose would hardly have talked. Who then was the anonymous poet, the blind Texas Homer of the tale? Who composed this epic of an event whose end no Texan ever witnessed? The source is the situation. The defenders, outnumbered some twenty to one, gave their lives for freedom. Like Patrick Henry, they set a higher value on liberty than on life. The idea that the heroes could not foresee the end and went inadvertently to their death was inconceivable to Texans of the day. In order to understand, they had to imagine the tale of the heroic moment when the decision to stay was taken.

The story of the Alamo, as we now have it, provides a rational and satisfying account of an otherwise inexplicable event. The heroic myth reconciles the people to their past. It also provides us with democratic heroes who are satisfyingly manageable: heroism is more tolerable in the dead, since the dead no longer constitute a threat to the living.

But heroism has never been merely consigned to the grave-yard or to public statues of our honored dead. Traditionally, educational institutions—in all societies, from the simplest to our own—have considered courage a virtue and the hero as exemplary, an ideal to be imitated. Education has prepared individuals in a democratic society to embrace the hero. In recent years, however, the encouragement of heroism has been abandoned in some educational circles, either from resentment of greatness or the suspicion that greatness is elitist. But in Texas the sense of the heroic survives. Young people still learn of heroes and see them as models for emulation.

Not only in Texas but throughout the United States, educa-tion—which our democracy counts among the rights and duties of every citizen—ought to present the heroic as exemplary. The philosopher Alfred North Whitehead has argued that moral education depends upon our recognition of the essential role of heroes in our life: "The sense of greatness," he wrote, "is the groundwork of morals." A surprising statement. Whitehead is claiming that morality, which establishes the norms for action, is grounded in an appreciation of greatness, which, by transcending the norm, intensifies one's motivation to attain it. Whitehead continues:

> Moral education is a fundamental education of the whole self into action or being. This is impossible apart from the habitual vision of greatness. If we are not great, it does not matter what we do or what is the issue.

And this sense of greatness, he holds, must be embodied in myth or story, rather than in some dry catalogue of moral virtues or handbook of duties held up for our emulation. "The sense of greatness," Whitehead continues, "is an immediate intuition and not the conclusion of an argument." The story of the brave defense of the Alamo presents a more powerful image of moral greatness than any obtainable through courses in ethical theory. An essential and traditional function of literature and art is to provide such immediate intuitions of greatness; hence the central role assigned to literature and art in liberal education.

Simply recall how liberal education has fulfilled this function in the past. Documents from the Boston school system a century ago make it clear that the inculcation of the heroic life was crucial to the curriculum: Macaulay's *Lays of Ancient Rome,* Milton's *Paradise Lost,* Scott's *Ivanhoe,* and *The Boys' Froissart* were studied in high school. Students would already have read in grammar school about the history of England and the United States. Such figures as Queen Elizabeth I, Henry V, Sir Walter Raleigh, Washington, Lincoln, and Jefferson were held up to the young as models to be emulated. The circulating library for the grammar schools included *Ivanhoe,* Towle's *Magellan,* Longfellow's *Evangeline,* *What Mr. Darwin Saw in His Voyage Around the World in the Ship Beagle,* versions of *Tom Brown* and *Robinson Crusoe,* and Gilman's *Magna Charta Stories.*

High school was considered the proper time at which to introduce mythology. Berens's *Handbook of Mythology* was, for instance, required reading. The Boston school board stipulated that Cooper's *Deerslayer* and *Pathfinder,* Longfellow's *Iliawatha,* and Herodotus on the Persian Wars were to be available in at least 35 copies per class.

In *McGuffey's Readers,* the dominant textbooks of American education in the nineteenth century (they began to appear in the year Texas gained its independence), the emphasis is less dramatic but no less edifying. The heroic is domesticated and brought within the purview of a child. Greatness becomes accessible. Examples of Roman generals and European kings, queens, and knights are therefore rare. The greatness is of a smaller scale, but its relevance has been democratized. A prudent, honest, confident George Washington, a steadfast, compassionate Lincoln—these appear in the company of wise grandmothers, sacrificing parents, and good children. The moral impulse behind

McGuffey's Readers is the same as that which produced a sign on the wall of the San Antonio YMCA in the 1930s: "Don't wait to be a great man. Be a great boy!"

Unfortunately for us and the age, our educational system has become less and less effective in transmitting this birthright of heroism, these patents of potential nobility. With the tragic eclipse of the belief that every educated person should have read certain books (the Bible, Homer's *Iliad*, and Plato's dialogues, to mention only three), we have lost that inspiriting greatness of which Whitehead speaks. When welcoming freshmen to Boston University, I ask if anyone knows what Achilles and Patroclus had in common with Jonathan and David. One of the few students who had heard of any of them pointed out that they were all dead. Not one knew what these heroic pairs had in common. In despair, I asked them, "Well, what do they have in common with Starsky and Hutch?" At last they knew what I was looking for. That the paradigm of male friendship for this generation of students is Starsky and Hutch measures the decline of our educational system and our culture. The students often asked, "What's better about these old versions of friendship? Why aren't Starsky and Hutch more relevant? Why isn't one hero as good as another?"

The falsity of the dogmatic assertion of moral and aesthetic equivalence is obvious to those who are truly literate. The Old Testament is not only sacred to three major religions, but a superb distillation of human experience, good and ill. It not only has heroes, but a wide and coherent range of heroes and villains alike. It is a continuous saga of heroism in a world created by a single supreme being.

And the heroes of Homer's *Iliad* display the basic modalities of human existence: the importance of learning from life—about ripening, the meaning of excellence, the nature of friendship, the necessity of loyalty and courage, the tragic solitude of our condition, and the inevitability of death.

None of this is now a part of the common experience—the common curriculum—of high school graduates. This means that typical freshmen entering college lack the texts of their potential humanity, even their spiritual survival. They will all face, possibly before they graduate, surely before they are thirty or forty, the loss of close friends or a family member, the loss of love, disappointed hopes. Ignorant of the heroes of ancient Greece, ignorant of Biblical heroes, ignorant of greatness, they will think themselves historically alone, confronting a new condition unaccompanied. They will not know David's lament on the deaths of Saul and Jonathan. David mourned:

> The beauty of Israel is slain upon thy high places;
>   how are the mighty fallen!
> From the blood of the slain, from the fat of
>   the mighty, the bow of Jonathan turned not
>   back, and the sword of Saul returned not
>   empty.
> Saul and Jonathan were lovely and pleasant in
>   their lives, and in their death they were
>   not divided:
>   they were swifter than eagles, they were
>   stronger than lions.
> Ye daughters of Israel, weep over Saul, who
>   clothed you in scarlet, with other
>   delights, who put on ornaments of gold upon
>   your apparel.
> How are the mighty fallen in the midst of the
>   battle!
> O Jonathan, thou wast slain in thine high
>   places.
> I am distressed for thee, my brother
>   Jonathan: very pleasant hast thou been
>   unto me; thy love to me was wonderful,
>   passing the love of women.
> How are the mighty fallen, and the weapons of
>   war perished!

Had Achilles heard David's lament, he might have said that such words would have graced the death of Patroclus. Achilles could not hear these words; we can. We can, but do not. Lacking these texts of greatness, we may then find ourselves dumb when we most need to articulate our grief, deprived of the company of those who have suffered greatly before us and like us.

So the answer to our first question about the nature of the democratic hero—the relationship between the great and the ordinary—is that each individual must imitate the great. It might be objected that such imitation is incompatible with individualism. In refutation, Goethe again comes directly to my point: "Let none be like any other; but let each be like the Highest."

Our second question concerns the relationship between the hero of force and those whom he protects or of whom he takes advantage. Consider the legendary lawmen of Texas, the Texas Rangers, who in their origins were quite different from what they are today. Their myth lives in bronze in the statue in the airport at Dallas, which proclaims "One riot, one Ranger." Behind this is the reality that created the myth. Because the Rangers are a part of recent history as well as of myth, we can compare the two.

The conduct and practice of the Rangers in those early frontier days bore little relation to their activities after the frontier was settled. Nor do I intend to denigrate the accomplishments of the earlier Rangers, who brought law and order into a region that was, without their presence, chaotic and violent. But to assess the early Texas Rangers and the myth that grew up around them, we must see them as they were, both good and bad.

Myth sometimes arises to ennoble the man of force whose actual deeds do not match the ideals and aspirations of his calling. I believe this is true of the Texas Rangers, and it can be acknowledged without disparaging the Rangers or losing sight of their accomplishments.

I am here using the word *myth* in the looser popular sense of something that ranges from illusion to falsehood. Later I will use the word in its deeper and more generous sense.

The mythical Texas Rangers emerge in Walter Prescott Webb's book *The Texas Rangers: A Century of Frontier Defense.* Webb reports a Ranger captain as saying, "No man in the wrong can stand up against a fellow that's in the right and keeps on a-comin'." Webb begins by invoking the chauvinism of A. E. Trombly's poem on the Texas Rangers, which includes the peculiar notion that Mexicans, Apaches, and Comanches are all "strangers" to Texas. Trombly versifies:

> Ask the Apache the why of his going,
> Ask the Comanche, he's not without knowing;
> Question the Mexican thief and marauder

Why his respect for the great Texas border;
Question them all, these beaten-back strangers,
White-lipped they'll tremble and whisper "The Rangers!"

With this invocation, Webb makes use of that debased sense of myth that reaches to falsehood. The mythic Ranger emerges in Webb's summation of the character of a Ranger captain of those days:

> The main requisite of the Ranger captain is intelligence. He is all mind, and his mind works, not only in emergencies, but ahead of them; he anticipates the contingency and prepares for it. As part of this intelligence he must have judgment, and it must be almost unerring. A Ranger captain, to be successful, must combine boldness with judgment.

Or, as Webb puts it more succinctly, "The mind of the great officer encompasses that of the outlaw." Of the Texas Rangers he might have said that the *actions* of a great officer also encompass the *actions* of a great outlaw.

To gain insight into the actual life and mind of the Texas Rangers of that period, we can consider two statements quoted by Webb from Ranger Ira Aten, charged with patrolling fences in West Texas. The first reveals the depths of his diplomacy and personal resource. Nothing, he says, "will do any good here but a first class killing and I am the little boy that will give it to them if they don't let the fence alone."

The second quotation reveals a rarely stressed aspect of the Ranger's function as double agent or double-crosser. Aten sounds not unlike a weary spy from one of John le Carré's novels, ready to "come in from the cold": "These are my last fence cutters whether I catch them or not. . . . We have had to tell ten thousand lies and I know we won't get away without telling a million."

Enough true stories of the Texas Rangers might incline us to agree with the novelist James Jones: "The world will not be civilized until the last brave man is dead." This, of course, is wrong, but it is a mistake we are tempted to make, a natural reaction to the example of flawed heroes. But we must not allow the flaws of heroes to obscure their real accomplishments. The Texas Rangers and other lawmen who brought peace and the rule of law out of unrest and the rule of the strongest were heroes, however flawed.

To conclude: Uncritical idealization of the hero of force produces a false version of reality—a version that denies all claims and perhaps even the humanity of the victims; it holds up the mirror, not to nature, but to the narcissistic ego.

Turning now to the third problem—the shadow cast by the hero—consider first the malicious envy aroused by the very existence of greatness. Many heroic myths and legends take account of this *ressentiment* by creating particular gods or men who express this dark shadow effect of heroism.

In the Norse myths, the wisdom of Odin, the giant-killing power of Thor, and the beauty of Idun are constantly threatened by the deviousness, envy, and malice of the god Loki. Homeric gods provide no single analogue to Loki, surely because they are less heroic. The envy and destructiveness concentrated in the figure of Loki are diffused throughout the Homeric pantheon.

All attempts of the Norse gods to banish, bully, or imprison the protean Loki are destined to fail. He is a consummate shape-changer, a completely unscrupulous liar who, like all such creatures down to the Frog Prince, has a way with women. On Ragnarok, the Day of Doom, Loki, out of sheer malice, will join with the frost giants, the fire giants, the great serpent, and the great wolf to destroy heaven and earth. For Loki the sense of greatness is not the foundation of morals, but a gradual evolution from moral indifference to evil on a grand scale—that is to say, to cosmic wickedness.

Loki, acting out of envy and malice, brought about the death of Balder, most beautiful and gentle of Norse gods. Loki, living in the shadow of a stronger, wiser, and more splendid being, hated Balder. Loki's threats frightened Frigg, Balder's mother, and she journeyed through the entire world, asking and receiving from every being she addressed a promise to help, and never to harm, Balder.

As Frigg was returning home she noticed mistletoe growing on an oak. She secured the oak's promise, and she started to ask the mistletoe, but thought "It's too small and soft to do harm." She entered Valhalla and told her son that all was well.

After Frigg's return, the gods played at throwing spears,

darts, swords, and axes at Balder. Only Hoder, Balder's blind brother, could not participate. All the others watched with amusement and wonder as their weapons veered and fell harmlessly at the feet of the laughing god.

A disguised Loki drew the whole story, including her oversight, out of Frigg. He then went to Hoder, handed him a dart made of mistletoe, and guided him to the right position. Hoder, glad to be able to join in the game, threw the dart. It failed to veer, and Balder fell dead.

Now, in light of the myth of Balder, look at the assassination of President Kennedy.

It is not perhaps too fanciful for us to recognize in Kennedy the figure of Balder—strong and beautiful—and in Lee Harvey Oswald a modern counterpart of both Loki and Hoder. Like Loki, Oswald killed out of resentment and outrage, moved by envy and hatred of what is strong, splendid, and successful. But Oswald was also, we may suggest, like Hoder, the hero's blind brother, deprived and disadvantaged, too limited to be a player in the great events of his time. Eager to participate, like Hoder he kills when the weapon is handed to him. The weapon, moreover, may have been handed to Oswald by a force impelled by Loki's envy and malice. Like Hoder, Oswald may have been a tool of a far greater force: in his case, Fidel Castro.

It is even more interesting to note that Oswald perceived himself as a kind of hero, a perception that might have been encouraged by some American myths. I think of the (perhaps apocryphal) attribution to John Wilkes Booth of the phrase *sic semper tyrannis* after his assassination of Lincoln. Booth, who had often played in Shakespeare's *Julius Caesar*, explicitly compared himself to Brutus. Can Oswald, in some confused way, have compared himself to Booth?

Oswald had probably never heard of Loki, but he certainly knew of Booth. Or he may have made perverse use of the myths of the Lone Ranger and Superman, popular mythical figures suggesting that to the individual everything is possible. Indeed the Protestant ethos, with its emphasis on individual volition, has encouraged such myths, and certain parables of Jesus are often misread accordingly. These elements of our culture support a romantic exaltation of the individual along with an ignorant and dangerous underestimation of the importance of institutions.

Regardless of the trappings, the essential message is this: The hero is self-sustaining and self-validating; whatever good or evil he does proceeds from nothing but his own will; the individual, through willpower alone, can transcend the social milieu on which he depends. Absent from these myths is the recognition that the foundation of moral responsibility rests on the inescapable dependence of the individual on the social structure that sustains him.

Influenced by these myths, a blind child like Oswald or any of today's terrorists may think of themselves as Lone Rangers, as messiahs, whose individual decisions can transform history and ensure victory for whatever they conceive to be good. These delusions too are a part of the shadow of the hero.

But besides the villain, the man of evil whether great or small, there is another being who lives in the shadow of true heroism: the antihero. By antihero I do not mean those who are motivated by resentment or envy in response to the hero. Neither Loki nor Lee Harvey Oswald, neither Tamburlaine nor Milton's Satan, are antiheroes. They are perverse heroes, evil heroes; however wrongly, however terribly, they *act*.

The same is true of Lady Macbeth and Richard III, who share a ferocious and devious energy that has its own kind of magnificence. When Richard III announces, "Since I cannot prove a lover . . . I am determined to prove a villain," or when Lady Macbeth, to further her husband's ambition and her own, says:

> Come, you spirits
> That tend on mortal thoughts, unsex me here,
> And fill me from the crown to the toe top-full
> Of direst cruelty! Make thick my blood;
> Stop up the access and passage to remorse.

—we are in the presence of vicious but not unheroic persons.

Nor by antihero do I mean those who from within a culture achieve an understanding or an approach to life that challenges what the culture considers heroic. I think of Job, for instance, refusing to accept the arguments of his comforters, or of Hamlet, often seen as a man whose intelligence and excessive self-consciousness render him unable to act, a prototypical hero of that elevated consciousness in which "the native hue of resolution is sicklied o'er with the pale cast of thought."

This is a dubious reading of Hamlet, albeit the prevalent one. Close reading of the play suggests that once he has not only satisfied himself that his uncle is his father's murderer, but also gathered evidence to justify his action before his mother and his uncle's courtiers, Hamlet acts with resolution and speed.

The figure of the antihero differs from all these, though like them it emerges in the hero's shadow. There are several kinds of antihero: Some are repelled both by the idea of greatness and by those who exemplify it; others are frightened by greatness; still others, bored. All antiheroes share a conviction that heroism is not for them, but rather a fate to be avoided.

Perhaps the best literary portrait of the antihero is Prufrock in T. S. Eliot's "The Love Song of J. Alfred Prufrock." A weak, sensitive, and timid man, but conscious of heroism in human life, he occasionally contemplates doing something that might, for him, amount to an heroic act. But constantly, with an ironic sigh, he sinks back into passivity:

> No! I am not Prince Hamlet, nor was meant to be;
> Am an attendant lord, one that will do
> To swell a progress, start a scene or two . . .

Prufrock knows that there is an "overwhelming question" but asks us not to ask it, and instead, in his stream of consciousness, we find a portrait of a failing society that he is convinced has no use for serious questions. When all is said and done, he is conversing with himself, alone. His final realization is the fading of his life and his approaching death. Not daring to disturb the universe, he draws back from the seductive forces of life beckoning the hero, the same sirens who sang to Odysseus:

> I grow old . . . I grow old . . .
> I shall wear the bottoms of my trousers rolled.
> . . . Do I dare to eat a peach?
> I shall wear white flannel trousers, and walk along the beach.
> I have heard the mermaids singing, each to each.
> I do not think that they will sing to me.

The mermaids sang to Achilles and to David, to Sam Houston and Dr. Frances Kelsey; terrible as their song may have been, they also sang to Hitler, to Stalin, and to Lady Macbeth. With unmistakable self-pity and resignation, the antihero says sadly, "I do not think that they will sing to me."

The spirit of the antihero dominated students in the 1960s and early 1970s. Motivated by foolish and jejune ideas like those presented in Charles Reich's *Greening of America* (if Prufrock is the finest literary embodiment of the antihero, Reich is surely its finest academic embodiment), many sat on hillsides like first-century Montanists, smoking pot and waiting for Consciousness III—people for whom the only law of nature was the second law of thermodynamics. They were living out the myth of the antihero. And the result could only be—can only be—Prufrock's discovery that one's time is gone, that one's mortality has presented its fatal claim. What they found was the opportunity to be preternaturally inconsequential, to achieve a precocious obscurity. Such a person lives, gropes, and dies within the shadow of the hero.

The tragedy of Prufrock and those like him is that the mermaids may in fact be singing to them, but they simply fail to hear the song. This is a tragedy for them personally; it means that they are forever prisoners of the impotence of irony. But it is an even greater tragedy for our democratic society, which must have leadership in order to survive.

There is truth, of course, in what Prufrock felt, truth in the antihero. Whitehead's notion of the completely developed man—a central idea in defining the democratic hero—must include the sense of how short our lives are, how bounded—of how little we actually matter.

Our consideration of the shadow of the hero brings us to a related question, central to the concept of the democratic hero. How does an individual, aware of his finitude, unimportance, and mortality, achieve that sense of greatness that is or ought to be the motivating force of life?

Regrettably for us all, the question is more apt to be evaded than answered. The most common means of evasion is to abandon consciousness altogether in the mindless pursuit of pleasure. In thrall to hedonism, cut off from past and future, a disconnected present is all that remains of human life. Even when hedonism is pursued with cosmic intensity, as Don Giovanni pursues it, it betrays the final emptiness of the antihero's existence, ending necessarily in futility. The poverty and paucity of his meaning negate any notion of the heroic.

Another method of evading consciousness of the problem is deliberate denial of individuality. The denier feels no envy of the heroic personality; he is beyond the shadow of any individual greatness. I have in mind the "Marxist hero." He renounces all claim to, indeed all belief in, individual effort or worth; unselving himself, he finds his place within the historical dialectic. History for him is made, not by individuals, but by dialectical forces operating through social classes. He submerges himself, not merely *accepting* his destiny as an obscure member of society, but also *seeking* this as his fulfillment. The Marxist theorist Plekhanov describes him well:

> He not only serves as an instrument of necessity and cannot help doing so, but he passionately desires this, and cannot help desiring to do so. This is an aspect of freedom.

Orwell could hardly have invented a finer example of doublethink.

The Marxist playwright Bertolt Brecht reveals much more of the truth of communism than he perhaps intended when a disappointed follower of his Galileo says: "Unhappy is the land that breeds no hero." Brecht's Galileo, who bears little if any resemblance to Galileo Galilei, replies: "No, Andreas. Unhappy is the land that needs a hero." Brecht's Galileo might be happy in a world in which the last brave man is dead—but only after the revolution. The triumph of the social utopia will, of course, depend not on those trapped in the dialectic of history, but on those individuals who direct an elitist party structure, who regiment the ordinary citizen into poverty in order to sustain armed forces that threaten the peace of the world and seek to extend the revolution of mass-man everywhere.

But for those who refuse to abandon either consciousness or individuality, who thereby reject the nostrums of hedonism and Marxism, the problem of the heroic remains and must be confronted. In his ordinariness, the democratic man must discover that sense of greatness on which moral growth and achievement largely depend. If he is not motivated by greatness in the abstract, he must be able to appropriate a model relevant to himself—a man like Jefferson, whose greatness includes a refinement and a reach that to some seems beyond that of the common man, or a man like Sam Houston, whose greatness was expressed not only in heroic appetite, ambition, and achievement, but also in a magnanimity and a common touch that endeared him to Indians, Mexicans, blacks, frontiersmen, and French aristocrats.

The democratic hero, as these examples show, must be a multifarious man. His consciousness embraces many things; he is a man who, as Pericles said, "does many things well." He is not, and cannot be, simply a man equal to other men. American democracy is founded, according to Jefferson, on a natural aristocracy based on talent and virtue. The democratic hero must steer a course between the worship of force and the rejection of violence. Finally, he must attempt to cope with all those shadows cast by heroes present and past, and by himself.

Here we come full circle, since the democratic man in his ordinariness must discover in himself that sense of greatness on which, as Whitehead says, moral achievement depends.

The democratic hero remains, as he must, a paradox. For all their greatness, Jefferson, Houston, and the heroes of the Alamo, like all other men, were subject to the "discourtesy of death"— the ultimate democracy. The democratic hero, like all heroes however great, shares the mortality and limitation that attend all human endeavor. He lives not only in the great light of his significance—of which he may, like Sophoclean heroes, be unconscious, though we are not—but also in the stark realization of his insignificance.

This duality is eloquent in the great chorus of Sophocles' *Antigone*, which emphasizes both the brevity of man's life and the glory of his accomplishments on earth:

> Numberless are the world's wonders, but none
> More wonderful than man; the stormgray sea
> Yields to his prows, the huge crests bear him high.
> Earth, holy and inexhaustible, is graven

With shining furrows where his plows have gone
Year after year, the timeless labors of stallions.
Words also, and thoughts as rapid as air
He fashions to his good use; statecraft is his,
And his the skill that deflects the arrows of snow,
The spears of winter rain; from every wind
He has made himself secure—from all but one:
In the late wind of death he cannot stand.

This dual insight comes to us also from the Bible, in the words of the psalmist who intones man's insignificance:

As for man, his days are like grass; as a flower of the field,
    so he flourisheth.
For the wind passeth over it, and it is gone; and the place
    thereof shall know it no more.

And from another psalmist, who celebrates man's glory:

What is man, that thou art mindful of him?
Or the son of man, that thou visitest him?
For thou hast made him a little lower than the angels,
And hast crowned him with glory and honor.
Thou madest him to have dominion over the works
    of thy hands.
Thou hast put all things under his foot.

Or, once again, from *Job:*

Man, that is born of woman,
Is of few days, and full of trouble.
He cometh forth like a flower, and is cut down;
He fleeth also as a shadow, and continueth not.

This duality also comes to us from the Gospel of St. Mark, where Jesus tells His followers that in the kingdom of heaven "many that are first shall be last and the last first." Mark also tells how:

There came one running, and kneeled to him and asked him,
"Good Master, what must I do to gain eternal life?"
And Jesus said unto him, "Why callest thou me good? There is
    none good but one, that is God."

This humility, the humility of Jesus as true man, must be set against the passage in the Gospel of St. John in which Jesus claims to be true God:

> Thomas saith unto him, "Lord, we know not whither thou goest;
>   and how can we know the way?"
> Jesus saith unto him, "I am the way, the truth, and the life.
> No man cometh unto the Father but by me."

This Christian paradox, expressing the union of incompatibles, reveals our nature as humbler than the lowest, but at the same time divinely exalted by our share in the life of God. Jesus, "very God and very man," as the *Book of Common Prayer* puts it, unites these opposites, reconciles human frailty and mortality with divine greatness and immortality. The least of men may be the Christian hero. There has never been a more democratic conception.

The duality of human greatness and insignificance confronted not only ancient Greeks and characters from the Bible, but also confronts twentieth-century Americans—most powerfully, I believe, in the climax of Arthur Miller's *Death of a Salesman.* This play, I was told by one of my professors at Yale, could not be a tragedy. Why? Because tragedies had to do with heroes, and Willy Loman was just an ordinary fellow who failed because he was a bad salesman. Yet for Miller the life and death of a salesman is worthy of high art. It is about *us*, and we should not be ashamed to read it and to weep honest tears of recognition.

We find ourselves on both sides of that climactic scene between Willy Loman and his son, Biff, where Biff, out of a life of failure, tells his father:

> Pop! I'm a dime a dozen, and so are you!

And Willy replies:

> I am not a dime a dozen! I am Willy Loman, and you are Biff Loman!

Then Biff, at the peak of his fury:

> Pop, I'm nothing! I'm nothing, Pop! Can't you understand that?

Biff collapses in tears, and Willy says:

> What're you doing? What're you doing? [He turns to his wife and asks] Why is he crying? . . . Isn't that remarkable? Biff—he likes me! . . . He . . . cried to me.

Then Willy, choking with his love, cries out his promise:

That boy—That boy is going to be magnificent!

We do not have to choose between Biff and Willy. Both are right. They are a dime a dozen, and they are magnificent. The great fact about human beings is that we are both dime a dozen and magnificent. If we believe only that we are magnificent, we become insufferably arrogant at best; at worst, Tamburlaines. On the other hand, if we believe that we are merely dime a dozen, we lose our reason for being, the motivation for excellence, and the ability to sustain the disappointments and losses inevitable in even the happiest and luckiest lives. Heroism is not only essential to democracy, it is essential to the life of every human being. The genius of democracy is found in this paradox: that we are all a dime a dozen and that we are all magnificent. The democratic hero is not an ideal beyond our grasp; it is relevant and compelling to each of us.

We know simply by looking about us that wisdom is within the reach of us all, for some of the simplest human beings are wise. Virtue is within the reach of us all, for some of the least educated are good. Happiness is within the reach of anyone, for some of the poorest are happy. There is neither positive nor negative correlation between intelligence, learning, and wealth on the one hand and wisdom, virtue, and happiness on the other.

The mermaids sing each to each, and they sing to each of us. But not all of us hear their song.

Why should we resign ourselves to insignificance and forfeit our promise of greatness? Unless, in the words of Augie March, "you want to say that we're at the dwarf end of all times, and mere children whose only share in grandeur is like a boy's share in fairy-tale kings, beings of a different kind from times better and stronger than ours."

But we do not live at the dwarf end of time, heroism is not the stuff of fairy tales, and our times can be better and stronger than the past. These affirmations require courage to live while confronting the ultimate indignity of death. But that ultimate defeat does not rob us of the hope of victory in life. Only by loss of nerve do we forfeit victory.

Our education should prepare us to stand in the tradition of our heroes ancient and modern. Facing the certainty of the worst, we can respond to the challenge of the best—because, of course, we are all a dime a dozen, and we are all magnificent. Education in a democracy must proceed from a clear understanding of this duality.

Education and Democracy in the Age of Television

T HE DISTINCTION between education in democratic and nondemocratic societies is critical and profound. In a society without respect for individual rights, true education is impossible. In an unfree society the educators' only sanctioned role is to deceive, to indoctrinate, and to intimidate. Their role is merely to train; they make each student into a functional part of the great machine of state—of Leviathan, to use Hobbes's apt term. They *train*, they do not *educate*.

In a free society, on the other hand, the educators' role is far more complex and demanding. Their aim is to awaken in their students the love of freedom and an understanding of the nature and conditions of freedom, and its importance in the pursuit of truth. Educators must also encourage in their students that self-restraint essential to a free society—that restraint which recognizes and truly respects the rights of others as the condition of one's own rights. They do not seek to produce human machine parts or components, no matter how complex. They seek to guide each student toward an ideal defined by the philosopher Immanuel Kant: the ideal of *autonomous* individuals whose freedom lies not in doing whatever they please, regardless of the consequences, but rather in their ability, by means of reason, to exercise their freedom in accordance with moral and social laws that define the conditions of fulfillment for oneself and all other members of one's society.

Many today wonder whether there are such laws. Today,

autonomy often means nothing more than various forms of will-fulness: self-indulgence, carelessness, and ignorance. Individuals are encouraged by governments, by organizations, and by charismatic individuals to sacrifice their true autonomy to political ideologies or religious cults. In a free society, it is the educator's duty to demonstrate the limitation and falsehood of such alternatives.

Even within democracies, the ideal of truth has become unfashionable in certain intellectual and political circles. In the minds of some of our most influential scholars, writers, journalists, and politicians it has been replaced by relativism. In a sea of relativism, fidelity to truth is replaced by ideological conformity. In literary theory no less than in political science, many intellectuals have adopted the notion that opinions are not to be grounded in fact but only sustained by the advocacy of the expert. Outside the sciences, there is a tendency among many intellectuals to denigrate the Socratic search for truth as hopelessly naive or confused. Any teacher who pursues the Socratic quest, who seeks through diligent study and investigation the likeliest account of the nature of things, is rejected and ridiculed by the modern sophists. The Socratic quest has been replaced by the relativism of the sophists. Having cast out Zeus, Whirl is king; we again hear Protagoras' assertion that man is the measure of all things—indeed that there are as many different standards of measure as there are classes or even individuals.

The notion that all truth is relative and that there are no values worth defending is often confused with the notion of academic freedom. In reality, the two are very different and indeed contradictory.

Every university depends on academic freedom, a concept implicit in the life of the mind from the days of Socrates. As an explicit concept, academic freedom can be traced to the principles of *Lehrfreiheit* and *Lernfreiheit*—freedom to teach and freedom to learn—embodied in Humboldt's reforms at the University of Berlin early in the nineteenth century.

Today, unfortunately, many assume that freedom to teach and learn involves freedom from values and the absence of perspective. This notion would have been nonsense to any of the great teachers at the University of Berlin: Humboldt, Hegel, Schopenhauer, Einstein.

No university can be value-neutral. Its very being presupposes a commitment to the search for truth. It is committed to logical thought and scientific method. The work of the university cannot be performed unless the individuals who do it are humble before facts and logic, willing to test their experience against the experience of others, and assiduous in avoiding or correcting for prejudice and irrationality. Freedom to teach and freedom to learn do not exist in a vacuum. They exist, as Kant correctly observed, in a moral context in which practical reason is primary. Scientists and scholars are obligated to subordinate themselves to the rules and procedures of rational thought. Unlimited freedom is an oxymoron, for there can be no freedom unless we observe the conditions that make freedom possible.

The university, in committing itself to the search for truth, beauty, and goodness—those transcendentals articulated as its goals by the medieval philosophers and theologians—commits itself to academic freedom: freedom to teach and freedom to learn. Therefore it cannot be value-neutral or indifferent with respect to the conditions by which academic freedom may be attained. The myth of value neutrality is a tenet of positivism, a philosophical theory of science advanced in the late nineteenth and twentieth centuries. Positivism promoted the doctrine of value neutrality despite the fact that the myth had been exposed and laid to rest centuries before the positivists rediscovered it.

Plato understood the interdependence of facts and values. How, Plato asked, can you know what a thing is until you know its value? How can you define a knife, how can you say what a knife is, without knowing what a knife is good for? Only when you know its purpose, its value as a cutting instrument, can you know what a knife is. How could one understand the nature of water if one did not know the essential relationship of water to life—the dependency of plants, animals, and humans on water? To define water merely in terms of the formula H_2O, without reference to water's presence in other substances, guarantees profound ignorance of the nature of water. Someone who knows only that water is H_2O and that prussic acid is HCN can distinguish between them as compounds but will not know that one brings life and the other death. It is the combination of water with other substances described by other formulae and the relationship of all of these to human life that reveal the true nature, including the value, of water.

The knowledge to which we ultimately aspire is knowledge of the goal of human life, and the conditions for human fulfillment. In the past, the belief that there were transcendent principles by which we should guide our lives helped give society a goal and an understanding of the human condition. Writing in 1830, Alexis de Tocqueville noted that in ages of faith, people concerned themselves with a distant supreme goal beyond this life. In doing so, Tocqueville wrote,

> . . .they learn by imperceptible degrees to repress a crowd of petty passing desires in order ultimately to best satisfy the one great permanent longing which obsesses them. When these same men engage in worldly affairs, such habits influence their conduct. . . . That is why religious nations have often accomplished such lasting achievements. For in thinking of the other world, they have found out the great secret of success in this. But in skeptical ages the vision of the life to come is lost, a problem that is exacerbated in democracies, where people are set free to compete with each other to improve their situations. In such a combination of circumstances, the present looms large and hides the future, so that men do not want to think beyond tomorrow.

Tocqueville thought it especially important that the philosophers and rulers in skeptical democracies should always, as he says, "strive to set a distant aim as the object of human efforts; that is their most important business."

Tocqueville did not specify the nature of the goals that need to be set in such ages. But for our age such goals must transcend the quotidian if they are to give direction and meaning to life, both for individuals and for society as a whole. Such goals must presuppose a respect for truth and human fulfillment. Lesser goals would by their immediacy and triviality leave individuals so immersed in day-to-day affairs that they would fail to consider the future and thus fail to ensure the conditions on which their and their children's future depends. That is, in a secular age in which few believe in a life to come, and in which for many God is, if not dead, at best indifferent, an ennobling and motivating purpose—some secular equivalent of the kingdom of God—is essential. In a secular age it is unlikely that such a vision can be grounded in anything other than free pursuit of truth for the sake of human betterment.

Tocqueville wrote in an age when philosophers were occasionally listened to, and in which television advertisers had not replaced philosophers, educators, politicians, and business-people as instructors to the populace on ethics or human goals. Today knowledge is fractured in collages of facticity that defy coherent organization. The assimilation of large bodies of facts into knowledge and the organization of large bodies of knowledge into comprehensive systems of thought are preconditions to the attainment of wisdom.

Educating people for autonomy has never been easy. First of all, it can be done only by teachers who are themselves autonomous—teachers capable of ruling themselves in accordance with their intellectual and moral responsibilities. Good teachers do not succumb to the temptation of telling their students only what will amuse, titillate, or distract them. Good teachers accept the responsibility of doing the extremely hard work that is required to discover the truth and to make that truth known to students.

But today even the best teachers face an unprecedented challenge because they will almost certainly *not* be the primary educators of their students. Nor will the primary educators be the student's parents or other relatives or mentors. In the United States, and to a lesser but increasing extent in most democratic states, children sit before the television set for more hours than they spend in the classroom. But only a small fraction of their time may be spent in viewing programs intended for their instruction. They spend most of their time being perversely educated or directly corrupted and stultified by programs produced merely to entertain. The educational "bottom line" of commercial television—whether in news, in entertainment, or in commercials—is profit.

Television is the most important educational institution in the United States today, and within a few years it will be the most important educational force in all free societies. And what does it teach? Consider first what it teaches Americans about violence. Can we seriously doubt that the experience of violence brought daily and hourly into the home contributes to violence in the streets? Since the beginning of human consciousness mankind has known what Aristotle later set down as the most fundamental fact about education: that children learn by imitating. Imitation is the dynamic of all education. Common sense alone tells us that the repetitive presentation of violence on television presents a violent model for imitation. Even if viewers do not commit the violent acts they have witnessed, the deluge of televised violence drowns their sensibilities; revulsion and abhorrence, our natural reaction to violence, are suppressed. We become reconciled to violence as though it were a normal part of life, as indeed it has become.

We now face the situation that Mark Antony prophesied when, standing over Caesar's dead body, he said,

> Blood and destruction shall be so in use
> And dreadful objects so familiar
> That mothers shall but smile when they behold
> Their infants quartered with the hands of war,
> All pity chok'd with custom of fell deeds.

This is already happening—violence has become so common-place that we no longer find it terrifying; worse, we find pleasure in watching it. The advertising breaks, moreover, extend the range of miseducation—and this miseducation, resting as it does on *misinformation*, is certainly more pervasive and perhaps more dangerous than Soviet *disinformation*.

The power of the media to educate for good or ill can be seen most conspicuously in the way television advertising and programming flood viewers of all ages with sexual images. This depends upon our first understanding that sex—the ultimate expression of intimacy between two individuals—is debased merely by being portrayed for many millions of third parties. But the viewer, who has perhaps no desire to peer into the bedroom, finds the bed dropped into his living room. He is invited to observe a violent orgy. In the global village, with millions of peeping Toms, sex can hardly be intimate; the viewer becomes, willy-nilly, a voyeur.

Additional instruction about sex is available from television advertising. One lesson is that any substance which can be tasted, sipped, swallowed, licked, chewed, or rolled around in the mouth—wine, ice cream, vitamins, mouthwash, coffee, cigarette smoke, toothpaste, orange juice—is an aphrodisiac. Other items, most of which should not be chewed or swallowed—kitchen cleansers, floor waxes, razor blades, major appliances, motorcycles, automobiles—are presented as having similar powers. Children, regardless of age, are thereby bombarded with sexual enticements that they are often too young to understand or, if they do understand, too young to cope with. Only a generation or two ago, society as a whole and parents in particular recognized that there is a period in human development when overt sexuality is inappropriate and positively harmful. Parents then went out of their way to protect their children from premature exposure to sex. Today, even if they wish to protect them, how can they?

What does indecently premature and promiscuous exposure to sex do to youngsters? What harm is it? Can there be any doubt that the preoccupation with instant sex along with the suggestion that sex is a readily available commodity rather than one of the most consequential aspects of human life is to an appreciable degree responsible for the growing number of unmarried teenage mothers and fathers in the United States?

Whether for commercial or artistic motives, whether intentionally or not, television educates its viewers in a system of values. It teaches us that violence is normal and enjoyable; that the pursuit of sweetness or nutrisweetness is more important than nourishment; that happiness is no more than instant gratification; that sexual intercourse is to be engaged in by casual strangers or even enjoyed as a spectator sport.

What is being taught is nihilism sweetened with hedonism. Television teaches us to seek pleasure wherever we can find it, whatever the consequences. And because pleasure is transient, this commercial "philosophy" is one of insatiability, a life of endlessly frustrated and unsatisfied desire.

Trained to expect instant gratification from food, sex, and images of violence, Americans are further trained to expect instant gratification from the news. If understanding of the news cannot be popped like pills or potato chips, we must at least try to achieve instant insight—bite-sized understanding; so broadcasters believe, judging from American television practice. The industry operates on the educational theory that the viewer's attention span is limited to 90 seconds. The conventional wisdom that 90 seconds defines the attention span of the American public may explain why in televised debates candidates are rarely given more than two minutes to elaborate an answer. Under such a format, it is not surprising that candidates have appeared to be dwarfs. Anyone is likely to appear inconsequential under such limitations.

The fact that any good teacher can hold the attention of students for 50 minutes is conveniently ignored. Television, by imposing the 90-second standard, is training American audiences to limit their attention span to 90 seconds; it thereby contributes to the illiteracy of those it should be educating. Consider the effects of this on Americans' understanding of world issues and matters of grave national import. Instead of presenting the news coherently, it has reduced the news to a form of episodic entertainment—the "miniseries of reality."

News treated as entertainment—the way it is presented today on television—involves a form of censorship. The president of the United States gives, let us suppose, a major speech. What happens? A commentator precedes the speech in order to "prep" the public by telling it in predigested form what the president is about to say. After the speech, a panel of commentators tells the public what the president has just said. In doing so, no commentator merely reports the president's words—that would be repetitive and therefore lack entertainment value. Instead, the commentators add their own interpretations and emphases. Next, politicians from the opposing party comment on the speech— but this is still not enough. Even more remote commentators are called upon to interpret the speech: Experts from other nations are summoned to tell us not only what our president said but what it means. Finally, to top things off, the network calls upon experts from the Soviet Union who comment on the president's sincerity and credibility. Can one imagine that during the Battle of Britain the BBC would have followed Churchill's speech "We will fight them on the land and on the sea . . ." by switching to Berlin for a comment by Dr. Goebbels? Would the radio have followed FDR's fireside chats with a commentary by Herbert

Hoover? Would our country have started to revive and rebuild if, following FDR's statement that "we have nothing to fear but fear itself," a series of pundits had come on to say how many different things there were to fear—joblessness, hunger, disease, and so on?

Like all of us, journalists are subject to the temptations of power. Power tends to corrupt them no less than it corrupts politicians. And as the fourth estate has become vastly more powerful through television, the journalists in the electronic media should be aware of their increasing vulnerability to corruption. Many journalists come to think of themselves not so much as objective reporters but as the loyal opposition. But this is not the proper function of reporters. The adversary relationship is not a relationship of objectivity. To be in opposition may be the duty of a politician or a party, but it is a violation of the responsibility of the journalist, which is to report on what happens as objectively and as dispassionately as possible.

The reporter's work should be like a pane of glass, flawlessly clear and unspotted, through which the viewer or reader can see the important events of the day. Today, the practice of "personal" journalism in news reporting has frequently sacrificed objectivity for entertainment and the personal gratification—and presumably the greater popularity of the reporter. This involves a conflict of interest that any good reporter would be quick to point out if he found it in a politician. The pane of glass is thereby dirtied and distorted. Too often we see and read not what actually happened or what was said, but the personal views of the fourth estate.

But distortion results not only from the practices of individual reporters; even worse distortion comes from the practice of *creating* the news instead of *reporting* it. It has always been the passion of news organizations to be "first with the news." In recent years, especially on television, this traditional imperative has degenerated into a scramble to report the news before it happens. Each month the government issues various economic statistics on unemployment, inflation, trade, the GNP, and the like. The broadcast news day begins, not with a report of these figures after they are released, but with an account of what various experts *predict* will be reported. "Today," the television reporter intones, "the government will report that the trade balance has deteriorated." Several years ago there was a period of about six months when, month after month, the experts— doubtless hoping against hope—predicted an increase in unemployment. Month after month the figures, when released, proved the experts wrong. Their errors did not, however, result in broadcasters seeking new experts who could provide more reliable forecasts. Nor did they abandon this exercise in soothsaying and return to the practice of reporting the news "as it happens"—which can only mean after it happens.

The most extreme, pathological, and damaging form of such soothsaying comes in reporting election results. Networks are not content to report the votes as they are counted. For thirty years, they have attempted, even while the polls are still open, to project final results on the basis of early returns. More recently they have begun projecting the results on the basis of so-called exit interviews before *any* votes have been counted. Once the evening network news has been broadcast on election day, Americans west of the Rockies go off to vote after the networks have already told them there is no point in doing so, because the result is already known.

Can one imagine a clearer instance of contempt for the democratic process? In Canada, where the right to a free election is held higher than the right of prophecy, news organizations are not allowed to report on voting until the polls have closed on the west coast. Perhaps the First Amendment prevents similar legislation in the United States. But nothing requires that networks place their profits ahead of a free election—an election conducted without the electorate's being intimidated by an anchor who says, in effect, "Go ahead and vote, but it doesn't matter." If network executives cared deeply about democracy, they would long ago have voluntarily stopped substituting this pernicious soothsaying for real reportage.

I do not question the legal right of the media to anticipate and distort the news. I oppose censorship of any kind, direct or indirect. I simply wish to ask: Can democracy, which depends on a people soundly educated on complex issues, and on the clear expression of the will of the people, survive the current self-indulgence of the media?

One fact is certain: If democracy does not survive, the free media will not survive either. All media are dependent on freedom for the fulfillment of their mission. They cannot with impunity compromise with those who would restrict freedom. And yet the American media, alert watchdogs against the faintest threats to freedom within America or within countries that are pro-American, are far less responsive to real threats to freedom elsewhere.

Why, every night, should not the media of a democratic nation report, in effect: "We wanted to cover the war in Afghanistan, but we could not because the Soviet government threatened to shoot any reporter we sent to the front; we would like to bring you pictures and stories about the Soviet gulags, but we are not allowed to go there and take pictures of them. We would like to bring you pictures of the conditions in Fidel Castro's prisons, but Castro will not permit it. We would like to bring you pictures from Nicaragua of ten of the worst political prisons in Latin America, including an underground prison near the Inter-Continental Hotel in Managua, where the Sandinistas detain and torture political prisoners. But despite the fact that we know this prison is next door to the hotel where our reporters stay, we cannot report on it"? These and other reports should be regularly filed, published, and broadcast from every place of repression and totalitarian rule in the world.

Consider the media's indifference to the suppression of Nicaragua's only opposition newspaper, *La Prensa*. Newspapers gave more coverage of the Sandinistas' decision to reopen it than they did to its closing. The Sandinistas have constantly harassed and censored *La Prensa*, but the fact is seldom reported. And when *La Prensa* was shut down, there was an embarrassing silence about this blow to free and independent journalism.

Few Americans were able to hear Mrs. Chamorro, the widow of *La Prensa*'s heroic editor Pedro Chamorro, to witness her quiet courage, her dignity and determination, her deep sadness at the extinction of this 104-year-old institution that had resisted and survived one dictator after another. I was in the Capitol building when Mrs. Chamorro was presented with a commendation by the Center for Democracy. In the presence of senators and congressmen of both parties, the commendation was presented by Democratic majority leader Senator Byrd. This event went unreported by the national media—treated as a nonevent involving nonpersons—an obliviousness of the media to the demise of Nicaragua's *La Prensa* that amounts to self-indictment and self-betrayal.

Many in the media increasingly appear not to value—at least for others—the freedom without which they themselves cannot survive. Their naïveté would be comic were it not so dangerous. In 1987, I watched one of the leading personalities in the news operation of a major network interviewing an expert on the prospects for arms control. The interviewer expressed the hope that the United States would make some impressive gesture toward the Soviets that would lead to a breakthrough. The expert doubted whether the Soviets would respond to such a gesture. They would have to, the reporter asserted, for their media would make them do it. This response illustrates what is meant by the communist term "useful idiot," and the anecdote, or, rather, the horror story, suggests the magnitude of the task facing those of us who would presume to educate the educators.

Since the media—not the primary and secondary schools, not the colleges and universities—have now become the chief educators of the American people, those working in television must assume the duties of educators as well as those of journalists and entertainers. If journalists and entertainers were not teachers, they would not be obligated to concern themselves with the question, "Am I corrupting the youth?" But that Socratic concern is central to any teacher. Can journalists and entertainers responsibly ignore the professional obligations that follow from their status—their manifest role—as teachers to the world?

The issue is not one of the law or of legal obligations. I am not suggesting that censorship or the curtailment of freedom of expression is the solution. The same freedoms guaranteed to Americans by the First Amendment to their Constitution are fundamental to democracy everywhere. Even if journalists write with reckless irresponsibility that may lead to disastrous consequences, including even the loss of freedom, they should be free to write as they please. But true freedom exists only in a context of self-restraint in which one limits his actions in recognition of the rights of others and in recognition of the social context on which all rights depend. People who would be self-governed must first of all govern themselves. That requires self-restraint by each citizen and especially by the educators of citizens.

Journalists already practice self-rule in matters where they are not bound to do so by law. Why does a journalist not reveal his sources? Not because of the law, but because he recognizes this as a moral obligation, or at least a prudential obligation— a protection for future sources of information. Self-restraint cannot be limited, however, to this matter alone or merely to journalists. All members of the media must sooner or later engage in self-restraint or they run the risk, because of the power and pervasiveness of their teaching, of destroying the society on which their livelihood and profession depend.

If we heedlessly trash the minds, indeed the very souls, of our children; if through reiterated models of violence and the false promise of endless instant gratification we produce generations incapable of self-discipline and restraint; if we encourage the development of insatiable men and women who put the pursuit of pleasure before the pursuit of happiness; if by shortening the attention span we create persons incapable of complex analysis and responsible judgment; if we distort events of the day, garble the words of our leaders, simplify the character of nations, positing a false equivalence between democratic and totalitarian governments—there can be only one result. A dictatorship may survive by virtue of the strength of one man and an army that stands behind him, but the survival of democracy depends upon the moral virtue and reasoning power of all its people and on their participation in government as responsible, understanding citizens. If the media fail to assume responsibility for their immense power to educate free men and women, how will democracy survive the onslaught of false and counterfeit values and false and counterfeit information?

Those of us who have made education our vocation, our calling, are in turn called upon to educate the future men and women of the media on their own true identity as educators and on the responsibility that follows from this fact. We are called upon to resist the entertaining but largely chaotic present and to teach that human knowledge and rational action must have a vector—a movement in some direction. To know enough to live decently as human beings, we must be free to follow evidence wherever it takes us. To follow the evidence, we must be capable of following the rules of logical thinking. Therefore, the educator cannot be value-neutral with respect to truth. The true educator must reject mere relativism on the one hand and ideology on the other.

Just as there is a difference between academic freedom and value neutrality, there is an equally profound difference between the rules of sound thinking and the constraints of ideology. The limitations imposed on thought by reason, by rational procedures, by scientific method, by facts, and by respect for the freedom and experience of others are not constraints but, rather, conditions essential to the enterprise of thinking. Ideology, on the other hand, accepts in principle and inevitably demands in practice that we overrule reason, ignore method, falsify facts, and constrain the freedom of others in the projection and defense of preestablished objectives void of any rational legitimation.

An ideology cannot be refuted by a counterideology. It must be exposed by those who are committed not to one ideology or another but to the search for truth. Within an ideological framework, there is no truth or reality or history—except the "truth," "reality," and "history" generated by the ideology itself. Therefore, in order to refute an ideology, one must subject all its claims to rigorous tests for truth.

To describe our relationship to the Soviet Union, for example, as a war between ideologies is, in effect, to declare the epistemological equivalence of the United States and the Soviet Union. If we grant the epistemological equivalence of the two societies, their moral equivalence follows in easy steps.

The conflict is really one between a brutal totalitarian ideology on the one hand and all free societies engaged in the pursuit of truth on the other. When asked why he left the Soviet Union, Michael Voslensky, author of *The Nomenklatura*, said it was because of his inability to change his views simply because the party had altered its ideology.

Anyone remotely knowledgeable about the history of the twentieth century will recall Stalin's reversal of his assessment of Adolf Hitler and Nazi Germany at the time of the Molotov-Ribbentrop pact when he established an alliance with the Nazis

(1939). This total reversal in the factual assessment of Nazi Germany and in the moral position taken toward it would be impossible in a society committed to the truth. It is totally consistent, however, with the Leninist position that whatever supports the revolution is true because the success of the revolution—at whatever cost in human lives and human suffering—is the only unalterable goal. In this instance, the alliance with Hitler gave Stalin additional time for war preparations and the opportunity to take Finland and half of Poland.

The substitution of talk about ideology for a discussion of the facts and of truth has been the source of widespread confusion and has led to the intellectual disarmament of the democracies. Those who beat the sword of truth into the plowshare of ideology can neither fight nor farm—neither defend their freedom nor feed themselves.

Because the university is committed to the development of human purposes and to the realization of human values, it is also committed to a few limited political objectives. The university, by its very nature, is committed to democracy, to that form of government that recognizes and defends the fundamental human rights of freedom of thought and freedom of expression. No university can be neutral or indifferent with regard to those nations that have imposed serious restraints on freedom of thought, freedom of inquiry, and freedom of expression.

Consequently, the absence of value neutrality with regard to freedom or the pursuit of truth is no shortcoming in a university. On the contrary, commitment to that freedom essential to the pursuit of knowledge is necessary for a university. Such a commitment is part of its definition.

Universities can thrive only under that form of government which protects and ensures the exercise of human freedom. Consequently, no university worthy of the name can pretend to be value-neutral in the assessment of the United States and the Soviet Union. If a university promotes the doctrine of moral equivalence between these two nations, presenting them as two equally valid systems of government or as two equally culpable parties in the history of our time, it repudiates the conditions of its very existence.

Whether we realize it or not, the doctrine of moral equivalence becomes a weapon in the hands of the enemies not only of the United States but of freedom. It turns the goodwill and openness of Americans—their honesty, their willingness to confess their sins and do penance for all their faults large and small, real or imagined—into a weapon for use by the Soviets. Those who teach this doctrine expect everything of us and little of the Soviets, thereby reducing us to an equivalent inadequacy. By means of this doctrine and their own naïve goodwill, free men and women are not only exploited but put their own free societies at risk.

It is therefore appropriate that a university, by its very nature committed to freedom, concern itself with the defense of the free world—and hence with defense issues. Universities worthy of the name, in whatever nation, should align themselves with principles observed always in theory, and generally in practice, by the free democracies.

This does not mean that we should disregard the deficiencies of the United States. It means rather that we are free, and indeed obligated, to recognize them and to call attention to them—because ours is the pursuit of truth, not of ideology. If our universities so educate our journalists and our citizenry that they come to prefer the success of the United States to its defeat by its enemies, educators will be doing no more than their job. They will be meeting the obligation placed on the university: to teach that freedom is the *sine qua non* for fulfilling the human spirit.

Academic Freedom and Civilization

WHAT ARE the essentials of civilized society? Not indoor plumbing, modern hospitals, or antibiotics; nor the stock exchange, large armies, or systems of rapid transportation. People have lived in civilized groups without any of these, and some societies in which all were present have been barbaric.

Alfred North Whitehead thought that civilization was "the victory of persuasion over force" and that civilization exists to the degree that ordered human life is achieved by means of rational persuasion rather than appeal to brute force.

At the most primitive levels, differences among people are resolved by force, and right is defined and enforced by the stronger party in physical combat. This can scarcely be the mark—indeed it is the antithesis—of civilized existence. As we introduce more and more elements of persuasion and tolerate fewer and fewer appeals to brute force in our achievement of social order and stable individual life, the skins of savagery are replaced by the clothes of civilization.

As long as a society—no matter how affluent or militarily sophisticated—appeals to force rather than to the consent of the governed in preserving order among its people, it is not civilized. A society in which public policy is set by one powerful man's unexamined views rather than by careful examination of alternative views and the adoption of the one that seems most reasonable and desirable is not civilized. Moreover, that individual who in private dealings with others gets his way by force—whether personal, economic, or physical—is not civilized. And, by contrast, the civilized society and the civilized individual proceed by rational persuasion, by pointing to facts and arguments, by seeing many sides of each question, and by acting on that proposal which most adequately takes into account the important truths in each divergent view.

This is not to deny that there is a civilized as well as a barbaric use of power. Ultimately, force may be required if order is to be maintained. But in a civilized society force follows the rational determination of policy and is never the justification of the policy it enforces. If an individual or a group rejects persuasion and decides on a course destructive to others or to society itself, it may be prevented from doing so by truly civilized force wielded by those who have persuasive, rational grounds for exercising it. Since the appeal to force is never totally abandoned nor the appeal to persuasion ever entirely effective, the difference between civilization and barbarism is a matter of degree.

Nevertheless, this difference in degree is also a difference in kind. The distinction between civilized recourse to power as a last resort and the wholehearted embrace of power as a way of life is a crucial one. Examples of this distinction immediately spring to mind: England under Churchill and Germany under Hitler; India under Nehru and the Soviet Union under Stalin; Al Smith in New York and Huey Long in Louisiana. Moreover, among our friends and associates we can distinguish those for whom rational persuasion and those for whom insensitive domination is the natural mode of self-expression.

But we should not be beguiled into thinking that civilization comes easily to either individuals or nations. The renunciation of power is one of the most difficult of human acts, and we may ask, without cynicism, whether power is ever voluntarily renounced. Alfred Adler and many other psychoanalysts have joined St. Augustine in insisting that man has a natural craving for dominion over others, and that, far from welcoming civilization, man, both individually and in groups, must be induced to strive toward it and readily departs from it at the first opportunity. The urge for and delight in power is so pervasive, basic, and corrosive as to justify Acton's famous observation that power tends to corrupt and absolute power corrupts absolutely.

This pessimistic view of mankind, well confirmed by history, is the orthodox position of both Christians and Jews, and it was shared by the American founding fathers. Given this accurate assessment of human nature, we have found only one satisfactory way to domesticate power: Divide it. Division of power characterizes the political history of the United States. Power was divided among the people by elections, and within the government by the creation of coordinate branches. In domestic life, power was divided through the emancipation of slaves and women. These developments mark victories of persuasion over force. When, in public and private life, power has been concentrated rather than divided, the tendency toward brute domination has increased and civilization has been retarded.

Civilization has waxed in those moments of history in which freedom has been permitted, in which divergences and differences have been tolerated, if not honored, and in which persons— even if prone to use brute force—have been opposed by their equals in power. When these conditions have been met, individuals have been compelled to strive for and maintain positions of authority by rational, spiritual, and artistic means. Civilization, to put the issue plainly, is expressed when the bullfighter is honored more than the slaughterer, the physicist more than the boxer, the poet more than the football player. The activities of the slaughterer, the boxer, and the football player are fundamentally brutal and power-oriented; hence their work, though valued, cannot deserve civilization's highest praise.

But what has all this to do with academic freedom? Almost everything. A university worthy of the name stands at the very apex of civilization. It is a community in which rational persuasion and recourse to artistic, spiritual, and intellectual achievement take precedence over the appeal to brute force. The power of a university is the power of mind and imagination in pursuit of truth, beauty, and goodness; it is not the power of muscles, money, or political influence. More than any other institution, the university exhibits the victory of persuasion over force; and it has tamed power through the historically successful technique of dividing the power centers. Power within universities is fractured to a degree unknown in other institutions. Each and every professor and student is a power center and asserts his or her freedom—his or her right to self-determination and to the determination of at least a part of what the university as a whole stands for and is. And the moral safeguard of individual self-expression, on which a university's achievement in persuasion depends, is academic freedom and the courage of free individuals.

Academic freedom is both a description of the ideal way of life within an academic community and a basic right claimed by all members of that community. Even the very words "academic freedom" have a power of their own, not unlike the magic word of childhood, "tickalock." It is "tickalock," "King's X," and other incantations that transform the games of childhood from games in which the swift and strong can always win into those in which each child has a fair chance. And it is in part the magic of academic freedom that helps free the community of scholars from domination by unqualified but powerful members of society (or occasionally members of the academic community itself) who lack civilized attributes: self-restraint; respect for freedom, independence, and difference; and delight in the high, difficult, and subtle art of rational persuasion.

It is easy for those not associated with a university to underestimate the importance of academic freedom. But I know from my efforts to recruit faculty that one of the first questions asked by a prospective recruit is: Does your university have genuine academic freedom? The question means: If I come, will I be free to develop in my own way, according to my own interests and my own best judgment? Will I be free of doctrinal domination by older members of my department? Will I be able to teach courses in which I am particularly interested? Will I be free to teach and discuss what I know best? Will I be able to teach without forfeiting my rights as a citizen to engage in the political and social life of my community, state, and nation? Very few scholars will accept a post unless all of these questions can be answered in the affirmative.

These questions, frequently asked in the 1950s and 1960s, are scarcely raised today. The turmoil of the late 1960s and early 1970s made it clear that the chief threat to universities is not from outside assaults on academic freedom. Today, there is virtually no interference or restriction on the actions or opinions of professors by politicians, boards of trustees, or influential business leaders. Sadly, it is now more likely that groups of students led by faculty will attempt to suppress the academic freedom of a professor or a visiting speaker whose views they oppose; that is, the major threat to academic freedom today is from its misuse by professors and students who engage in what can only be accurately described as academic license. When the exercise of academic freedom degenerates into academic license through a professor's disregard for the rational procedures essential to the work of the scholar, academic freedom is lost and the integrity of the university is threatened.

In the public mind academic freedom is often identified with professorial tenure and job security. But this is a serious confusion. In the first place, students no less than faculty members have a right to academic freedom. Good students want the right to invite a provocative public figure to their campus. They want to hear all points of view and to argue with those who present them. They want to attend lectures by professors free to express their own views and not merely the safer views of others. They want their university to extend all the rights of citizenship to all students. They want the opportunity to experiment with ideas and movements and to gain wisdom through relatively harmless undergraduate excursions into folly. They want to examine many things and to hold fast to that which *they* find sound and true. They want, in short, the same independence their parents wanted at the students' age, and in the name of academic freedom they have a right to it. In the words of President Dodds of Princeton, "Ideas should not be made safe for students, but students should be made safe for ideas."

The difference between academic freedom and tenure is visible, again, in the fact that any good university guarantees its instructors academic freedom as soon as they arrive, whether tenured or not. Before receiving tenure, faculty members should expect to be evaluated individually over a period of years on their knowledge of their field, their respect for reason, their promise of originality, and their effectiveness as teachers. Regrettably, there are many institutions in which procedures to guarantee careful evaluation on these issues are lacking. But few universities would deny the appropriateness of this procedure.

Professors come to the campus, not with the assurance of tenure, but with the understanding that, if dismissed before being tenured, it will be due to contingencies of which they are aware from the start: The term of appointment has expired and there is no tenured position available; failure to evidence real excellence in research and teaching; or having been guilty of acts of moral turpitude. It is difficult today to give precise meaning to the concept of moral turpitude. Dismissals or resignations by mutual consent are still effected in cases of established criminal conduct, persistent drunkenness in class, or flagrant sexual harassment of students or colleagues. But by and large a teacher's private morals are now regarded as irrelevant to his professional status.

No beginning faculty member expects to wait for tenure before enjoying academic freedom. Academic freedom for both students and members of the faculty is guaranteed not by tenure but by the integrity of students and faculty.

Tenure does, however, provide a safeguard for the academic freedom of tenured faculty. By limiting the grounds and specifying the procedures under which tenured faculty may be dismissed, tenure regulations directly protect all tenured faculty members. (Administrators, who rarely have tenure in their administrative posts, often ensure job security by accepting tenured appointments as professors.)

Generally, tenured faculty cannot be dismissed except for cause—that is, incompetence, some serious breach of behavior, or termination of the department or school in which they serve. If an administration proposes to dismiss a tenured faculty member, it must inform him or her and state the grounds for its decision. Faculty members then have the right to legal counsel and a hearing before a special committee of faculty members empowered to decide whether their academic freedom has been violated. Although the administration is not bound by the committee's findings, it realizes that rejection of an adverse finding would have serious consequences. The general faculty might, in such a case, vote to censure the administration, and the American Association of University Professors (AAUP), after inquiry, might blacklist the university.

No administration takes lightly the threat of censure by its own faculty. The AAUP, however, has lost a good deal of its moral authority in faculty–administrative relations by becoming a trade union, and thus a legal adversary of the administration. In so doing it has forfeited its position as an arbiter and has become an antagonist. The AAUP still tries to do both, but its normative pretensions are no longer taken seriously. This is a loss both to it and to the academy.

Faculties are also aware—or should be—that academic responsibilities go hand in hand with academic freedom. Although a faculty will not tolerate restriction of its right to free speech in and outside the classroom, it should also recognize the obligation to speak and act in a manner befitting a member of an academic community—with reasonable taste, accuracy, and fairness.

The concern of academics for their own free speech does not appear to be endangered, but their general concern for the free speech of others does. It is much diminished from what it once was. While there is still general support of the right to dissent along currently fashionable lines, the right to dissent along unfashionable lines is increasingly denied. Jeane Kirkpatrick, Adolfo Calero, Caspar Weinberger, and other dissenters from academic orthodoxy have been howled down by mobs occasionally led by faculty members. Sometimes, as in the case of Dartmouth's handling of the *Dartmouth Review*, it is obvious that the right to dissent has been perverted into an Orwellian right to support the politically correct. From all accounts over the years the students who publish the *Dartmouth Review* have been guilty of serious lapses of taste and civility. They are lapses analogous to those routinely tolerated and often praised when performed by left-wing students. Indeed at Dartmouth left-wing students have erected illegal shanties, which they refused to remove when so ordered by the college authorities. They occupied college buildings. But none of them was reprimanded, much less suspended.

It is sometimes supposed that attacks on academic freedom usually issue directly from the central administration. This is almost never the case. Attack is far more likely to come from colleagues—from a department head who, along with other senior professors, finds the opinions or activities of one of their colleagues offensive; or, perhaps, from alumni who, because they are influential, suppose they are also wise and competent to decide what is or is not in the best interests of the university; or from trustees or regents whose success in business leads them to imagine that they are educators and uniquely qualified to set the course of the university; or, in a state university, from governors or legislators, or perhaps alumni of the university, who for some trivial political advantage prevent the appointment of an outstanding candidate to the board of regents.

Attacks on academic freedom also come from students—for instance, from a student who, moved more by fear than love of freedom, tries to discredit the university. It was at one time not unusual to find students who were good at decorating floats and organizing pep rallies, but like apathetic Germans of the 1930s did little or nothing when some of their classmates were denied basic civil rights. This was succeeded by a period in which youthful idealism and the search for justice were quickly replaced by the pursuit of power, and reasoned argument by coercion. In the late 1960s, students proved themselves particularly susceptible to the corrupting influences of power. Some were willing, not merely to protest, but to steal, commit arson, kidnap, and murder.

In these, as in most instances, the administration finds itself caught in a crossfire between those who would harm the university by curtailing its freedom and those who would militantly defend the free life of the university against any infringements.

The general public would perhaps be shocked to hear controversy praised for its own sake; to the man on the street this might seem decadent. Shouldn't the university support and defend truth rather than controversy? The question brings us to the heart of the matter. The strongest support of all freedoms, including academic freedom, is the historical fact that for mankind open controversy between different points of view is far better than the uncontested presentation of only one.

In the advance toward civilization, people have learned that "time makes ancient good uncouth," that the self-evident truths of the past are the patent falsehoods of the present. People have begun to regret that the greatest benefactors of mankind are so often punished or destroyed by those very people they are trying to help. Socrates, Jesus, Galileo, and Billy Mitchell are only a few of those who were punished and whose contributions were rejected as heresy or impiety by those who claimed a monopoly on truth and goodness.

The reflective student of history knows the full extent of the danger incurred when controversy is stifled and opinions alleged to be false are suppressed. Without controversy and argument we have no way of discovering which opinions are true and which are false; and this is dangerous. John Stuart Mill said it best:

> But the peculiar evil of silencing the expression of an opinion is that it is robbing the human race, posterity as well as the existing generation; those who dissent from the opinion, still more than those who hold it. If the opinion is right, they are deprived of the opportunity of exchanging error for truth; if wrong, they lose, what is ever as great a benefit, the clear perception and livelier impression of the truth produced by its collision with error.

The attempt by our forebears to suppress the opinion that the world moves around the sun cost Galileo his freedom and Giordano Bruno his life but did nothing to promote knowledge or virtue and greatly restricted the exercise of freedom and intelligence. When men are free, truth and knowledge prosper; without argument, diversity of opinion, and varieties of approach to truth, there can be neither freedom nor truth. Consequently, faculty acquainted with these basic historical facts and committed to the pursuit of truth acknowledge their respect for freedom, argument, and diversity of opinion as the soundest means of approaching truth.

It follows, of course, that professors have faith in the power of truth to win in the free marketplace of ideas, in Justice Oliver Wendell Holmes's phrase. Like our founding fathers, university professors should have that confidence in reason and truth bequeathed to all of us by John Milton, whose *Areopagitica* offers a persuasive denial of the right to censor and destroy books:

> As soon kill a man as kill a good book. . . . Though all the winds of doctrine were let loose to play upon the earth, so Truth be in the field, we do injuriously by licensing and prohibiting to misdoubt

Her strength. Let Her and Falsehood grapple; whoever knew Truth put to worse in free and open encounter?

University professors and students should say with Milton: "Give me liberty to know, to utter, to argue freely according to conscience above all liberties." And, like Milton, they should understand that "Where there is much desire to learn, there of necessity will be much arguing, much writing, many opinions; for opinion in good men is but knowledge in the making."

Dedicating the University of Virginia, Thomas Jefferson made a statement that I have no doubt would be welcomed by both the faculty and the administration of all universities: "This institution will be based on the illimitable freedom of the human mind. For here we are not afraid to follow truth wherever it may lead, nor to tolerate error so long as reason is left free to combat it."

A university—whether publicly or privately funded—cannot pursue the truth and advance knowledge unless it can proceed in freedom with toleration of all points of view and with vigorous criticism of each. The toleration of all points of view must not, however, lead to the absurdity of a relativism that holds in principle that there is no truth and that every opinion is as good as any other. This doctrine totally blurs the distinction between truth and falsehood; an institution pursuing this policy could not honestly be called a university.

There are, however, those who believe that state universities and their faculties are bought and paid for by tax dollars and should therefore be subservient both in doctrine and program to the state's elected representatives; and there are those who also believe that independent institutions, financed in part by philanthropy, should be subservient to their governing boards. This viewpoint was put succinctly by a faculty member at a state university:

> To me it is elemental that just as any business can survive only by giving its customers services or products they like, so also can the university survive only so long as it operates in a manner compatible with the social order in which it operates and in a manner acceptable to citizens whose tax payments make its very existence possible.

The implicit assumption is that a university is just another business, that its faculty are hired employees, and that both business and employees must please the customers. We can hear the motto being intoned in the background: "The customer is always right." But this view is mistaken: A university is not a business, faculty members are not hired hands, and the people are not always right. The people establish a university in order to be guided and instructed by it, just as they expect to be guided rather than pampered by a professional consultant.

[handwritten margin note: Church too ?]

A university is the treasure-house of civilization in which the attainments of the past are kept alive. But it is also the community's fountain of youth and, as George Bernard Shaw observed, "It is all the young can do for the old, to shock them and to keep them up to date." A university must always be free to appear "unreasonable" to the public since new insights frequently appear to be unreasonable. As long as a university hopes to fulfill its function in the discovery and embodiment of truth, it must dare to seem unreasonable in the eyes of the public. The public, in fact, demands just that when it establishes a university. A man who goes to a doctor is prepared to be hurt, for there are few painless cures. Likewise, the public must be prepared to be "hurt" when it summons a university into existence, for the faculty of a university may at times condemn public opinion as prejudiced ignorance, public art as trash, and public morality as shameless compromise and duplicity. The ability of the university to assume this role depends, of course, on its living up to its highest ideals.

Whenever a university is *subjected* to the public will, whether in the name of the majority or on the principle that the customer is always right, it is destroyed. Its existence depends upon its achieving excellence in the sciences, arts, and humanities that far transcends the general norm. If it is not permitted to *lead* and *instruct* the public in these matters and to *expose* that public, or that part of the public which is its student body, to the exhilaration of free inquiry, it cannot be a university at all.

[handwritten margin note: church ?]

True, regrettably few business, professional, and working men and women enjoy as much freedom as professors and students. The restrictions that once prevented clergy from departing from orthodoxy to assert their own divergent points of view are now generally relaxed. Indeed, in many contemporary theological circles, a new orthodoxy has arisen: that there shall be no *orthodoxy* except that there shall be *no* orthodoxy. How free is the clergy today to withstand the pressures urging them to abandon orthodoxy in support of a contemporary cause? Although less restricted now than in the past, would a banker, even today, feel free to participate with quiet dignity in a civil rights demonstration? How free is a tobacco-state senator to oppose cigarette advertising? How free is a newspaper editor to ignore the paper's advertisers when writing editorials? How free are the children of the poor to get a good education? How free is a labor leader to consider the problems of featherbedding in an age of automation? And how much time have those outside a university or an academic think tank to consider long and deeply those issues on which their minds are open? The degree of freedom exercised by professors and students does indeed surpass that exercised by the public at large.

But why should academics have more freedom than others? The answer is simply that they should not. But it does not follow that we should therefore curtail the freedom of professors and students. Our university communities—which are beach-heads of freedom—should be cherished, protected, and emu-lated. Academic freedom does not exist to give job security to professors; it exists, rather, as an expression of the continuing movement of humanity toward goals of truth and persuasion.

II

LESSONS IN SCHOOL

Poisoning the Wells of Academe

No ONE REALIZED it at the time: On December 2, 1964, higher education in the United States had just reached the zenith of its public esteem and entered a downward course. It had begun its upward climb after October 4, 1957, when the launch of the first *Sputnik* and subsequent Soviet technological and scientific successes began to be seen as a judgment on America for her financial neglect of educational institutions and the McCarthyite abuse of intellectuals. The sudden triumph of Soviet science and technology was now seen as a vindication of Adlai Stevenson and other "eggheads" who had argued in favor of free inquiry and research untrammeled by ideological restraint.

The congressional reaction to *Sputnik* was rapid enactment of a national legislative program to support education and research at all levels. The budget of the National Science Foundation (NSF) was rapidly increased, and major NSF grants were allocated to universities for the stimulation of research and teaching. The National Defense Education Act of 1958 provided scholarships, not only in the sciences, but in the social sciences as well, and led eventually to the development (by Jerrold Zacharias and others) of new elementary and secondary curricula in science, mathematics, and language.

At all levels, the scholar, the research scientist, the teacher, and the student were honored with rising esteem and rapidly increasing salaries and stipends. In the fall of 1957, as the moon completed its last semester in solitary orbit about the earth, mean faculty salaries for full professors ranged from $7,900 to $11,300 in 39 institutions surveyed by the AAUP. By 1964, those salaries had been increased by more than 50 percent (and academics began to have the unfamiliar experience of meeting people socially who earned less than they!). Even those teaching in elementary and secondary schools prospered by comparable percentage increases in salary. From 1957 to 1965 the total expenditure on public elementary and secondary education almost doubled. Wherever one looked, whatever the measure, education had received a vote of confidence and had prospered. On commencement day 1958, 437,000 degrees were conferred; by 1964 the total was 614,000. Even more impressive were the figures for doctorates: The last pre-*Sputnik* class had numbered 9,000; by 1964 there were 15,000 PhDs.

By the mid-1960s there was a national consensus that education provided the solution to social no less than financial and military ills: The Peace Corps, the Job Corps, Operation Head Start, and civil rights legislation were all political embodiments of academic ideas. By 1965 it was generally assumed that the national treasury would be diverted in significant measure to the support of educational institutions on all levels, because they were clearly perceived as a national resource and their development as a national goal.

Although increases in support were to continue to the end of the 1960s, the upward vector then began to flatten, and by 1970 what had been perceived as a national asset had become something of such dubious merit that more than one politician tried to gain office by campaigning against it. From the first seizure of a campus building at the University of California at Berkeley on December 2, 1964, this conversion took just four years. Although it might seem obvious now that the right of free speech carries no corollary guarantee of taxpayers' subsidy, and that no such guarantee can be extracted by force, we probably should not blame university president Clark Kerr for having failed to articulate these points with decisive clarity. After all, higher education in this country has no Distant Early Warning system, unless it be California itself.

The message of the Free (and the Filthy) Speech movements was not missed everywhere. Commissions made up of faculty,

students, and administrators were established at many universities and colleges to develop codes of conduct that would protect
academic freedom by securing peace and order on campus.

But the concern to meet the crisis presaged by events in
California was unnoticed at several other universities that were
overwhelmed by the crisis. Unfortunately, these set the pattern.
Grayson Kirk of Columbia and James Perkins of Cornell could
not claim to be surprised, since Clark Kerr's unhappy exit from
the University of California should have been their clear and
early warning. They were good men, but following the riots at
Berkeley they failed to bring their faculty and student representatives together to prepare for conflict on their own campuses.
They operated from an aloof standpoint that made the danger
seem unreal. When the crisis came, they were incapable of
careful discrimination between privileged free speech and
prohibited criminal action; unsure of this distinction, they were
incapable of decisive action on the basis of it. Neither assumed
the role of educator to explain the political, moral, and legal
issues at hand to his students and faculty and to urge on academic
grounds their constructive response to rational persuasion. Not
only did Grayson Kirk fail to explain that trashing his Columbia
office was no cultural achievement; for whatever reasons, he took
no counteraction against the occupiers of the Columbia buildings. He permitted the friends of trespassers to supply the
trespassers with food. He himself supplied them with electricity
and water; later he complained that they had used the electricity
to copy confidential documents. James Perkins at Cornell, torn
between his Quaker background and his legal training, sat on
the ground and bantered with students while his campus was
held at gunpoint. Thus he forfeited the confidence and respect
of faculty, students, and public. These good men did less than
they could have to preserve free speech and discussion, to prohibit
arson and criminal trespass, to discourage unlawful assembly
and unlawful use and concealment of firearms.

I am not speaking from hindsight. In 1966, for example,
President Norman Hackerman of The University of Texas at
Austin appointed a special committee, composed of students and
professors from law and other disciplines, to develop a new set
of rules and regulations for student affairs. Because there was

expert legal guidance, this code met all the requirements of fairness and due process; and because there was responsible student participation, the legitimacy of the revised rules was generally recognized. The administration, moreover, accepted the responsibility to assume an educative role by entering into confrontation with students whenever direct meetings were needed; administrative and faculty positions were presented, and those who proposed to disrupt the university were denied their strategy of misinformation. Frequent meetings of the faculty assured consultation and full discussion between faculty and administration on potentially disruptive issues. As a consequence, there were no serious disruptions on the campus of The University of Texas at Austin.

Many administrators, however, failed in the period from 1965 to 1968 to make clear the special character of the university as a free marketplace of ideas, and the conditions on which the freedom of that marketplace depends. With revolution in the wind, they might well have recalled the words of Edmund Burke:

> Men are qualified for civil liberty in exact proportion to their disposition to put moral chains upon their own appetites. Society cannot exist unless a controlling power upon will and appetite be placed somewhere, and the less of it there is within, the more there is without. It is ordained in the eternal constitution of things that men of intemperate minds cannot be free . . . .

In the inaction of these university presidents, "Operation Pander" was established and quickly set a pattern for vacillation emulated by administrators across the nation, just as the mindless behavior of Mark Rudd and his band of militants found student imitators as Rudd traveled across the country lecturing on desecration as art. Violence stalked the campus in what has sometimes been called a triumph of social involvement by students, but which was in fact largely a burlesque—often a cruel one—in which students and faculty of radical persuasion, like cuckoos, laid eggs in the nest of the black civil rights movement and hatched such dubious birds as the Free Speech Movement and such slogans as "Student Power" and "Student as Nigger." Because those who were threatened by the military draft sensitively recognized the folly of the Vietnam War, we should not overlook the means chosen by some activist students to express their opposition to the war—occupying buildings, bringing firearms on campus, destroying manuscripts of books, assaulting and kidnapping university officials, and murdering at least one student.

The academy—which had successfully resisted the politicization of its academic program and restrictions on academic freedom and discussion from without—failed to resist politicization from within. The remarkably thoughtful, scholarly, and impassioned discussion of U.S. policy in Vietnam and in the Dominican Republic that was the subject of the early teach-ins gave way to mass meetings, rhetorical overkill, and disruption. Faculty and students in one university after another, by adopting statements on the Vietnam War, attempted to legislate political and moral orthodoxy by the majority vote of the minorities present at the meetings. There began gradually to emerge a kind of ideological license that would ultimately threaten to enslave the academy and destroy its freedom.

Academics developed a novel meaning for the term "political crime," which had once meant an action rendered criminal solely by its political content, but which now came to mean a crime—however vicious—justified by its political motivation. This new definition of political crime found swift adoption not merely on college campuses but throughout the world, as hijackers, kidnappers, killers, and Watergate "plumbers" justified their contempt for law through an inappropriate appeal to political motivation. A man jailed merely for opposing a government can be truly described as a political prisoner. A man who is jailed after he has attempted the assassination of a government official is *not* a political prisoner. He is a criminal who may have committed his crime from a political motive.

Not only was political crime given a novel meaning; the concept of academic freedom was transformed. Once, it entailed an immunity for what is said and done by dedicated, thoughtful, conscientious scholars in pursuit of truth or the truest account. Now it came to entail, rather, an immunity for whatever is said and done, responsibly or carelessly, within or without the walls of academe, by persons unconcerned for the truth. Reckless, incompetent, frivolous, or even malevolent persons promulgated ideas for which they could claim no expertise, or even committed deeds for which they could claim no sanction of law.

At the same time, there arose the notion that there was no freedom to be wrong and that right could be determined by the voice of a mass meeting, however poorly attended. This was the ideological license articulated by Herbert Marcuse. Against the concept of a free marketplace of ideas in which contrasting ideas are tolerated, he proposed to permit only a "liberating tolerance":

> Liberating tolerance then would mean intolerance against movements from the right and toleration of movements from the left. As to the scope of this tolerance and intolerance: . . . it would extend to the stage of action as well as of discussion and propaganda, of deed as well as of word.[1]

The academy at large did not recognize that Marcuse was nothing more than the Joseph McCarthy of the left. It has paid a fearful price for its failure to proclaim a plague on McCarthyism in whatever guise it appears.

The significance of this widespread adoption and support of ideological license should not be overlooked. Nor should it be minimized merely because the worst effects of this kind of politicization have been reduced by a later generation of administrators who reject the notion that a forcible blockade of a college building is any more peaceful than the blockade of a country. They came to recognize that there can be a civilized use of force in which a thoughtful, rationally constituted civilian authority, after sustained efforts at rational persuasion, calls in police power to restore order among those who are simply lawless. As a result of this recognition, our campuses have returned for the most part to a state of apparent civility not disturbingly worse than that which obtains outside. But it would be foolish to imagine that we have thereby become "depoliticized." The open campus may exist once more, but it is difficult to assert that it again provides a free marketplace of ideas.

Academic freedom originally had no other purpose than to ensure this free marketplace in which controversy in the pursuit of truth might flourish. Although the general public has long been shocked to hear controversy praised for its own sake, and although Marcuse and the radical left used their ideology to license doctrine and limit controversy—hence both made common cause in urging the university to support and defend their versions of revealed truth rather than controversy—neither the right nor the left met the arguments of the traditional defenders of academic freedom. The strongest defense of all freedoms, including academic freedom, lies in the historical fact that open controversy between alternative points of view is far better for mankind than the unopposed presentation of dogma. In the words of Justice Holmes:

> But when men have realized that time has upset many fighting faiths, they may come to believe even more than they believe the very foundations of their own conduct that the ultimate good desired is better reached by free trade in ideas—that the best test of truth is the power of thought to get itself accepted in the competition of the market, and that truth is the only ground upon which their wishes safely can be carried out.

The reflective student of history knows the full extent of the danger inherent in stifling controversy and suppressing opinions alleged to be false—the danger that, without controversy and argument, there is no means of distinguishing true from false opinions. Truth-finding is a kind of adversary process, and competition for intellectual favor has remained and should remain the method for proceeding. Truth-seeking is secured and sustained by the presence of academic freedom, which ensures toleration of all points of view with vigorous criticism of each.

But there are further conditions for a free marketplace of ideas that have received scant attention, not because they were not required and expected of all members of an academic community and of all those who respect academic freedom, but rather because they were taken for granted. They are conditions that guarantee academic responsibility, and only a few have been singled out for examination by the AAUP. The tendency of academics to introduce extraneous material into the classroom has prompted the AAUP's warning that intrusion of such material runs counter to academic responsibility. But nowhere in the AAUP position on academic freedom and responsibility do we have a statement prohibiting the falsification of evidence. The

AAUP simply took for granted—as did Holmes—that well-poisoning in the academic marketplace is forbidden. Prompted by a profound, almost pietistic respect for truth and the truest account, and an absolute abhorrence of anyone who would falsify evidence or even be careless in its use, no one thought such warnings necessary or appropriate.

The free marketplace of ideas can be destroyed or damaged in many ways—by disruption, shutdown, false advertising, false pricing, negligence, and well-poisoning. The AAUP's silence on these important threats to academic freedom originally stemmed merely from the high-mindedness of its membership and its leaders. But more recently the AAUP has shared fully in the intellectual corruption that accompanied the politicization of the university, and its adventure with unionism made matters still worse. A union is required to defend the interests of its members with little or no regard for external standards; the AAUP as a labor union found itself defending the indefensible in a way that the AAUP as a professional organization would have found abhorrent.

But in the AAUP's golden age, the organization did not foresee the necessity to argue the obvious. Had a committee of the AAUP ever proposed in a draft statement on academic freedom and tenure such language as "Members of the profession should not falsify evidence," the annual meeting would have howled this down as a gratuitous insult to the honor of the profession. It had always been assumed within the profession that its members would observe the highest standards of civility, objectivity, and fidelity to the search for truth, but one can no longer make this assumption.

Yet, of all the threats to the free marketplace of ideas, perhaps the most serious is the threat of well-poisoning. Such well-poisoning can be carried out in many ways, making a pure well polluted, and a polluted one deadly.

Sometimes political zeal leads a usually careful scholar to carelessness and rhetorical distortion that he would usually avoid and despise. Noam Chomsky, for example, has written:

> Three times in a generation, American technology has laid waste a helpless Asian country. . . . The systematic destruction of a virtually

defenseless Japan was carried out with a sense of moral rectitude that was then, and remains today, unchallenged. . . . In Korea the process was repeated, with only a few qualms. It is the amazing resistance of the Vietnamese that has forced us to ask: What have we done?[2]

Chomsky is an excellent linguist and philosopher of language. How do we explain, then, this simplistic and distorted rendering of history by Chomsky the historical commentator? This Chomsky never asks whether America's three Asian involvements are comparable: He simply asserts that they are, when he should have known better. Suppose that we grant that Japan—which introduced at Nanking in 1937 the annihilation bombing of civilians and pioneered the concept of total war against humanity that was brutally developed by the Luftwaffe at Warsaw and Rotterdam, the same Japan that imposed heavy losses on the United States at Pearl Harbor, Guadalcanal, Tarawa, Iwo Jima, Okinawa, and the Philippines—is correctly described as a "defenseless Asian country."

And let us suppose for the sake of argument that the bombings of Hiroshima and Nagasaki—thought at the time to have saved millions of American and Japanese lives that would have been lost in the invasion of the islands of Japan—were unnecessary and that by some stretch of logic and historical knowledge we can conclude that the United States engaged in "the systematic destruction of a virtually defenseless Japan." How does this explain Chomsky's failure to distinguish the action in Vietnam and Japan from the action in Korea, so that in his eyes our defense of South Korea constitutes one of the three times in a generation that American technology has laid waste a helpless Asian country? There is no plausible way to deny that the Korean War began with the invasion of the South from the North. The people of South Korea, quite unlike the people of South Vietnam, had no doubts about their loyalty to their government or about their opposition to communism. They fought hard and well beside the forces of the United Nations that had come to their assistance. Chomsky fails to mention that the American involvement in Korea was supported by a United Nations mandate, that the United Nations condemned the action of the North Koreans and called upon member states of the United Nations to come to the aid of the South Korean government. He fails to mention that President Truman restricted American military activities to the limits imposed by the United Nations mandate, and that when General Douglas MacArthur repeatedly overstepped those limits to the point of questioning the supremacy of the civilian authority, Truman relieved him of his command, an action politically disastrous for the president and his party alike.

When an intellectual proceeds, as Chomsky does here, to rewrite history and to use his interpretations as if they were historical data, he pollutes the well of the intellectual marketplace. Whether or not this is intentional is beside the point. I would not argue that Chomsky's political writings justify his exclusion from the marketplace, but they call for counterargument and analysis. His views should be subjected to relentless scrutiny and criticism.

Chomsky's normal care and scholarly restraint are more flagrantly cast aside in his *American Power and the New Mandarins* (1969), in which he attributes to Truman these sentiments, alleged to have been proclaimed in 1947: "all freedom is dependent on freedom of enterprise. . . . The American system can survive in America only if it becomes a world system."[3]

Chomsky gives as the source for the quotation D. F. Fleming's *The Cold War and Its Origins*. In this work one finds only Fleming's account of a speech Truman gave at Baylor University on March 6, 1947. What is not to be found there is precisely the remark in question, that all freedom is dependent on freedom of enterprise, but rather a paraphrase: "[Truman] explained that freedom was more important than peace, and that freedom of worship and speech were dependent on freedom of enterprise."[4]

One also finds, in quotation marks and cited from J. P. Warburg's *Put Yourself in Marshall's Place*, the statement from which Chomsky adapted the remark about the desirability of the American system and the necessity of its worldwide diffusion. I say "adapted," for Chomsky's version changes tense and mode— a curious slip for so distinguished a linguist—so as to suppress the fact that the quotation is indirect.

In a review of Chomsky's book, Professor Arthur Schlesinger noted this conversion of paraphrase into quotation, an exposure subsequently given wider currency by Lionel Abel in the pages of *Commentary*. Chomsky's rejoinder was that although conversion was "careless and inexcusable," the paraphrases were accurate and perceptive, and no real harm had been done. Schlesinger replied that they were neither accurate nor perceptive, and the two paladins continued to fill the Letters column for some months with their increasingly ill-tempered accusations and rejoinders.[5] We can do no better than to follow Schlesinger's suggestion to look at the Truman speech itself.

The paraphrased material derives from two separate passages:

1. "There is one thing that Americans value even more than peace. It is freedom. Freedom of worship—freedom of speech—freedom of enterprise. It must be true that the first two of these freedoms are related to the third."
2. "But if controls over trade are to be really tight, tariffs are not enough. Even more drastic measures can be used. Quotas can be imposed on imports, product by product and month by month. Importers can be forbidden to buy abroad without obtaining licenses. Those who buy more than is permitted can be fined or jailed. Everything that comes into a country can be kept within limits determined by a central plan.

   "This is regimentation. And this is the direction in which much of the world is headed at the present time. If this trend is not reversed, the Government of the United States will be under pressure, sooner or later, to use these same devices to fight for markets and raw materials. . . . This is not the American way. It is not the way to peace."[6]

The question is not whether these passages are accurately paraphrased in the versions given by Fleming and Warburg. It is, rather, whether they are so patently and precisely equivalent that no man of sense would care whether he had read the original or the paraphrase. Now, whether any paraphrase ever meets such a standard may well be doubted. But surely these do not.

Even if one considers Chomsky's conversion of paraphrase into quotation accidental, his cavalier insistence that it makes no difference is sharply at odds with his admission that the conversion was "careless and inexcusable." In any case, it is this sort of carelessness about evidence that characterizes the negligent academic well-poisoner. Rational discussion of foreign policy and sober assessment of the nation's strengths and weaknesses are made impossible when scholars resort to such means.

Another well-poisoner, Professor Howard Zinn, once observed in the forum of an "underground" newspaper—one wonders what Sartre and other survivors of the French underground Resistance would make of this thoroughly dishonest appropriation of the term—that it was a deficiency of philosophers that they "are sometimes annoyed by the intrusion of facts into comfortably vacuous generalities." He then took me to task for having claimed that Martin Luther King, Jr., "emphasized the importance of showing respect for lawfulness at the same time that he refused to abide by a specific law." Commenting on my statement, Zinn said:

> That is a gross distortion. It is true that King went to jail rather than escaping—but it isn't at all clear that he did this out of any overall respect for "lawfulness"—rather than out of tactical and dramatic motives, or simply out of lack of choice. I doubt that King would criticize Angela Davis or Daniel Berrigan, who carried their defiance of authority beyond that point of arrest, who refused to surrender to the government because they believed its activities did not deserve respect. It is true that King urged respect for his opponents, and love for all fellow beings, but it is not true that he "emphasized . . . respect for lawfulness." I knew Martin Luther King, and was with him on occasions of civil disobedience, in Alabama and Georgia, and it is a disservice to his memory to twist his views so as to omit what was by far his chief emphasis: resistance to immoral authority.[7]

Let us see if "an intrusion of facts" will disclose who has "twisted" King's views. After all, Martin Luther King was an articulate exponent of his ideas, and it is (to say the least) curious that Zinn, trying to prove what King must have thought on so central an issue, cites not one word from King himself. If we go no further than King's "Letter from a Birmingham Jail," we readily see why Zinn may have preferred to invoke King's memory rather than his words.

> In no sense do I advocate evading or defying the law as the rabid segregationist would do. This would lead to anarchy. One who breaks an unjust law must do it openly, lovingly, and with a willingness to accept the penalty. I submit that an individual who

breaks a law that conscience tells him is unjust, and willingly accepts the penalty by staying in jail to arouse the conscience of the community over its injustice, is in reality expressing the very highest respect for law.

That is the clearest possible evidence that Martin Luther King himself believed in the distinction that Zinn calls a "gross distortion." It is testimony available in one of the most accessible of King's writings.

Nor is this the only direct quotation from the letter that contradicts Zinn's distortion. King insists:

A law is unjust, for example, if the majority group compels a minority group to obey the statute but does not make it binding on itself. By the same token a law in all probability is just if the majority is itself willing to obey it.

Now Zinn observed in his piece that "John Silber did not even seem to be embarrassed as he invoked the name of Martin Luther King." Why should anyone be embarrassed to be caught expounding King's views honestly and *accurately?* The more pertinent question is: Was Zinn embarrassed in so shamelessly distorting and degrading King's ethical position?

Wherever Zinn was in Alabama with Martin Luther King, it was not in the cell in Birmingham. There is no reason to believe that Zinn is a more reliable exponent of King's views than King himself. King did not win a Nobel prize for his advocacy of lawlessness, but for his passionate crusade for human dignity within the context of law and love. We can see very clearly who it is that has done King's memory a disservice by poisoning the well and cheapening the standards of discourse.

Sometimes the well-poisoner victimizes himself as well as the academy. In May 1968 Lawrence Caroline, a promising young member of the philosophy department of The University of Texas at Austin, crowned a series of irresponsible speeches, lectures, and activities by stating, before a crowd of some 2,000 students, that there were five concentration camps in the state. He said that while he was not concerned about their existence, he could understand if his black brothers suffered from paranoia because of them. When I asked him to identify the concentration camps, he was unable to do so. In fact, he had deliberately lied in order to make a rhetorical point before a large group of students, to whom, as a professor, he owed a very special responsibility. Did the philosophy department, of which he was a member, then rise up and condemn him for having violated the basic principles of rational inquiry, namely, that he had willfully and knowingly distorted the truth? Not at all.

The chairman of the Board of Regents, however, was less complacent. At a meeting of the Regents, he offered a motion that Caroline be dismissed forthwith, supporting his proposal with chapter-and-verse quotations from the AAUP's Statement on Academic Freedom and Tenure. I was present at the meeting, and successfully argued against this course of action.

A year later, Caroline's contract was up for renewal. The philosophy department was deeply divided on the issue, not least because of evidence that contrary to his claims Caroline had made no progress on his doctoral dissertation. It approved a contract renewal by a margin of one vote. The department chairman recommended against renewal, and as dean I affirmed his recommendation, forwarding it to the Regents.

In the passionately political ambience of the late 1960s, Caroline's case was all too common. Nor is it unheard of today. Many young scholars find the siren call of political activism irresistible, largely abandon their scholarly work, and, caught up in the passions of the moment, drop all pretense to intellectual integrity. Lawrence Caroline badly miseducated his students and was himself a casualty of an ideological invasion of the campus. I wonder what would happen today if the fabricator of the Piltdown skull were a member of the faculty of an American university. I daresay his fraud, if exposed, might nonetheless be excused—provided that he claimed it was done for some political or other high-minded purpose.

The story of Lawrence Caroline has a happier ending than might have been expected. In 1987, he wrote me that as a result of his departure from The University of Texas he made contacts that led to his return to the Judaism of his youth. He joined the Lubavitch movement, a Chassidic organization, and found a new and far happier life as the director of a religious school. He expressed gratitude for "the opportunity to make amends for the damage I did then. In retrospect," he wrote, "I too would have tried to remove me from the university."

If it is difficult to extend the benefit of doubt in the Caroline case, the well-poisoner in the next case leaves us no choice. He *tells* us that he is poisoning the well. When I was dean of the College of Arts and Sciences at The University of Texas at Austin, I received the following letter from a young faculty member:

> Dear Dean Silber:
>
> I enclose an article which I have submitted to *The Daily Texan* [the student newspaper at The University of Texas]. In fairness I thought you should see it. I say in fairness, because the article is definitely not fair. I made no attempt at objectivity. I aimed at a gut-level response that would cause a confrontation and lead to rational discussion later on.
>
> I did not intend personal vilification. You have become a negative symbol; hence, I must oppose you.
>
> Yours for a better University

When I received that letter, I immediately sent a copy of it to the editor of *The Daily Texan* with my comment: "If you wish to publish this article, I think you should publish this letter as the author's comment on it." The editor of *The Daily Texan*, a fair-minded student, returned the article to the professor. Whereupon I received a second letter from the professor, in which he whined: "I only sent you my letter for your information. I did not intend that you should do anything about it."

When a faculty member behaves in this fashion, he achieves ultimate corruption. Having no power of self-control within, he must anticipate the imposition of control from without—in this case at the hands of a fair-minded undergraduate student. And if the faculty as a whole does not have ways and means at its disposal to deal with corruption in its own professional ranks, it must expect to be disciplined either by the administration or by the public.

It is both deplorable and dangerous, however, for outsiders to be called in to refine or reprove a university, or for an administrator to reprove a faculty member. These tasks are properly the job of an autonomous, self-respecting faculty.

I am deeply committed to the autonomy of the faculty and

the university. But we should stop misusing the concept of autonomy. Since *nomos*, or law, is its fundamental root, *autonomy* does not mean willfulness or capriciousness or "doing one's own thing." One is autonomous only when one acts according to law that has been self-prescribed. Kant, who introduced "autonomy" as a technical term in ethics, had the genius to see that a moral community depends for its very existence upon the lawful behavior of each individual by virtue of the person's own respect for law. Instead of being coerced to cooperate within the lawful framework of a society, each morally sound individual cooperates in it because of a personal decision to do so—hence, autonomously. But when autonomy is used simply as a synonym for willfulness, for the most irrational and antinomian activity—then obviously it is being misused, and its misuse must be stopped.

Despite the fact that one hears frequently about the "repression" of radical faculty by "reactionary administration," it appears that well-poisoning rarely gets the poisoner into any trouble whatever and may (if done with adequate attention to public relations) advance him in the profession. That this extraordinary state of affairs should obtain is largely due to our almost universal acceptance of an absolute concept of academic freedom, namely, that the academic can say whatever he pleases about whatever he pleases, whenever and wherever he pleases, and be fully immune from unpleasant consequences.

Present tenure policy encourages anyone to become a sophist rather than to accept even the most attenuated form of Socratic testing. When tenure functions as sinecure—as it almost always does—it does not necessarily ensure academic freedom; it may, rather, encourage academic license and abuse.

If a faculty member is guaranteed absolute immunity from the consequences of telling lies, the search for truth is inevitably made more difficult. If the system does not encourage the utmost accuracy in recording facts and the utmost rigor in developing arguments, the procedures of sound scholarship lack all support beyond that of the integrity of the individual scholar.

This problem is exacerbated whenever the university becomes politicized. There is ample evidence that when academics engage in what they perceive as political speech, scholarly responsibility is cast to the winds. Professor Chomsky is an obvious case in point. Although at present the distorting ideologies in the academy are of the left, they can just as easily be from the right. Recall the degeneration of the German universities into seedbeds of Nazism. Not even Martin Heidegger, steeped in German idealism and the philosophy of Kant, was immune to the blandishments of National Socialism. Thus, when the academy immunizes scholars from the consequences of their work, how shall truth be defended—not only from inadvertent error, but from frivolous or malicious distortion?

There is a sense in which untrammeled academic freedom is the intellectual equivalent of inherited wealth. Having it does not ensure that one becomes fat and sloppy, but it requires a certain amount of character to reject the life of ignoble ease. Intellectually, such a life is not the absence of thought (any more than the material life of ignoble ease is the absence of activity, for it may be characterized by frenetic doing). It is, rather, an abandonment of the mind to its own devices. Such an abandonment means that its victim remains exiled to the world of the sleeping, particular to each sleeper, and never enters that world of the waking that Heraclitus tells us is common to all. One of the dangers in providing men with immunity from all consequences of what they say is an increased risk of such abandonment, potentially in the guise—far more dangerous than overt irrationalism—of rational thought. Lysenko, after all, managed to secure from Stalin the right, in effect, to publish without the risk of exposure by the scientific community. The result was not to the advantage of Soviet genetics or Lysenko.

The absolutizing of academic freedom with its concomitant disregard for academic responsibility has been in part the inadvertent consequence of tenure that, inadvertently, has come to function as sinecure. No matter what revisions are made in tenure rules and practices, tenure can never protect or guarantee academic freedom, which should be exercised and enjoyed by all faculty, whether tenured or untenured, and by students and administrators as well. Academic freedom is protected and guaranteed by the courage of individual professors, by individual administrators who protect individual members of the faculty, and by individual students. If they express their freedom responsibly, they will not expect immunity from criticism or public disapproval; they will recognize these risks as one of the essential conditions of responsibility. Provision of seven-year terms as basic units of academic employment might, for example, even in the absence of any tenure, effectively protect free men from almost all capricious firings in the heat of specific controversies without immunizing them from the risks that ensure academic integrity and responsibility. Ultimately, however, the academic neither needs nor deserves a greater protection for his or her political freedom than that afforded the ordinary citizen. There is (and in my opinion should be) a price for glory.

Another cost of our unmoderated American standard of academic freedom is an increasing difficulty in maintaining even the most footloose standards of academic duty as obligations increasingly fail to be correlative to rights. The marketplace of ideas is corrupted by a variety of ideologies that are not especially political. It is not unknown for a professor to begin the year by announcing to his students that no one will receive less than a B in his course. (I wait in vain to hear that some student has responded by asking the professor if he is afraid he can't hold the class without pandering in this way.) It sometimes even happens that a professor turns in a grade list of a large class with all As. It would not take an excessively suspicious nature to suspect that such a list is a perjured document, nor a very demanding one to doubt that its author has failed to make a careful and honest assessment of the students' work. Suppose that the administration were to call such a teacher in and say: "Look, you know as well as we that your students are performing at different levels. Awarding honest grades is a part of your job, and if you don't start doing it, you are going to be dismissed for nonperformance of contract . . ." In any inquest on such a termination, it would doubtless be argued that grading, being a professional duty, is protected by academic freedom, and that if a teacher believes the A–F scale to be fascist and repressive, academic freedom will protect his refusal to use it. And doubtless many faculty, themselves careful and honest graders, would endorse this procedural defense of a colleague.

What is being abandoned here is a condition on which the development of scientific truth depends, namely, the expectation of gradually increasing competence among students and the reservation of positions in graduate schools and in the professions for those who have clearly demonstrated extraordinary ability. The movement toward pass/fail (or pass/no record) grading, led in the past decade by students and younger faculty, is in part a move against the intellectual elitism on which any significant scientific and scholarly achievement must depend. It is largely a transparent effort by the middle and upper-middle classes to protect themselves from downward mobility. Behind the egalitarian clichés lies hidden a conflict of interest that must be relentlessly exposed. Do we wish to waste the facilities of medical schools to educate any person not extraordinarily gifted? Do we wish to admit to graduate school in physics any person incapable of handling differential equations? Music schools are not troubled by the egalitarian thrust: One plays the violin or one does not. The elitist (not to say repressive) demand that the concertmaster of the Boston Symphony Orchestra play the notes as they appear in the score, at the tempo set by the conductor, cannot easily be dismissed by egalitarian rhetoric.

It is only natural that professors who don't believe in grades may stop reading papers very carefully. This condition accounts for the success throughout the country of paper-writing factories like "Termpapers Unlimited" and "Quality Bullshit," and the use of their fabrications in virtually every major university. Such fraud that makes a mockery of every academic ideal can rarely succeed where professors grade their own papers with an eye to tracking the intellectual development of each student. Firms such as these have counterfeited the very medium of exchange in academic life. And some universities have been guilty of more than simply providing an atmosphere in which students are tempted to dishonesty. They have refused to take decisive action to expose the fraud and root it out where discovered. They have been willing to drink from a poisoned well and seem oblivious to the dire consequences. When Boston University led the successful legal fight to put these firms out of business in Massachusetts, we discovered in their files the names of customers from every major college and university in the Boston and Cambridge area. When we checked with other universities, we found that they were not interested in having the names—they intended to do nothing about it. At first, we felt some righteous indignation, since the Boston University administration had passed the names to our several faculties and asked for action to end the abuse. Although the majority of students found guilty were disciplined and a few had to leave the university, we found the faculties of two schools remarkably tolerant toward those who had offended. In one case, a young woman who had used several store-bought papers was about to graduate with honors. She was required to write an additional paper in one course and her grade was lowered in another. But even after admitting her use of purchased term papers, she was allowed to graduate with honors!

These are examples of academics who refuse to do some part of their duties and, by negligence or deliberate action, disrupt the marketplace of ideas. But there have been widespread examples of academics who refuse to do any part of their duty whatever, and participate, for example, in the thoroughly dishonest practice of the "student strike," in which students stop going to class and demand full credit for being absent. The term "strike" in this context is preposterous. When workers go on strike, they lay down their tools and forfeit their pay. Professor Richard Pipes has pointed out that when students go on strike, they lay down their brains, but what do they forfeit? Nothing, if they can help it. Even more dishonest is the practice of the faculty voting itself a paid holiday under some such label as "moratorium," "days of rational discourse," or "strike." That such paid holidays voted by beneficiaries thereof amount to a raid on the institutional treasury should be obvious, but their proponents never cease to swell with honest pride in the degree of concern and involvement such paid vacations demonstrate. More recently, when students have been less prone to such irresponsibility and more concerned with their studies, they have been castigated for their apathy.

Reed College was the scene of what must be a canonical example of this demand to be irresponsible on full salary. A teacher there suddenly discovered that his principles forbade his coming to campus at all. He withdrew to his house, where he founded something called "the College in Exxxile" (going Exxon several better, he always spelled it with at least three x's). There, from midnight to three, alternate Tuesdays, he taught classes having little to do with the curriculum of the college. Because his bungalow would not accommodate the sophomore humanities lecture, he would sit in a car on the frontier of the campus and lecture over shortwave radio, illuminating the work of Flaubert by reading from a Mexican comic-book life of the author. Let us suppose the administration finally called him to task and told him: "You will not get paid until you start operating on campus at regularly assigned hours. Take the matter up with the AAUP if you wish, but remember who signs your paycheck in the meantime." He would have found defenders—themselves quite innocent of such methodological fopperies—who would have argued that the scheduling of classes is a professional matter, not to be tampered with by petty academic bureaucrats.

In this case, he was not even put to that racking, but merely required to pick up his paycheck in person. He found that a man must live, and submitted. The monster Custom lent a kind of easiness to his next indulgence, and the next, till use indeed did change the stamp of nature. His Parthian shot was to rent a large billboard near campus and garnish it with a photograph of the acting president and the query, "Would you buy a used college from this man?"

But in most cases, university officials, troubled alike by the prospect of AAUP investigation and radical disruption, tend to let the innovators go their merry ways, free to deny Caesar even a widow's mite. And in each case, we see the notion of academic freedom, designed to shield the marketplace of ideas, used to close it down entirely. These closures have at least the merit of being overt. Others are more insidious.

It is becoming increasingly difficult to discuss highly controversial ideas on the American campus. There is no better example of this than the controversy surrounding the work of professors Jensen, Herrnstein, Bronfenbrenner, Eysenck, and Shockley. Each of these scholars has been in some way harassed by those opposed to what they think are his ideas.[8] In 1972, when Professor Bronfenbrenner spoke at Boston University (under police protection after I had refused the demand of a faculty member to cancel his lecture), strident members of the audience demanded that he recant his former errors. In a scene reminiscent of a Moscow purge trial, he obliged. At the London School of

Economics Professor Eysenck was physically assaulted at a lecture, and at one major university after another, Shockley has been denied a platform at the last minute. The argument employed by those who would silence these scholars has generally been that their views are impermissible. This argument in favor of censorship gains sophistication in its formulation by Professor Charles Isaacs of Staten Island Community College. He informs us that there should be no right to debate when truth is known, and that the truth is that racism—which he dogmatically identifies with Jensen's and Shockley's alleged intelligence differential—is wrong.[9] Racism as the expression of prejudice and persecution directed toward racial groups certainly is wrong. But just as wrong is Isaacs's prejudice against and persecution of those engaged in open, unimpeded search for truth on controversial subjects, which he seems to fear more than respect. One wonders what Isaacs would say if Shockley claimed that Isaacs had shown himself to be an intellectual storm trooper who ought to be hounded out of the profession. When one denies free speech to others, how shall one retain it for oneself?

Without exploring the complex ramifications of the controversy, it is possible to raise a number of important questions hanging on its resolution. Suppose we were able to measure a significant difference in IQ between blacks and whites. First of all, we might develop once and for all a *reductio ad absurdum* of the concept of IQ as a measure of intelligence independent from environmental influences. If this be a myth, it is clearly one best put to rest—the sooner the better. Second, we would almost certainly observe a substantial range of overlap between blacks and whites, a circumstance that ought to be sufficient to render absurd any pride of intelligence in either race. Third, if IQ were recognized as not only a reflection of native intelligence but also (as it almost certainly is) an effect of environmental influences, then the IQ differential between blacks and whites would itself be a measure of the cultural deprivation of blacks and a way of quantifying for Congress and the state legislatures their obligation to take remedial steps in providing equal opportunity for the black community. No racist implications need follow from the rigorous scientific examination of the concept of IQ. Racism, after all, resides in treating individuals as if they were a category. Refuse to do this, and what you believe about that category becomes irrelevant.

And yet Chomsky himself has argued that because there is no *decent* reason for wanting to know whether there is an IQ differential among races, and because racists will exploit any evidence that there is, Herrnstein and others ought to cease and desist, turn to some less controversial avenue of inquiry.[10] As it stands, the academic community's implicit acceptance of Chomsky's argument and complacent acceptance of interruption of free discussion and inquiry is yet another disruption of the marketplace.

Further, the thoughtful discussion of the efforts of Jensen, Herrnstein, Bronfenbrenner, and others should result in a sustained examination and reevaluation of the methodology of the social sciences, which, by ignoring the interdependence of most social variables, and aping methods more appropriate to physics, leads perhaps not to truth but to error. The refinement of social science methodology might be one of the scientific gains of discussing these issues. Herrnstein needs to be opposed by colleagues worthy of him—by serious scholars—not by rabble-rousers.

Christopher Jencks, author of *Inequality* (1972), should also be opposed by someone who can examine with him the limitations of a methodology that cannot escape the egocentric predicament. Jencks reaches discouraging conclusions about the efficacy of education, primarily because he cannot measure the effect of the presence and absence of education in the individual. Instead, he must measure different groups of individuals, and because he is dealing with different individuals, he must confront the influence of such a vast array of variables that his conclusions must certainly be in doubt. The lack of sophistication in his methodology is a subject worthy of most careful examination. His political views and his moral principles, so far as I can discern, are beyond reproach—and whether they are or not is beside the point.

In recent years there has arisen the related question of the wares to be bought and sold in the academic marketplace. Some examples are obvious. A university begins, as it so happens one did, by offering credit for a course in judicial astrology—that is, not in astrology as an historical phenomenon that has had and continues to have cultural significance, but astrology as a "science," its scientific pretensions unchallenged by the annihilating refutations they have received over the centuries. Or a university, in a burst of ecumenism, appoints a voodoo priest-in-residence. Are these, perhaps, so mad that we can look forward to a time when sanity shall have returned, and such schools will wonder what they were doing?

More subtle, altogether more fashionable, and more likely to endure is the growing fad for the use of the computer in social science research. This could be seen, if investigators write (or at least understand) their own programs, as no more than a highly efficient way of storing and retrieving data. But when, as is too often the case, the investigators rely blindly on someone else's programming, there is grave danger that they will lack an intellectual grasp of the meaning and significance of the data used, of how it is derived, and what weight should be put on it. When data are pulled together through computer technology by a variety of highly abstract and remote techniques, the intellectual grasp of them can become so attenuated as to place their value substantially in doubt. Happily, this is changing dramatically. The microcomputer revolution has placed programming languages at the disposal of scholars. They can now rely on themselves in using computers, and thus now know what they are doing.

Implicit in our increasing reliance on the computer are the fallacies that output equals data and that data equal knowledge. It is likely that Descartes was right to insist that one has no assurance of truth unless one can grasp the entirety of argument in intellectual intuition, or see it (as Descartes would say) in the natural light of reason. What we fondly call a "knowledge explosion" is probably not even an explosion of data but, rather, of printout. That we should have become unsure not merely of the quality of our knowledge, but its very location, is a measure of the degree to which the marketplace has been disrupted.

It is not so clear that this disruption has begun to attenuate the conditions requisite for science, but they have been made precarious. The willingness to follow truth close on the heels wherever she leads us, the insistence on having the evidence and all the evidence, the remorseless comparison of idea with idea, the necessary distinction between idea and act, the very belief in an external reality common to all, accessible to all, have been put at hazard by a failure to insist upon academic responsibility.

The community outside looks in at the madness and doubts whether the university, after all, is an institution worthy of any special admiration. It requires no subtle understanding to know that a community in which intellectual questions are settled by force has, at least partially, relapsed into barbarism. The community outside may not know whether the right to free inquiry is essential to science, but it knows that there is no honesty in voting yourself a paid holiday and calling it an act of conscience. The cab driver who understands the connection between his driving and his income looks at an academic moratorium and wonders what sort of con artists inhabit the groves of academe. The welder, accustomed to carrying on his political activity after hours, looks with disgust at the boondoggle called the Princeton Plan, a quaint operation under which Princeton University declared a vacation for some days prior to the election so that students and faculty could campaign for the candidates of their choice. He sees here a community of aristocrats who consider their political activity ever so much more valuable than that of ordinary mechanics.

Such abuses must be corrected if the academy is to regain the respect and confidence of the community on which it depends. The academy must free itself of enslavement by ideological license. Freedom is attained not in the absence of constraint, but through internal acceptance of those responsible limits on which the fulfillment of freedom depends. If the faculty cannot correct themselves, they must not be surprised to find interference from without—through gross neglect or direct intervention. The public at large may yet demand a great and perhaps tragic moment out of Dostoevsky, when all academics, like Raskolnikov, are forced to kneel at the crossroads and kiss the ground.

The Dean as Educator: His Doing and Undoing

T HE INTEGRITY of the academic enterprise is in the hands not only of individual professors, but also of academic administrators—above all, in the hands of academic deans. Although this responsibility does not exhaust their role, it defines a significant part of it. Full understanding of deanship requires that we know who and what a dean is. My philosophic bias favors self-knowledge as a point of departure—and a brief phenomenological investigation should assist our efforts to grasp the decanal essence.

The jokes told about deans are revealing. A perennial one is that "a dean is a mouse growing up to be a rat"—a definition produced by an academic Thersites.

There is also the story, probably originated by a college president, about the professor who was called to duty in World War II and took a military leave of absence from his academic post. When he returned to the campus after the war, he was told by his department chairman that he had been reported dead and his position filled. The professor objected vigorously and went to see his dean. The dean told him the same thing. Finally the professor went to the president who said that, unfortunately, the facts were exactly as reported. The professor, a veteran used to the coarse vocabulary of the soldier, said, "Well, I'm a son of a bitch." At which point the surprised and elated president exclaimed, "Well why didn't you say so? We have a vacant deanship."

The edifying power of these stories becomes more apparent, moreover, when they are supplemented by a phenomenological description of the scene that typically follows the selection of a new dean. At his first reception, the new dean meets a member of the faculty. The faculty member takes the dean's hand in one (or in post-LBJ days perhaps in both) of his or hers and says, "Congratulations, or should I say, Commiserations." This is followed by a phthisic laugh. The faculty member exhibits the Jack Horner syndrome, thinking "what a good," or at least, "what a witty boy am I." The new dean forces a smile, since this remark has accompanied every expression of congratulation, and he is beginning to wonder if some of the students were perhaps right to complain of widespread senility in faculty ranks. But the new dean plays the game, replying: "Thank you very much. I appreciate your good wishes." The faculty member now adds, with an expression of deep personal concern: "You have a terribly difficult if not impossible job." "Yes," answers our new dean—who, now serious, speaks from the heart—"but with your help and the help of your colleagues I'll do my best to carry on."

Examining this conversation from the detached perspective of a phenomenologist, or from my vantage point as a full-grown rat, I note that the new dean is a humbug. Persons who have used every last ounce of energy, intelligence, imagination, and political skill to ensure their selection as dean now act as if a terrible burden had been thrust upon them against their will. By a process of instant metamorphosis, the Machiavel has become the Suffering Servant.

Today, however, we must be honest in all things, not just in lending or advertising, but also in deaning. To any young man or woman aspiring to become a dean I must point out that there never was a dean who did not want to be one. And, more central to our discussion, there is no greater correlation between wanting to be a dean and being qualified to be one than between wanting and being qualified to serve on the Supreme Court. We do not hear so much about our academic mediocrities simply because administrative appointments do not usually require confirmation by either a faculty or student senate.

A further complication. Incompetence is a mask sometimes worn by many of the most gifted and effective deans. They follow the example of Lucius Junius, who under the last of the Roman kings was reputed to have escaped, by feigning great stupidity, the death visited upon other members of his family by the suspicious King Tarquin. His tactic gave rise to his nickname Brutus, meaning "stupid." Later members of his family, including the assassin of Caesar, wore the slur as a badge of honor.

Incompetence, of course, is also the refuge and sole talent of genuinely incompetent deans. But feigned incompetence is the practiced deceit of persons who must deliberately submerge all signs of intelligence, imagination, and moral concern in order to disarm or disorient opponents, increase harmony, and encourage congruent, if pathetically slow, movement toward their administrative goals. In short, the typical dean, whether a success or a failure, competent or incompetent, suppresses every vital sign in order merely to survive or to successfully realize his or her objectives. On being informed of the death of almost any dean, Dorothy Parker might have asked, as she did when told that President Coolidge had died, "How can they tell?" To hide one's light under a bushel may run counter to the teachings of Jesus, but it is the modus vivendi *and* the modus operandi of the prudential dean.

To conclude these phenomenological descriptions, I must comment on the dean's status as a member of the faculty. Clearly, if the dean is to be an educator, he or she should also be a member of the faculty. Most deans or ex-deans (I prefer to describe myself as a post-dean) believe that there is no radical separation of faculty and administration, since administrators are recruited almost exclusively from the ranks of the faculty and the faculty usually have the strongest single voice in the selection of administrators.

But this is a naïve and mistaken belief. The moment faculty members accept deanships, their faculty origins are utterly forgotten. One of the sad discoveries awaiting newly appointed deans is that within twenty-four hours they acquire a new set of enemies and a new set of friends and forfeit the right to speak as a faculty member.

While new deans feel and think of themselves as completely unchanged, their most difficult task is that of adapting to the faculty's new perception of them. The point can be illustrated by a letter from a respected colleague of mine commenting on the way in which I handled a faculty meeting. She wrote:

> First and foremost, so much of what you *once* could say and do when you were Philosophy Professor John Silber you cannot now say and do, simply because you are Dean. "I have not changed," you say, "I know I am the same person," you repeat over and over again. Unfortunately, all this is vain, for, to the faculty, you are no longer the man, John Silber. You are the *Dean:* The Administration; the Establishment; the Oppressor of Academic Freedom (although you might have been its strongest defender as a staff member, that is all forgotten); the Representative of not enough funds, of heavier teaching loads; Hatchet man; Flunky of the President and the Board—in two words, *The Enemy.* That analytical and logical mind must now be diversified into channels of a public relations expert, a program development solicitor, a loving father to student needs, a Solomon, if you wish.
>
> Everyone loves the underdog. Remember, to your faculty friends you are the authority—*The Enemy.* There were times in your meeting when friends and other staff members took exception to being identified too closely with administrative-cooperative projects which could be considered proof of the power structure's attempt to cope with the problem. There was nothing personal in the dissociation. It is just the unconscious desire not to be considered in an alignment with the power structure—that is tantamount to selling out and being seen as a tool of the Establishment.

This response helped me to understand that no matter how much administrators may continue to feel like faculty members— no matter that they continue to publish, teach, and counsel students; no matter that they were named to their administrative posts largely because of faculty support—the faculty will no longer accept them as one of their own. Deans may just as well accept this fact as a part of their job description. The irrationality of this faculty attitude is beside the point; it is a part of the reality that any dean must face. They are exceptionally fortunate if they have a loyal colleague who will alert them to this fact.

There is some consolation, of course, in the fact that faculty irrationality works in two ways. Thus, although the new deans' appointment strips them of faculty status, they are welcomed home as the returning prodigal as soon as they leave administration. And if they are fortunate enough to be fired, not only are they welcomed back, but their professorial virginity is restored as well.

This leads to metaphysical speculation on the inscrutability of the faculty. Why do so many faculty members prefer their colleagues' martyrdom to service in a worthy cause? Why do they favor Polycarp over Peter? Why don't faculty members— at least those in the English department—agree with Holden Caulfield in *Catcher in the Rye* that it is harder and better to live for a cause than to die for one?

I have an idea that the irrationalities of the decanal order are all traceable to the faculty origins of the deans. Faculty irrationalities are but symptomatic of the human condition, a part of the reality of the situation, one of the ties that bind the academic community to the general community, and, perhaps, a thread on which to develop communication between the two!

As a philosopher, moreover, I must refuse to be intimidated by irrationality. If academic deans arise from and may return to faculty ranks, then we must not allow ourselves to be confused by irrationalities of class distinctions. If we look behind the ideologies, we find that the academic dean is a faculty member—a professor, a teacher, a scholar—who is called upon for leadership in the academic community. Surely this is a call, not merely or even primarily upon faculty to manage, but a call upon educators to educate!

Today academic deans in many American universities are tempted to see themselves merely as administrators or managers with no special competence as educators. A few notable failures in academic administration have induced some boards of trustees and politicians to call for professional managers rather than educators in our administrative posts. In times of uncertainty and stress, the man on horseback has many disguises and many appealing qualities. It is my conviction, nevertheless, that educators belong in academic deanships because university management not directed by genuine educational understanding and purpose must fail.

I do not argue that *every* dean must necessarily be recruited from academic ranks—that is, I acknowledge the possibility of a Grandma Moses of higher education. But if someone from a

nonacademic background succeeds in being a good dean, it will
be due to the native genius of a folk educator rather than to the
strengths of a skilled manager. And if academic deans fulfill no
more than their job description—if they merely fill the chair but
fail to meet the educational demands of the office—they are
substantially worse than a merely managerial counterfeit whose
innocence of academic matters at least supplies an excuse. But
we should not overlook the fact that high-level qualifications in
management and education can be found in the same individual.
And the possession of that combination of abilities is the mark
of an outstanding candidate.

Before considering what is required of the dean who
transcends the job description to become an educator, let me
examine the important question of the dean's doing and undoing.
Sadly, from the day they first take office, many deans are undone
by nothing more oppressive than their own overriding concern
not to lose their deanship. For fear of being undone, some deans
pursue a course disastrous for their colleges and themselves; that
is, they stay in office by doing as little as possible and trying to
camouflage their want of ideas or educational policies as respect
for faculty autonomy. Occasionally, they may explain the
"negative sum" of their "administrative input" as the consequence of their faithful observance of the "prioritizing" of the
university president. But no excuse compensates for a wasted life.
A dean who would not be undone by his or her failure to do
must recognize that longevity may prove the prolonged undoing
of a dean who does nothing.

A corollary must also be noted. Deans may lose their jobs
and be undone precisely because they have done their jobs
exceedingly well. Some reforms, for example, cannot be carried
out without making the reformer dispensable. Indeed the vigor
and impatience of a dean or college president may be disastrous.
The late J. Herbert Hollomon presents a case in point. On
accepting the presidency of the University of Oklahoma, he
published in *The Making of a University* his plans for the reform
of the university. Informed of his plans, all of his adversaries
united to remove him. While it is no great honor to be fired from
a job, there may be good and sufficient reason for congratulating
the person who has been willing to use the full powers of his or

her office to accomplish worthy goals without compromise or concern for one's own future in office. In short, the doing of the job may lead to a dean's undoing, which may be a fair indication of just how much he or she has done. A firing, a failure to be reappointed, death, or a variety of other proximate causes may terminate a highly successful career. Just as longevity in office is no proof of success, so brevity in office is no proof of failure; in some cases it may be the very price of success.

Some years back I was interviewed for the presidency of a small college. In the course of my visits I met a disgruntled and aggressive faculty member whom I recognized as a man far better qualified than I for the presidency of that college. By trying to lead the college into needed reforms without the power base of the presidency and without the support of the ineffective incumbent, he had failed in his efforts at reform (beyond the remarkable upgrading of his own department) and exhausted the wide faculty support he had once enjoyed. I conveyed my observations to the chairman of the search committee. I added that the man's faculty support would reappear as soon as he was made president, and that it would take an outsider at least two years to accomplish what the internal candidate could do at once. But I failed to persuade. A total stranger, from outside, who had no enemies precisely because he was a stranger, was chosen, and promptly failed. The internal candidate whom I had recommended then accepted a much more demanding administrative assignment at another institution where he enjoyed the advantage of anonymity. The point is clear. An administrator may exhaust his usefulness on one campus and be forced to move in order "to make his marble good" on another campus where the opposition that inevitably confronts innovators and reformers has not yet formed. (The idiom refers to that happy moment of childhood when one wins his first game of marbles with his brand-new agate shooter. As the late eminent philosopher J. N. Findlay once observed, using this idiom, it is a pity that the game of marbles no longer plays a central role in the life of children.)

To summarize, deans may be undone because they have done very well, or by skillfully doing nothing; that is, they may fail either by perishing brilliantly or by surviving without accomplishment. For many years I did not know of a single instance

in which a do-nothing dean or a dean who was graciously incompetent was removed from office prior to death or the age of
mandatory retirement. I am now aware of several examples.

I therefore conclude that if deans are concerned merely to
serve until retirement, their realistic course should be that of
doing well by doing nothing or as little as possible. On the other
hand, if one is not a prudential but an idealistic dean who aspires
to greatness, then one must be prepared to risk brief tenure as
the possible price of introducing improvement and change into
the university, which is among the most conservative of institutions. But the daring dean may take solace from the fact that
the scene and circumstances of a debacle may provide the
occasion and energy for a new adventure. With good luck the
dean may anticipate full support from a self-confident president
who understands that a president's reputation is enhanced or
diminished in proportion to the effectiveness of deans.

What about the positive role of the deans as educators—their
doings? Although most deans properly come from faculty ranks,
scholarly credentials do not guarantee decanal competence. One
may be a leading scholar and a brilliant teacher in a discipline
without ever having thought about the full scope of education
or the role of educational institutions. But these concerns are
essential to competent deans, and selection committees should
be concerned with examining the educational philosophy of those
who aspire to deanships.

But note that I do not propose that deanships should be the
preserve of those trained in schools of education. Just as war is
too important to be left to generals, education is too important
to be left to educationists. A school of education may turn out a
splendid educator, just as a theological seminary may turn out
a saint. Neither result is likely, however, since no program of
instruction can guarantee the production of either. The test is of
the individual, not of his degree.

The test may take the form of a series of questions. We might
ask scholars who aspire to deanships what they have to teach the
faculty, students, administrators, trustees, and the public. If they
have nothing to teach them, why should they pretend to be
educators? If they have, let us examine their views.

Deans who are doing their jobs in the normative sense must

have the imagination to put themselves in the place of all their constituents as they consider the activities and the goals of their college. If they put themselves in the students' place, they will immediately become impatient with the complacent indifference of so many faculty members to the confusion and lack of coherence in their college's educational programs.

Deans will acknowledge at once that, from the students' perspective, a problem of relevance exists. But they will have to analyze the situation on their own campuses before knowing the nature of the problem. The problem of relevance varies from campus to campus. Although it has a common core—the search for meaningful existence in a chaotic, post-Christian civilization—its features will vary according to the educational and social background of the students, the extent of their intellectual interests, and the quality of the institution, its faculty, and its degree of emphasis on oral or written publication.

The thoughtful dean will understand that relevance in higher education is not a problem for which students or faculty members, administrators or parents, either individually or collectively, are to blame. The problem has its origin in a highly complex network of historical, cultural, and socioeconomic forces.

Part of our problem arises from the various temptations to which professors are exposed, and the increase in the number of noneducational services they are asked to perform—opportunities or demands not merely or even especially to teach, but to consult for industry, government, and private research institutes. These external distractions have tended to reduce the coherence of the educational program.

Another part of the problem stems from society's practice of prolonging adolescence without providing students "a piece of the action" until they are in their middle twenties or early thirties. When John Kennedy became the youngest man to be elected president, he was ten years older than Alexander the Great at the time of his death. Kennedy was also substantially older than many of our founding fathers at the time of their greatest service to our republic. At 23 John Quincy Adams, for instance, was admitted to the bar; at 27 he was appointed ambassador to the Netherlands. At 26 George Washington was a colonel; at 37 he sent protests to the king. At 20 Alexander Hamilton was lieutenant colonel and secretary to George Washington; at 25 he represented New York in Congress, and at 32 he was named secretary of the treasury. Jefferson began the practice of law at 24 and wrote the Declaration of Independence at 33. Is it any wonder that present-day students and young professors are impatient?

Our age is often said to be an era in which youth is worshipped. But, in fact, our time is characterized by its willingness to be led by older men and by its insistence that young men and women bide their time. The problem is made more acute by modern medicine, which has prevented death from opening opportunities for the younger generation at the time when their energies, aptitudes, and ambitions call for expression and responsible action. And what modern medicine had not yet accomplished, Congressman Claude Pepper ensured by legislation— legislation that, in the name of ending age discrimination, legalizes age discrimination at the expense of the young. Pepper's reforms forced universities to introduce stringent evaluation of older faculty to justify their termination for cause. Formerly, a humane policy allowed burnt-out professors to retire with dignity at 65. Even without Pepper's reforms, universities were and still are fully empowered to continue the tenure of outstanding professors for as long as they are productive.

The problem is further compounded by the fact that universities and colleges, along with high schools and elementary schools, are left to provide instruction once offered by the church or the family. If colleges and universities are loath to provide instruction in ethics and in the obligations of citizenship and parenthood, we will surely become a society of intemperate citizens contemptuous of law, and a society of parents negligent in the nurture of their children. Parents increasingly, when income permits, abandon their children to kindergartens or nursery schools, and when income does not permit, leave them unattended. And college experience comes far too late in a person's life to provide an adequate foundation for moral conduct. Ethics, if it is to be taught at all, must be taught from the start. For ethics is, to an extraordinary degree, a matter of habituation in a moral ethos.

Increasingly, college students confront the discrepancy between the ideals proclaimed in our society and the practices of individuals in business, the professions, and government. They do not need to be investigative reporters to observe the hypocrisy of the elders who should be their mentors. The opposition of college students to the war in Vietnam resulted in part from their witness of the contrast between our society's ideals and its practices. This contrast also fueled the resentment of students, black and white, over racial discrimination on and off campus. These concerns and distresses are shared by most of their elders as well.

It is a time when simple answers are patently false and sound answers difficult to come by. In such a time men and women, young and old, are tempted to abandon reason in favor of anti-rational, simplistic programs that satisfy our hunger for certainty even as they defy our powers of comprehension. We have seen a wave of anti-intellectualism rise to the breaking point before us. The student left inadvertently recruited the student right, and extreme campus movements provided encouragement and support for opposing right-wing movements over the country as a whole. Relevant irrationality has been, and is, far more attractive to young minds than irrelevant rationality. Now that students are more serious than in years past, their irrationality is more dangerous.

The charge that contemporary students are more apathetic than the students of the 1960s calls for examination. In part, the complaint expresses the frustration of 1960s students who are now members of university faculties and the longing of their student epigones for a golden age they never knew. What is referred to as apathy is in part a renewed commitment to the process of learning, which is encouraged by a growing recognition that the student reform movements of the late 1960s and early 1970s failed to produce a workable political agenda and thereby exposed the folly of expecting instant solutions to complex social problems.

It seems clear, then, that colleges must now assume responsibilities they have traditionally avoided. Instead of striving to be impersonally objective, they must strive to be objectively personal. And they must experiment and innovate while carefully looking over their shoulders to discover failed and sometimes fatal historical antecedents for some of the proposed "innovations."

As educators, deans must take the lead in curricular revision; they must encourage their faculties to provide the essential ingredients of a coherent world view whose creation must be the work of each student. And they must encourage each student to find coherence and meaning through diligent study.

The issue of relevance is not really of recent origin. In the 1930s, Robert Hutchins, one of the greatest educators ever to become president of a major university, addressed this issue with a major reform of the curriculum at the University of Chicago. Even then, Hutchins correctly saw that the demand for relevance was in truth a thirst for meaning. Full of hubris, Hutchins attempted to direct the professionalized and disconnected activities of the Chicago faculty into a coherent pattern of coordinated ideals and objectives. Though not entirely successful, his efforts were heroic.

Granted that no synthesis can or should be imposed on faculty or students, the program of a college must nevertheless make sense. At the very least, the college must concern itself with the unfolding of individuals. It will be concerned with developing graduates who are not tempted by suicide, whether chronic or acute, but who will confront life with passion, with joy and delight at the prospect of human existence, and with courage to cope with its contingencies and disappointments.

The purpose of the liberal arts college is well expressed in an essay by Professor Neil Megaw:[1]

> The College . . . offers certain basic courses for students taking pre-professional training in other colleges and schools of the University. It has a few pre-professional programs of its own. And it prepares many students for graduate studies in the various disciplines. These functions, however, grow out of its central purpose: To create an environment in which each student can advance toward his or her individual version of a liberal education.
>
> What is a liberal education? Precisely because such an education liberates the individual, setting free the distinctive powers of this particular man or that particular woman, it is notoriously hard to define in general terms. It obviously means more than knowl-

edge. At the very least, it sharpens the student's perceptions of his world and of himself, and both broadens and disciplines his understanding. At its very best, a liberal education is the way of life of a whole human being, toward which college provides only a beginning. . . . In four years, finally, the student can hope to achieve a measure of that intellectual independence and creativity that is his ultimate goal: The individual mind defining its freedom in significant action.

The dean must exercise leadership by siding with students in their insistence on improved teaching at both undergraduate and graduate levels. In many universities, deans must educate their faculties on the central importance of teaching and encourage by salary and promotion those who teach well. When faculty members argue that the quality of teaching cannot be judged objectively, the dean must ask: How, then, is the objective assessment of published writings possible? Perhaps the chief reason why books and articles are used more frequently than teaching to assess scholarly competence is that senior colleagues will read the books and articles by younger nontenured faculty members but will rarely visit their classes. Assessment of published writings would also be thought of as subjective if no one bothered to read them. Indeed, I have heard of one case in which published writings were evaluated without being read, on the rationale that the journals in which they appeared would not have published inferior material.

To those faculty who object to having their teaching evaluated by faculty colleagues or students on the grounds that visitations violate the character of the student-faculty relationship, the dean must explain that the classroom is not the sanctuary of a mystery religion in which secret rites are performed. The classroom is essentially public. A student conference in the professor's office might well be privileged, but not the educational transactions of the classroom itself. A useful analogy is the work of lawyers in a courtroom. Lawyers who refused to allow their clients or others to observe them in action in the courtroom would put themselves out of business. To the argument that classroom visitation by other faculty or administrators violates the dignity of the teaching profession, Professor Francis Hart of the University of Virginia sagely replied, "What a curious concept of dig-

nity . . . to be ashamed to be caught at one's work!" The idea
that lectures should not be open to examination by colleagues or
administrators violates the concept of the open marketplace of
ideas—the public nature of scholarship. No doubt faculty
aversion to such examination arises in part from their reluctance
to be judged. They are pious folk who say, "Judge not, that ye
be not judged." They carry senatorial courtesy to new heights,
in many cases perpetuating intolerable incompetence.

Evaluation of teaching, which is best initiated by the faculty,
can only be completed by the students. As dean I assisted students
in their efforts to produce a course evaluation; when they needed
money to perfect their methods or to publish their results, I gave
them all the support I could. Still, it is the faculty that should
assume the main burden of faculty evaluation.

An effective dean must also reject the false antithesis between
teaching and research, even while accepting the practice of
"publish or perish." This is because publication may occur either
on the page or in the classroom. Each is necessary to the academy
and, if based on sound knowledge, each is worthy of respect and
support. Just as scholars can hardly respect publications that they
are not allowed to read, neither should they respect a colleague's
teaching unless it can be witnessed and evaluated. There can be
no doubt that professors and others engaged in teaching will
improve their teaching when they discover that their oral "publication" will be examined and evaluated by colleagues and
students, and that good teaching will not only be respected but
rewarded.

In order to improve teaching we must also increase our respect
for good teachers. When we reward in rank and in salary
colleagues who concentrate on research and writing to the neglect
and detriment of students, we send a clear signal to all faculty
members that teaching is at best of secondary importance. Those
colleagues who devote themselves to research that leads not to
written but to oral publication in lectures and seminars of
inspiring quality must be rewarded no less handsomely than those
who excel merely in their written publications. And we should
also recognize that true excellence is rare, whether in oral or
written publication.

Justice Felix Frankfurter, reminiscing about Professor James

Barr Ames of the Harvard Law School, spoke eloquently of the importance of teaching: "He was a wonderful teacher, and original mind," said Frankfurter, "and he illustrated, to a degree unexcelled by anybody I ever knew anything about, the conception by Socrates of a teacher, that of a midwife. Ames was the midwife of minds." When Ames died, Frankfurter praised him to his roommate, Morris Cohen, who would later distinguish himself in philosophy. Cohen thought the praise was exaggerated and said: "After all, what is the deposit Ames left behind him? He hardly wrote anything." To which Frankfurter replied:

> What he left behind him is that which Pericles says in his funeral oration is the most important thing. His deposit is in the minds of men. He excited and touched more first-rate minds in the profession of the law, I suppose, than any man who ever had pupils. Dean Ames would rather spend hours with a student than write a legal essay that would immortalize him.

Because it is easy to mistake the permanence of the printed page for importance, and the transience of the spoken word for trivia, deans who care about the health of their institutions must guard against such confusion with all the power of their office.

In the defense of teaching, the dean must pay careful attention to the allocation of resources. He must call into question the inverted pyramid of costs in higher education and insist that resources are allocated to each constituency in accordance with its needs. Why, for example, should it be assumed that graduate education is intrinsically more expensive than undergraduate education and therefore deserves more support? For some fields of study that require complex machinery and expensive materials, this assertion is obviously true. But why should more be spent on the education of graduate students in English, history, or philosophy, for example, than is spent on the education of undergraduates in those same fields?

When do students face the greatest needs? Obviously, as freshmen. Freshmen in large lecture courses, even when superbly taught, are frequently denied any personal contact with their professors. Often in such classes, papers—if any are required—are cursorily graded without comment, and examinations are limited to multiple-choice questions. In all their courses, freshmen need tutors who will read their papers with care and concern, tutors who will scrupulously criticize style, method, and thought.

Most irrationally, freshmen are frequently denied access to professors, and abandoned to inexperienced teaching assistants who, though competent in their graduate specialty, may be unprepared for teaching freshmen. This is not to decry the use of teaching assistants. When teaching assistants are apprenticed to outstanding teachers who instruct them largely by example in the art of teaching, they may, in one or two semesters, become well prepared to teach sections of elementary courses on their own. Often they bring to their teaching an enthusiasm that may be lacking in more experienced professors. And their proximity in age to their students makes them somewhat less intimidating to students and enables them to elicit student participation more effectively than is possible for older and more intimidating colleagues.

If more of our academic resources were spent on freshmen and sophomores, advanced undergraduates and graduate students would be far more able to study on their own. Graduate professors would not then have to spend so much time on their supervision.

Courageous deans, in order to improve the quality of teaching, must also be prepared to call faculty members to honest self-assessment of their teaching methods. For example, the seminar method is frequently misused. When professors come to class with no understanding of what they intend to accomplish, and without having made advance assignments to focus the attention and preparation of students, it will almost certainly be a seminar in boredom, as the discussion meanders from one *ad hoc* comment to another, sans argument, sans direction.

There are seminars in which the professor does little more than audit, adding no more than an occasional comment in an atmosphere of relaxed cordiality. Such seminars are not as educative as the informal sessions of conversation to which Alfred North Whitehead on occasion invited his students. When I was a graduate student at Yale, Professor Paul Weiss carried on Whitehead's traditional open house. But even though these evenings were more educational than many seminars for which academic credit was given, Weiss never suggested that these be counted as part of his regular teaching load.

Faculty members unwilling to prepare adequately for class have a ready rationalization in the specious claim that they are really only concerned with allowing maximum student participation. And in order to reduce the claim of students on their time, they argue in favor of extremely small classes on similar grounds. The dean must be willing to challenge these rationalizations—to point out that seminars, no less than lectures, call for careful planning and vigorous participation by the professor. Moreover, seminars require a critical mass of prepared and articulate students. If the students are extraordinarily good, five will be sufficient. If they are inadequate, no number will produce a critical mass. Ten to fifteen students are usually required even in colleges and universities of the highest quality.

The dean's call for honest self-assessment must include the students no less than the faculty. Students can be as much humbugs as deans or faculty members. And since the students pay tuition, they especially are owed an education. If they insist on the right of revolution, they deserve to know its corollary: that the revolutionary had better win. And if, out of professed concern for the tragic events at Kent State, they propose the cancellation of final exams and graduation, they must ask themselves whether this can alter the situation with which they are concerned, or whether they are merely campaigning, out of pure self-interest, for release from their academic duties.

The courageous dean must also be willing on occasion to educate the president. If, at times of student unrest, the president refuses to fulfill the role of educator, arguing that the dignity of the office precludes direct involvement with students, it may be up to the dean to remind the president that there is very little dignity left in an office after it has been invaded by students. Instead of worrying about dignity, administrators—presidents, provosts, or deans—should represent their office in the most effective way by infusing, whenever possible, educational content into moments of physical encounter.

In short, it is a part of the dean's responsibilities to speak, publicly and privately, to all constituencies—students, faculty, administration, trustees, and the public—on both the realities and the ideals of liberal arts education. Part of the university's reason for being is to mediate the ideal and the actual—and the academic dean is essential in this mediation. Faculty and students should understand their dependency on the public, which has little sympathy for adolescent self-indulgence or adult irresponsibility and can express its disaffection from the university by withholding support. At the same time, trustees and the public should be aware of the concerns of youthful idealists and the aspirations of faculty, which it is the purpose of the university to nurture.

In addressing trustees and the public, the dean must convey something of the magic and confusion of youth, the fragility of the academic life, the excitement of rule by persuasion rather than by force; and, perhaps, if deans have the vision, something of the form and substance of the times. They must seek to convey how students, through the difficult search for truth, begin to discover their true selves. As Nietzsche says in his essay "Schopenhauer as Educator":

> How can a man come to know himself? He is a dark and veiled thing; and if the hare has seven skins a man could skin himself seventy times seven and still not say, "This now is yourself, this is no longer husk." Besides, it is an agonizing, dangerous enterprise to dig down into yourself and descend forcibly by the shortest route down the shaft of your own being. A man may easily do himself such damage that no doctor can cure him. And besides, why should it be necessary, since everything bears witness to our being—our friendships and hatreds, our looks and our handshake, our memory and the things we forget, our books and the strokes of our pen? But there is a way of performing this crucial inquiry. Let the young soul look back upon its life and ask: What up to now have you truly loved? What has raised up your soul? What ruled it, and at the same time made it happy? Line up these objects of reverence before you and perhaps by what they are, and by their sequence, they will yield to you a law, a basic law, of your proper self. Compare these objects, see how one completes, enlarges, exceeds and transfigures the others, how they form a ladder upon which you have so far climbed up toward yourself. For your own true nature does not lie hidden deep within you, but immeasurably high above you, or at least above that which you customarily take to be yourself.

Your true teachers, the men who formed you and educated you, revealed to you what is the true original sense and basic stuff of your nature. . . . And that is the secret of all education and culture; it does not give artificial limbs, wax noses, or corrective lenses—rather, that which can give those gifts is merely a caricature of education. Education, on the contrary, is liberation, the clearing of all weeds, rubble, and vermin that might harm delicate shoots, a radiance of light and warmth, a loving, falling rustle of rain by night.[2]

When deans understand that "education is liberation," they find themselves and their role in the academic community is to clear away "all weeds, rubble, and vermin that might harm delicate shoots." They remove the obstacles to personal fulfillment that beset both students and faculty; they help to create a context in which the individual may emerge. This is a context, moreover, which, made vivid by an effective dean, can engage the imagination and support of parents, trustees, and taxpayers.

Above all, Nietzsche's portrait of the ideal teacher should stir the imagination of deans who are educators. In this ideal they may find their role as the teachers of those who teach and learn. There can be no major undoing of the work of deans who fulfill their role as educators.

Tenure in Context

Discussions of tenure rights in the American university have been marred by failure to examine the similarities and differences in the functioning of tenure in various institutions. This failure to consider the contextual framework has given rise to fundamental confusions. None is more glaring than the confusion of tenure—its role and function—with academic freedom, or the vague notion that in academic circles tenure functions in a manner radically different from that in business or professional life.

My purpose here is to take a modest first step toward correcting this failure. As a philosopher, I would characterize it as the absence of adequate phenomenological examination of tenure and of its relation to academic freedom. Full discussion would require a book, but even a phenomenological sketch will, I believe, measurably advance our understanding of the problem.

When the average business executive, carpenter, cab driver, lawyer, or surgeon discusses some "wild-mouthed professor" or a professor who is negligent or unresponsive in his or her duties because of psychological depression, alcoholism, premature senility, or some other cause, or even some responsible academic exponent of a system of thought that outrages folk wisdom, these professional, business, and tradespeople will likely say, almost in unison, "If that man were in my field, he'd be fired."

The cab driver, surgeon, carpenter, lawyer, and business executive are firmly convinced that survival in their occupations depends upon continued productivity at a high level, that they are caught up in competitive or professional forces that ensure competence and efficiency, and that professional and financial disaster awaits those who, for whatever reason, fail to meet rigorous expectations. But they believe that university and college professors, public school teachers, and everyone in civil service have tenure in a sense that is denied them. They believe, moreover, that academic tenure has destroyed responsibility and performance and that vitality, efficiency, and competence in their own fields are largely traceable to its absence.

Every college and university president knows that, outside the academy, these are the prevailing dogmas. Every university administrator with at least two months' experience has been repeatedly told, "Professor X should be fired," and, what is more, "He would be fired if universities and colleges operated on the same principles as the rest of American society." This charge is usually made, first, because of the prevalent business attitude toward academics and, second, because university administrators usually respond inadequately or confusedly to such charges.

Without bothering to consider the nature of tenure and how it operates in social and industrial life, the university administrator typically claims that the incompetent or irresponsible professor cannot be fired because he or she has tenure. The administrator discusses tenure as if it were a sinecure or a magic property like the protective waters in which Achilles was dipped or the charm with which Brünnhilde shielded the body of Siegfried—in short, as if it were an absolute bar to the severance of a professor, his reassignment, or the curtailment of his professorial activities. To excuse either the administrator's evasion of responsibility or inability to give substantive answers to the questions asked by trustees, the administrator has encouraged the mistaken belief that academic tenure functions as a sinecure— that is, as something radically different from the tacit forms of tenure that flourish in professions, businesses, and unions.

If we examine these other contexts, however, we immediately see the absurdity of the distinction. Consider the manner in which surgeons must deal with incompetent or less than fully competent performances by their colleagues or by student physicians. In the surgical services of a teaching hospital, quality is in part ensured by an exercise known as Deaths and Complications, a weekly review of all hospital cases in which unexpected developments or death occur. In a typical session a case is presented; then students and the surgical staff are asked questions concerning procedures that were followed.

Suppose, for example, an infection develops after a cesarean birth. What caused the infection? Investigation indicates that it resulted from the removal of a normal appendix in conjunction with the cesarean section. Is it wise or foolish to complicate a straightforward cesarean with an appendectomy? Was the pedicle of the appendix cut too short? Should the combining of operations be recommended in any case? and so on. The purpose of the discussion is to educate students and sharpen the skills of practicing surgeons by expanding their experience through examinations of the experience of others, as well as to censure constructively those who have made mistakes in order to improve professional performance. This is a humane but stringent examination of human judgment, aimed at its refinement. Deaths and Complications provides a review group in which professionals and students can severely criticize one another without running the risk of ostracism or more severe penalties.

If one surgeon provides far more cases for discussion than any other, how do the teaching faculty, residents, and affiliated surgeons remove him? Only two courses of action are open. Deficient surgeons can be removed, but they then may go to less demanding hospitals where they can practice without supervision. To avoid this, colleagues recommend retaining the deficient surgeon and protecting the surgeon's patients by assisting in operations.

Doctors who graduate from a medical school, complete their residency requirements, pass their boards, and enter practice are almost never denied tenure. Occasionally, surgeons are persuaded to change their fields from surgery to general practice or some specialty less likely to endanger the lives of their patients. Basically, however, surgeons have tenure in the sense that they have a right to continue the practice of surgery indefinitely—a right, barring criminal activities, virtually impossible to rescind. Moreover, the medical profession has rarely been willing to apply severe sanctions to doctors who are alcoholics or addicted to drugs.

So much, then, for the notion that in medicine "a man like Professor X would be fired."

The situation in legal practice is similar. Imagine, for instance, the partners of a law firm meeting to discuss another partner. The discussion goes as follows: "Bill's alcoholism has gotten steadily worse for the last five years. It's been almost five years since he has been able to meet a client effectively for more than two hours at a time. Everybody knows that he drinks too much. It's time we asked him to withdraw from the firm." And the typical reply is: "But how can we just get rid of Bill? Admittedly, he's an embarrassment to the firm. But he's brought in at least 15 to 20 percent of our clients over the last twenty years. We still have several clients who swear by him, and all the clients he brought in would resent our tossing him out at age 55 after 30 years' service and 20 years as a partner." The partnership might insist on reducing Bill's share of its income. It is extremely unlikely, however, that they would leave him severely embarrassed, either socially or financially. And we are all aware of the difficulties involved in removing a judge whose performance is publicly acknowledged by the legal profession to be defective.

So much, then, for the myth that in law "a man like Professor X would be fired."

We also know that in every business minor and major failings are tolerated at all levels, from executives to janitors. Except in times of severe financial strain, corporations and family businesses retain their employees—particularly high-placed employees—by overlooking or resigning themselves to their various shortcomings. Examples are legion and notorious; we all know of them. When a man is fired, we can assume either that he had been with the firm for a short time, that he had been detected in flagrant wrongdoing, or that his firing will be seen as irresponsible or unjust. Arthur Miller's *Death of a Salesman* is, in part, an indictment of the callow inheritor of a family business who met none of the obligations his father owed to older employees. An executive of one of the largest insurance companies remarked that, of its several hundred salesmen, no more than 30 to 40 percent could be expected to produce at a reasonably high level.

This level of performance, he observed, was standard for the industry and had remained unchanged over several decades.

So much for the myth that in business "a man like Professor X would be fired."

In carpentry, plumbing, and taxi-driving, the situation varies, depending upon whether the individual is a self-employed entrepreneur or the employee of a firm. If the latter, his case is covered by the preceding discussion. If the former, the tenure obligations of the self-employed entrepreneur will be personal obligations to employees, if any, and to the entrepreneur's dependents. Thus tenure characterizes many relationships usually overlooked in discussions of the subject.

Properly understood, tenure is a relevant aspect of all human relationships—an expression of the human need for order and certainty, and a condition of the fulfillment of responsibilities reasonably expected, not only of institutions, but of individuals.

Though far from complete, my sketch leads persuasively, in my opinion, to the conclusion that tenure is an expression of the human concern for continuity and stability in personal, social, professional, and business life. Tenure, whether formal or informal, is an expectation of continued employment, of relative permanence, that grows with each year of service in the minds of employers and employees. It is the expectation, rising with the passage of time, that severance or alteration of service will not occur. It is also the moral conviction that employment must not be altered or terminated capriciously, that these things will occur only if changed circumstances justify their occurrence. Tenure may be seen in part as a contextual variant of the principle of nonparasitism: "One who serves must be served" and "for unto whomsoever much is given, of him shall be much required." Both maxims express the basic human need for coherence and continuity in human associations.

Typically, on the first day of a job one is impressed with the uncertainty of continuance. The newcomer is on trial: Probation is the mode of employment. A secretary's probationary appointment begins on the first day at work. But for an airline stewardess, probationary appointment begins with the first day in stewardess school. For surgeons, probation probably begins prior to admission to medical school, certainly with the commencement of residency. By the time surgeons have passed their boards and are licensed to practice independently of supervision, their practice is no longer probationary but tenured. Surgeons have tenure in their license and also in their institutional positions. They can continue to practice surgery for as long as they live unless someone can prove—and proof is extremely difficult—that they are incompetent or guilty of flagrant malpractice, or unless malpractice premiums consume so much of their income that practice is no longer worthwhile. Lawyers' probationary appointments begin either with law school or on joining a firm. Gradually their probationary mode becomes a permanent relationship expressed by membership in the firm or by joining the partnership. A similar relationship characterizes participation in consulting firms. The large group of associates are, like assistant professors, on probation, while the partners function in many ways as tenured faculty.

Tenure functions in all institutions as a rising expectation of continuity or permanence. The burden of proof for continuance is gradually shifted from the employee to the employer. New employees must demonstrate their value to their institutions; the firm must demonstrate to old employees that it is justified in insisting on reassignment, reduction of duties, or severance. Tenure functions on a continuum, and tenure claims are partly a function of the claimants' power within their profession. At the height of an employee's powers, he or she reaches a zenith of tenure expectation. As an employee's powers decline, there is growing reasonableness in a call for removal. Removal after long service must reasonably involve either reassignment or adequate retirement or disability benefits if the employer is to be free of the charge of exploitation or of parasitism in relation to the employee.

The number of years required to establish a tenure claim will vary according to the nature of the institution and the demands of the job. A janitor might establish a weak tenure claim within a few weeks or months on the basis of competence and a very strong claim within five years on the basis of satisfactory service. A surgeon, by contrast, would need eight or nine years to sustain a claim on the basis of competence, and by that time would already have given substantial service.

Grounds for alteration or termination of employment must likewise vary according to the nature of the institution and the responsibilities of the employee. In some fields and professions tenure, once acquired through years of increasing competence and service, is not likely ever to be lost by a conscientious and healthy participant. (Law, architecture, retail sales, interior house painting, and cabinetmaking are examples.) In other occupations, however, the claims of tenure decrease as surely as they increase through the natural rise and decline in the effective performance of jobholders. And in some professions skills are so specialized that reassignments are almost impossible to arrange. Professional baseball and opera are two obvious examples.

Nor are tenure claims and rights apt to be standard even within a single profession. The musician's profession, for instance, is incredibly varied. The concertmaster may look forward to long tenure, whereas a coloratura must resign herself to a much shorter career. A well-managed opera company must acknowledge tenure claims by members of its orchestra that are substantially more enduring than those of its singing staff. But the economics of opera production are such that no company, unless subsidized, can guarantee future employment or properly reward prior service.

Tenure within institutions is not totally dissimilar to the claims made on one another by members of a family. In this context, we may see a kind of tenure imposed on the self-employed individuals who insist on continuing to work for themselves (granting tenure to themselves as their own employee) as a condition for meeting the obligations they owe to other members of their family. They cannot rid themselves of these obligations (except, perhaps, in a merely legal sense, or in an empty physical sense through abandonment or suicide) simply by deciding to disown their offspring and divorce their spouses, since they have claims markedly similar to tenure (once again as expectations of continuity) in relation to themselves. Even in our friendships there is a slowly rising claim analogous to tenure; responsible persons do not make or terminate friendships suddenly or capriciously. Severance of these associations requires justification.

The concept of tenure in its most systematic manifestation

may be found in Japan, where much of the industrial system is viewed as similar to an extended family. The imperfections in most of the tenure relationships in our society stem from the absence of this extended family concept. What we find wanting is a general system of retirement and insurance that provides dignified options for those who, through natural processes of physical, mental, and motivational decline, are no longer capable of maintaining their effectiveness in highly competitive or professionally demanding contexts. In societies such as Japan's, simple firing is comparatively rare. This drastic extreme is usually avoided by means of reassignment, retirement, or hospitalization. And, ideally, reassignments and retirements are arranged within a context that successfully preserves the dignity and self-esteem of the individual.

In light of this cursory examination, we must conclude that tenure exists as a claim of continuance and as a demand of immunity from arbitrary termination of most human relationships, whether private or institutional. Tenure is grounded ultimately in a human expectation that there be continuity in life, that there be a *quid pro quo*, that associations among individuals and between individuals and institutions be orderly rather than chaotic, responsible rather than capricious.

Tenure exists in universities and colleges, not because of the American Association of University Professors, but rather because of human nature. When a businessman says, "In business, we would fire a man like Professor X," he talks tough but misstates the facts. All of us in all professions, institutions, and personal associations come to terms with relative degrees of competence and responsibility. Incompetence and irresponsibility no less than their opposites are a part of the human condition.

If this analysis of tenure is sound, why is there a widespread belief that tenure functions differently in academic communities? The responsibility lies, I believe, both with academic administrators and with the AAUP. I have already mentioned the confusion that has led academic administrators to explain, "Professor X cannot be fired because he has tenure." But nothing in the concept of tenure precludes firing; tenure precludes only capricious or arbitrary firing. If a tenured professor fails to meet the demands and responsibilities of his position, he may be fired or reassigned for cause. If tenure were interpreted as an absolute bar to dismissal or reassignment, it would lose its distinctive meaning and become something approaching sinecure. Unfortunately, college and university administrators have frequently invested tenure with just that meaning.

The AAUP influenced administrators in this direction through laudable but sometimes misguided efforts to protect academic freedom. And neither the AAUP nor the academic administrators have unraveled the confusions that led them astray or have sought perspicuous and effective means of pursuing their common goals. They failed to inquire into the relation of tenure to academic freedom. They never asked whether the principles and procedures that protect the one are compatible with the protection, or even the existence, of the other.

The transformation of tenure into near sinecure was not the original intention of the AAUP but, rather, the inadvertent result of a number of maladroit efforts to defend and protect academic freedom. The history of the transformation of academic tenure into near-sinecure is a topic worthy of study by our best historians, but for my purposes here a sketch must suffice. At a time when the public was hostile to and intolerant of evolutionists, secularists, economists, psychoanalysts, sociologists, or indeed of any professor whose views differed from local public opinion, the AAUP perhaps decided that the successful defense of all members of the academic community from capricious dismissal was impossible. Unable to defend all, in 1915 the AAUP suggested that the positions above the rank of instructor be tenured after ten years of service, subject to removal for cause. By so doing, the AAUP unquestionably increased the effectiveness of its protection of academic freedom for tenured faculty. It also stimulated public recognition of the need for academic freedom, even though it did little to clarify the latter concept among either professors or the general public.

In 1940 the AAUP decision to lower from ten to seven years the period of service at which tenure claims are made may have derived from numerological instincts. Or perhaps the example that guided the AAUP leadership in arriving at this number was Jacob's seven years in service to Laban. Or it may have been the political judgment that by 1940 a larger subset of professors could be defended against arbitrary dismissal. Whether guided by numerology, biblical precedent, or political tactics, the AAUP could reasonably argue that a professor who had worked seven years for a university has a *bona fide* claim to tenure—that is, a reasonable expectation of continuance and immunity from capricious removal—on the basis of service. Such a professor might reasonably assume, moreover, that if he had not shown some promise of meeting minimal expectations of competence, he would have been separated from the institution at an earlier date. Although the seven-year rule distorts the essential character of tenure by disregarding its continuum features—that is, by overlooking the gradual rise in the expectation of continuance— the AAUP tenure rule, as formulated in 1915 and modified in 1940, did not absolutize tenure as an unqualified right to continuance. On the contrary, it clearly provided that faculty members could be dismissed for cause.

As formulations of bare principles, there is little to contest in the AAUP statements on academic freedom and tenure. The academic community was fighting for its life—for the freedoms to teach and learn according to sound principles of intellectual inquiry. The AAUP tenure rule offered a significant defensive weapon against the arbitrary firing of faculty—that is, against the destruction of teaching and research capabilities through enforced conformity to the dominant views of local communities, no matter how ignorant or prejudiced. The 1915 Declaration of Principle and the 1940 Statement of Principles on Academic Freedom and Tenure were undeniably helpful.

As formulated, however, AAUP principles provided scant protection of academic freedom for nontenured faculty or students. (Universities occasionally use AAUP procedures to defend academic freedom of nontenured faculty. This defense has been limited, as far as I know, to cases that involve political rather than strictly academic issues.) Moreover, scant attention was given to elaborating the concept of academic responsibility. Little was said about those institutional conditions or levels of faculty performance that might provide reasonable grounds for faculty dismissal or reassignment; and procedures for evaluation and assessment of competence in teaching or scholarship were not developed to guide faculties or administrations in deciding issues of continuance, separation, or reassignment. But during those early years, when all academic communities were chastened by marauding bands of religious and racial bigots and, in addition, experienced the pressures of economic austerity compounded by intermittent economic depressions, faculty were, almost without exception, highly responsible; hence these shortcomings went unnoticed, and there was no pressing need for correction.

To enforce its tenure rule, the AAUP developed a trial procedure and a common law tradition of cases whereby the rule was interpreted on the basis of precedent. Actually the AAUP's trial procedure may have been a more effective weapon against arbitrary firing than the tenure rule itself. The trial procedure guarantees every tenured faculty member subject to possible removal or reassignment the right to a hearing before a jury of faculty; the jury determines whether administrative action is justified. The professor is granted most of the traditional protections of legal due process, including the right to counsel, the right to confront witnesses and cross-examine them, and the right to a transcript of the proceedings.

At the time the AAUP first proposed its trial procedure, it was not unreasonable to suppose that most violations of the rights of faculties would be politically motivated. Although the first AAUP Committee on Academic Freedom and Academic Tenure, formed in 1915, intended to formulate principles and procedures that would provide universal protection of intellectual freedom in universities, its concern as expressed in recommendations was more limited. Initially, the AAUP did not intend to conduct investigations of alleged violations of academic freedom, but during its first year it did so. Perhaps because at that time most cases involved attacks from outside the university, the AAUP selected the adversary system. Although the adversary process and the jury system are crude instruments in the search for truth, they are remarkably effective in the defense of political freedom. We should not overlook, however, the serious limitations of the adversary system—agonistic both in conception and operation—in the context of a community as subtle, organic, and dependent on mutual respect and persuasion as that of a college or university.

Nor should we overlook a much more serious defect in the AAUP trial procedure that is justified by neither Anglo-American law nor the experiences of the AAUP. The AAUP jury panel does not function as an impartial body concerned primarily with determining the most reasonable and just course of action. Factional and class-oriented, it is designed to defend a member of the clan from outside interference; and it views all administrators, staff, trustees, and alumni as outsiders. The AAUP has entirely overlooked the fact that nearly all academic administrators are also faculty members or former faculty members. Thus the unity or harmony essential to academic life is jeopardized by the AAUP's reliance on an adversary process whose divisive qualities are exacerbated by the use of guild-oriented or directly partisan juries. That these disadvantages and risks are historically offset by concern for academic freedom should not blind us to the serious problems caused by defects in trial procedures.

The AAUP, I am convinced, has not used its tenure rule and its trial procedure merely to protect academic freedom; instead, it has used the trial procedure to defend the seven-year tenure rule itself. In its local chapters and nationally, the AAUP has come to the defense of anyone who has taught seven or more years. No issue of academic freedom may be involved. The administration may have, at the professor's own request, extended an appointment beyond six years in the not inhumane hope that he might complete the long-awaited book, two or three articles, or demonstrate the outstanding teaching that might justify his continuance. The administration will nevertheless be told by the AAUP that the professor has tenure. But the meaning of tenure has changed. The AAUP asserts that the professor has an absolute claim on continued employment, in effect, a *sinecure.*

The result is that the seven-year rule no longer serves as the dividing line between probationary and tenured employment. It has become, instead, the line that divides probation from a status that may approach sinecure. The AAUP now puts so many obstacles in the way of removal or reassignment of professors and imposes such severe penalties on most institutions that dare to recognize tenure in its true meaning that administrators have acquiesced in the virtual transformation of tenure into sinecure. Largely because of the AAUP's forfeiture of its role as a professional organization in its drive to become a union, the seven-year rule is increasingly a dead letter. Universities substitute a ten-year rule, or declare certain positions to be off the tenure track, and the sky does not fall. The AAUP has sold its birthright of moral authority for the pottage of misguided trade unionism.

Ironically, the concept of sinecure is not merely different from that of tenure, but incompatible with it. Sinecure is either present or absent: It does not function on a continuum of fluctuating expectations reflecting the growth or decay of competence or the rising claims of service. All of the complexities and subtleties characteristic of the concept of tenure are lacking in the concept of sinecure. They are likewise absent from the concept of tenure as transmuted by the policies and practices of the AAUP.

By making seven years the absolute limit of probationary employment, the AAUP imposes a uniform standard on all colleges and universities and on all departments and faculty without regard to the crucial differences that essentially alter the way in which the concept of tenure functions in these various contexts. Much can be said for the AAUP tenure principle. But we have to recognize that a principle needs to be supplemented by human intelligence, imagination, and judgment in its application, and that the mechanical application of a rule or principle destroys its value.

By specifying a uniform deadline within which the ax of severance must fall or tenure be granted, the AAUP has in practice forced each academic administrator—whether senior faculty member, department head, dean, or president—to disregard the natural laws of development in the lives of individual professors. Some young men and women mature early, making important contributions in their fields and teaching effectively by the time they are thirty. Given a junior teacher's tested character and demonstrated achievement, senior faculty and administrators can responsibly (though, admittedly, not always accurately) predict his or her future development. Other academics are still—even in their mid-thirties—groping about in uninteresting, unimaginative, or even psychopathological ways. These individuals likewise pose no problem for administrators;

their association with the college or university is usually terminated long before the AAUP-dictated crisis year.

But no administrator can effectively apply the AAUP rule to young teacher-scholars with six or eight years of service, who, while ineffectual, confused, and indeterminate either in character or intellect, are so in ways that, far from being pathological, are healthy, exciting, and in some cases suggestive of genius. In the case of these individuals on whom the future of a great institution may often depend, the rigid code of the AAUP poses an intolerable dilemma: The university must decide either to commit more than $2 million in lifetime salary to a person whose character or intellectual promise is uncertain or to fire these highly promising individuals. Neither course is defensible.

Harvard has partially avoided the rigidity of the seven-year up-or-out rule and has made tenure decisions on its own terms and at its own pace in disregard of the AAUP. Normally, tenure is not granted at Harvard to fledgling scholars; they usually serve from one to nine years without being tenured. Tenure is granted more commonly to fully established scholars at the time of their appointment to the faculty. Although the AAUP has been reluctant to censure Harvard for disregarding its seven-year rule and has occasionally extended an indulgence even to Princeton or Yale, the AAUP has never recognized the validity or wisdom of these deviations. And it has been adamant in the enforcement of its rigid expectations in less prestigious institutions.

When I came to Boston University, one of the first cases that came to my desk was that of a professor who had been denied tenure by his department, his chairman, his college, and his dean. Looking at a record that could charitably be called undistinguished, I concluded that the evaluators were right. But the professor was appealing on the ground that because he had served for more than seven years without being given notice of nonreappointment, he had under the AAUP rules earned tenure *de facto*. Boston University had subscribed to these rules, and it was obvious to me that his interpretation of them was correct. Accordingly, I overruled all the decisions from the department on up and recommended that the Trustees award him tenure, despite his lack of distinction. Several years later, I found myself reading a document calling for my speedy removal from office.

One of the items in the indictment was that I overruled departments and colleges on matters of appointment and tenure. Seeing the name of the professor in question shamelessly affixed to the indictment, I was reminded that no good deed goes unpunished.

The natural laws of personal development by which mathematicians and lyric poets often reach peak achievements in their twenties or early thirties, while historians and philosophers, by comparison, crawl along at a snail's pace, have no place in the reckoning of the AAUP. All faculty members must develop in goose step. Instrumental musicians and vocalists must march with composers, composers with literary critics, who in turn march with mathematicians marching with sociologists and psychologists. This uniformity, though rigid, might be tolerable if it were not so totally contrary to human intelligence and aspiration. Far greater flexibility that takes the complexities of human nature into account is called for; and the insistence of the AAUP on rigidity and mechanism where flexibility and intelligence are required is most unfortunate. This rigidity represents a substantial violation of the academic freedom of nontenured faculty; its modification is long overdue.

Mechanical uniformity in the application of the AAUP tenure rule violates the legitimate claims—and the academic freedom—of institutions, as well as those of individuals to be different and to develop in ways that require substantially different applications of the tenure principle. A university with a vital program in the arts, for example, must employ artists—vocalists, instrumentalists, composers, dramatists, actors, painters, and sculptors—whose careers develop, flourish, and decline according to very different time frames. Such a university cannot abide by AAUP tenure rules that fundamentally distort its proper and justifiable institutional aims. Any school of fine arts that rigidly adhered to the seven-year tenure rule would soon decay as the vigor of its faculty declined, or commit itself to a continual turnover of young nontenured artists incapable of conveying to students the power of seasoned artistic judgment. A university that ignores the performing arts and is wholly preoccupied with the purely theoretical and intellectual aspects of the arts may suffer slightly less under the uniform AAUP rule, but it cannot escape the pressure that favors intelligent differentiation.

The time required for the development of creative power is ineluctably various. Why, then, should different programs and different institutions be forced into rigid conformity on this basic issue? Why should we stifle the peculiarity or genius of personal and institutional identity? Why should we ignore the motivational vitality that comes from pursuing highly individualized goals whose realization calls for flexibility and changes of pace?

The AAUP, I fear, may have become so preoccupied with the defense of tenure and so rigid in the application of the seven-year rule that its tenure principle no longer serves as a protector but rather as a destroyer of academic freedom. The seven-year rule drives young scholars in overworked fields into wanton production of the obvious, the unnecessary, or the speciously innovative. Well aware that they must make their mark within six years, young faculty rarely have the time to think, explore, speculate, and grow in silence and privacy. Young faculty members are not allowed to ripen at their own pace and thereby to produce something worthy of oral publication in the classroom and written publication in books or articles. The seven-year rule too often rewards fast and flashy scholars rather than scholars whose power develops at a slower pace but more profoundly. It thus encourages frantic productivity of fashionable trivia, and this in turn pollutes the marketplace of ideas and lends a bogus dignity to busywork.

Neither scientific nor literary invention can be commanded. While some pressure may be useful, the pressure to meet the demands for sinecure within seven years is destructive of all that is best—most sensitive, imaginative, creative, and profound—in many young academics. If the AAUP and faculty members are responsive to the realities of tenure, they will avoid absolutizing the seventh year; rather, it will be simply an important nodal point on a rising scale of tenure expectations, after which severance becomes decreasingly reasonable though not impossible.

The tenure rule, through its rigidities, clearly limits the academic freedom of a college or university to develop not only its younger faculty and its own specialties at their own proper quantitative level, but also its ability to respond to changing educational needs and the financial reverses that many face. Institutions must have academic freedom to pursue their own distinctive institutional goals. Hampshire College, for example, has deliberately focused on innovation and experimentation. Toward this end, it has avoided tenure appointments altogether, maintaining a probationary, transitory relationship with every faculty member. The policy is humane; it is openly declared and practiced; and its influence on the Hampshire campus is significant. This free expression of academic purpose should be protected rather than inhibited by a tenure rule.

Institutions that eschew all permanent ties with faculty and operate on a purely probationary basis, like Hampshire College or like Harvard with its younger faculty, must pay a price in loyalty and commitment to the institution. But they gain options for change and guarantees of quality that are lost to colleges and universities that promote their young faculty to tenured posts.

Far more serious, however, is the damage done to public and professorial understanding of academic freedom when we claim that tenure is essential to its survival. This commonly held view is ambiguous and in part mistaken. (The cliché was reiterated by the president of a distinguished college who said: "I am not about to defend tenure. It needs no defense by me; it is necessary to the climate of freedom which sustains intellectual life in the college.") Although tenure (whether functioning properly or as sinecure) has actually protected academic freedom, it is clearly not necessary to its existence. How could tenure, held only by *some*, be the basic weapon in the defense of a right claimed by *all* members of the academic community? Students, instructors, and assistant professors have the right to academic freedom and must exercise that right to be worthy of their responsibilities. The best nontenured faculty members assume the risks of speaking their minds to the best of their knowledge and competence quite without the protection of tenure. And academic freedom can clearly exist on a campus where there is no tenure, as shown by Hampshire College.

But even a sinecure fails to guarantee the exercise of academic freedom, simply because some professors with virtual sinecures are more concerned with salary advances or with administrative appointments than with the faithful exercise of their academic duties. Academic freedom, properly exercised, requires courage. Where courage is present, academic freedom will be exercised with or without tenure; where courage is absent, the sound and vigorous exercise of academic freedom is impossible. And when tenure becomes virtually a sinecure, as it has under the AAUP interpretation, it encourages irresponsibility—not academic freedom, but academic license. Thus, tenure may inhibit or corrupt, as well as enhance, the realization of academic freedom even by tenured faculty.

Tenure has, of course, been moderately useful in protecting established scholars in their intellectual deviance from the conformists of their discipline. Sigmund Freud, for example, would have been a likely candidate for dismissal had he not possessed professorial and medical tenure. Even so, his pursuit and elaboration of novel ideas required great courage and independence. Professor Nikolai Hartmann, the renowned German philosopher, remarked that were it not for the pressure of the neo-Kantian school in Marburg (where he was employed initially as a nontenured assistant), his own philosophical development would have been substantially different. He admitted to a human weakness that pervades academic circles—the fear of deviating from established lines of disciplinary orthodoxy.

But limiting the vigorous defense of academic freedom to the ranks of the tenured faculty has unfortunately left the nontenured faculty exposed. Infringement by tenured professors of the rights of the nontenured to develop their intellectual interests according to their own professional judgment—that is, the censuring of the nontenured faculty from the standpoint of doctrinal orthodoxy as defined by the senior professors of a department—represents by far the most serious and most frequent violation of academic freedom in our colleges and universities.

Any professor can cite numerous examples of this abridgment of academic freedom. In philosophy, for example, departments dominated by logical positivists and linguistic analysts have frequently denied appointment or promotion to young philosophers with primarily historical or metaphysical interests, no matter how able. In psychology, experimentally oriented departments have frequently refused appointment or promotion to clinical psychologists; clinically oriented departments have denied appointment to experimentalists; and departments dominated by behaviorists have sometimes gotten rid of experimentalists and clinicians who would not accept the reductionist formulas of behaviorism. Political science departments have frequently been captured by Marxists or Straussians who frequently impose an orthodoxy on the members of their department. And English departments are notorious for their rejection of creative writers—novelists, poets, playwrights—who do not produce the usual critical clichés for the usual scholarly journals.

"Doctrinal orthodoxy" may be too grand a description of the demands sometimes made by senior professors of their younger colleagues. Too often the senior professors demand nothing less than conformity or deference to their own prejudices. Anything so exciting or dignified as the resistance of Newtonian physicists to the disturbing implications of the Michelson-Morley experiment for Newtonian theory is rarely involved. Rather, I have in mind the all too common decision by senior professors to remove an able young person whose outstanding teaching and scholarly promise expose their own deficiencies. Resentment is an academic vice, perhaps *the* academic vice.

If we recognize that the guild masters impose doctrinal orthodoxy, and that senior professors demand deference from their juniors, we must then recognize that these are genuine infringements of academic freedom, and that academic freedom is severely restricted for all but the most courageous or naturally conformist of the nontenured faculty. The AAUP has never defended academic freedom from this more subtle coercion practiced by academics themselves or recognized that such coercion, though of very common occurrence, is a violation of academic freedom.

There is, nevertheless, a place for doctrinal bias. A Methodist school of theology, for example, has every right to restrict faculty appointments to practicing Christians. But if a department or college exercises the right to a doctrinal bias in the pursuit of its educational goals, it should openly admit the restrictions it places on academic freedom and inform faculty members of these limitations at the time of their appointment.

How are nontenured faculty—the younger faculty with minimal claims to tenure—to be protected from intellectual censorship? I acknowledge the difficulties inherent in the problem. It seems clear, nevertheless, that some review procedure ensuring that assessments include responsible but nonmainstream points of view is essential in protecting younger faculty from the doctrinal censorship of their own colleagues. In such reviews, administrators have an essential role to play. A vigorous dean can often prevent the dismissal of an able young scholar simply by insisting that members of his department justify their decision. By producing evidence from leading scholars and critics in praise of the young scholar's written efforts and by adducing student evaluations in support of his or her excellence in teaching, the dean should be able either to persuade the department to change its decision or to feel justified in overruling it.

If we believe that the adversary process and common law are the only effective means in the academic community, we overlook the power of rational persuasion. My experience as an educator suggests that senior professors often change their minds when confronted by a substantial body of evidence supporting the appointment or promotion of a controversial faculty member. This experience is not without exception, however, for in order to secure the appointment of three internationally eminent classicists, I had to appeal beyond the Department of Classics at Boston University to the international community of scholars, to an *ad hoc* committee of world-famous classicists to justify the appointments. It would have been irresponsible of me as president to allow modestly qualified and resentful members of that department to prevent its improvement.

On the other hand, there is no reason to defend the intellectual novelty of individuals who cannot present deviant ideas in a way that is reasonably convincing to fair-minded and competent critics. But in the appointment of faculty, we can rarely expect to be absolutely certain of the soundness of any decision, for the recognition of talent is an aleatory science.

No university can effectively pursue its own educational goals, enhance the development of individual faculty members, and ensure the academic freedom of all faculty and students while acting in accordance with current tenure procedures and policies. Those procedures ignore the contextual variations of human life, individual and social and, as we have seen, they frustrate the highest ambitions and potentialities of individuals within academic communities and academic institutions themselves.

What conclusion should we draw from this? We must recognize the human need for continuity and reward for long and loyal service. We must also recognize institutional need to remain solvent, innovative, and responsive to students. Administrators, faculties, and the AAUP must develop a tenure policy and procedures that serve these essential needs. If the AAUP is ever again to play a relevant role in academic life, it will have to recognize the folly of its misadventure with trade unionism and reestablish the almost majestic moral position it once held. Failing this, it can play no part.

The "Private" Sector
and the Public Interest

H IGHER EDUCATION is bedevilled by a number of super-
stitions, of which a misunderstanding of tenure is one. But
perhaps the most dangerous of these is the belief that there is
such a thing as a private college or university. There is not. Until
we realize this, the financial crisis that now threatens American
higher education cannot be resolved. The fact of the matter is
that virtually all so-called private institutions are open to the
public, serve public needs, and are gravely influenced by public
deliberations. Some argue that only those institutions owned by
the government are public, but that is as ridiculous as arguing
that because our airlines are not owned by the government, there
is no public air transportation in this country—as ridiculous as
believing that because the telephone companies are privately
owned, the telephone system is not public.

Public education in the United States, throughout its history,
has been predominately private in sponsorship. From the first
colonization until the Revolution, virtually all education beyond
the high-school level was available only in privately sponsored
institutions. By 1800, only three states had sponsored any sort of
higher education. Passage of the Morrill Act in 1862 was the first
national initiative for taxpayer-supported universities. Since the
"private" institutions are really public, in the sense that they for
many years constituted almost all of public education and
continue to train and educate a disproportionate number of our
nation's trained professionals, we should cease to speak of public

and private higher education. We should speak rather of privately sponsored versus taxpayer-supported institutions, or of *independent* as contrasted to *state* institutions.

To believe that present-day independent colleges and universities are citadels of privileged affluence that ignore the public interest in educating the poor and the minorities is to embrace a superstition. The achievement of equal opportunity in a democratic society requires that no qualified student be denied an education because he cannot pay, and any college or group of colleges that restricted education to those who could pay for its cost would betray a fundamental ideal of democracy by limiting education to the affluent.

The question is not whether the state-operated schools have contributed to equal opportunity, for they have; nor is it whether they should continue to, for they must; it is, rather, whether the independent schools have made a similar contribution, and if so, how it can be continued.

One way to show the dedication of the independent schools to the ideal of equal opportunity is to show what they have been doing for the education of minorities. The education of these minorities is often thought to provide a special justification for subsidies in the state sector. If we limit our view to New York City, with its atypical combination of high minority population and open enrollment, there is merit in this assumption, but if we look at the country as a whole, we will see its falsity. In St. Louis, 11.4 percent of the undergraduates at the University of Missouri are from minorities, but so are 11.5 percent at "private" Washington University. And "private" Saint Louis University outperforms both schools with 11.9 percent. And further east, none of the branches of the University of Connecticut (7.9 percent overall) approaches the minority proportion at Yale, which is 13.4 percent. Nationwide, in 1984 (the last year for which figures are available), 18 percent of the students in the independent sector belonged to minorities; the figure for the state sector was barely higher: 20 percent. Given the advantage possessed by the state sector in the form of subsidized tuition, the independent sector's performance is remarkable. Moreover, a large proportion of the minority students in the state sector attend two-year colleges. In 1984 the independent sector enrolled 22.5 percent of all students in higher education, but 32.5 percent of all minority students enrolled in four-year, degree-granting programs.

These figures are not attained by chance. Boston University, for example, in 1988–89 devoted 26.4 percent of its financial aid for freshmen to minority students, who make up 18.7 percent of its freshman class. The proportion of minority students educated at "private" Boston University is higher than that at every state-owned school save two. In absolute numbers, "private" Boston University educates more minority students than any "public" college or university in Massachusetts.

Another useful measure of the public importance of the "private" sector is revealed in the number and range of degrees earned there. In 1950, the independent sector enrolled 50 percent of college and university students and awarded 50 percent of bachelor's and postgraduate degrees. By 1986–87, the independent schools enrolled 2.8 million students, but the major expansion in the state sector had cut the independent schools' share of enrollment to 22 percent. Even so, they awarded 32 percent of all degrees, a disproportion even more marked when it comes to professional degrees. The independent sector in 1987–88 awarded 60 percent of the professional degrees earned in the country. Over the past 40 years, a *majority* of the doctors, dentists, and lawyers in this country have been educated at little or no cost to the taxpayer. After vast expenditures for professional training in the state sector, the independent sector still trains more than half of the members of these three key professions.

The examples could be multiplied, but the conclusion would remain: The independent colleges, with limited resources, have set a standard in the education of minorities rarely equaled by the state sector. In view of their remarkable sensitivity and responsiveness to the problem of educating minorities, and their responsibility through graduation and certification for most members of the learned professions, the independent colleges are as entitled to be thought of as "public" as are schools owned and operated by the government.

Some hold that the state educates more cheaply than do the independent colleges and universities, a notion that gains wide credibility because taxpayers know they can send their children to a state-owned institution and pay substantially less tuition than would be required by an independent institution of comparable quality. Few taxpayers note that the difference is not one of cost, but of price. Tuition is the *price* charged by state institutions and may be as little as one-tenth that of the independents. But the *cost* of education in the two sectors must be approximately the same, for the state cannot buy goods and services more cheaply than anyone else. The cost of education in comparable institutions is comparable. In 1985–86, current expenditures at state colleges and universities, nationwide, totaled some $63 billion. Since the state sector educates about 10 million students, the average cost within it was $6300 per student. This figure is slightly lower than the average tuition in the independent sector, which was $6600. However, the $6300 state figure excludes capital expenditures; in 1984, capital outlays for higher education by the state amounted to $460 a student. The expenditure in the state sector is thus $6760—$160 per student higher than the average tuition in the independent sector.

But the important issue is not relative costs, but the fact that the independent sector provides educational services out of funds that are largely voluntarily raised. It provides education for the public in exchange for very few of the taxpayer's dollars. If a man stood on the corner selling authentic dollar bills for two cents each, from the point of view of his customers, he would operate at 5000 percent efficiency. If he raised his price to thirty cents a dollar, he would lose no customers, nor should he be criticized for his rapacity or inefficiency. That man on the corner stands to his customers in the relation of the independent colleges and universities to the taxpayer.

Whenever an independent university or college educates a resident of its state, that state's taxpayers are saved whatever it would have cost to educate that student in a state school. Boston University educates some 3,700 residents of Massachusetts every year. To educate them at the University of Massachusetts would cost taxpayers at least $23 million. In 1986–87, some 2.8 million students were enrolled in independent colleges and universities throughout the nation. Their education relieves the taxpayer of at least $16 billion annually that would have had to be spent to educate them in state schools.

An independent college or university is a goose that lays

golden eggs on a ration of a few pennies from the taxpayers. The fable warns us against killing any goose whose eggs exceed in value the cost of its ration. There is more than one way to kill a goose, and slow starvation is sure. The goose would thrive on no more than thirty cents' worth of ration per dollar's worth of egg; and the policy of slow starvation is absurdly shortsighted.

A state college or university is no golden goose. For every dollar of services it provides to the public, it charges the taxpayer the full dollar. Fair perhaps, but it is no bargain. Any legislature that shifts the taxpayers' educational business from existing independent colleges to newly created state colleges shows about as much sense as a man who roasts and eats his golden goose and then buys his golden eggs at the bank.

Whenever it is proposed that independent colleges must be helped by an infusion of public funds, critics of the scheme propose conditions that would convert the independent colleges into wards of the state. Usually these conditions reveal suppositions about the independent sector that are totally misleading. For example, proponents of the state sector speak of the need for the independent sector to accept strict audit and fiscal restraint before receiving substantial tax money. An orgy of peculation and waste impressive even in government would be required before the taxpayer could be a loser at current or prospective levels of tax support for independent higher education.

Ironically, independent schools are usually held to more demanding standards of accounting than the state schools. The budget document of an independent university details all its expenses, while the budget of a state university may represent only those expenditures that have not been squirreled away in other state accounts. In Massachusetts, for example, higher education debt service, retirement, and group insurance payments, totaling hundreds of millions of dollars, are reported separately in the state budget.

When taxpayers look at the budget of one of these institutions, they are deceived; yet, this deceptive standard of accounting is being urged upon the independent schools as a price of taxpayer funding.

Nor is there much evidence of any widespread or substantial waste in the independent sector. Substantial waste is not possible for any but heavily endowed colleges. Independent universities *must* eschew deficits, for there is no way they can survive them. Banks honor overdrafts only in wealthy accounts. Once their savings are gone, universities that spend more than they earn face bankruptcy as surely as private citizens who behave in the same way. Only the state institutions, drawing on the presumably bottomless well of the public treasury, or the handful of independent institutions that draw on large endowments, can run deficits. New York University, one of two independent schools to run a series of huge deficits, was finally forced to face reality and settle accounts by the sale of an entire campus. Columbia University, the other, drew down a very large endowment by $100 million. In the state institutions, tuition income falls far below expenses as a matter of policy, and the taxpayer makes up the difference.

When an official of a state system tells the independent schools that they must learn to be as accountable as the state schools, we may be misled still further. An independent college or university, to a far greater degree than a state institution, is accountable in the marketplace. Its budgets inevitably assume a certain enrollment; any failure to achieve it will inevitably lead to deficit, and any series of substantial deficits will inevitably lead to disaster. Independent colleges and universities, like any other business, face the possibility that their product may not attract customers. This danger is not mitigated because a university seeks no profit, or because its product is by nature intangible and freighted with purposes and values beyond the merely financial.

Ten years ago we might not have understood Dr. Johnson's dictum, but now we can all agree that the knowledge that one is to be hanged in a fortnight concentrates the mind wonderfully. The economist Paul Rosenstein-Rodan named the effect of this knowledge "the tremble factor." It is a dreadful but essential benefit to the independent sector, and the state sector has rarely faced it. One of the most effective uses to which the tremble factor has ever been put was in the building practices of ancient Rome. For when the scaffolding was removed from a completed Roman arch, the Roman engineer stood beneath. If the arch came crashing down, he was the first to know. His concern for the quality of the arch was intensely personal, and it is not surprising that so many Roman arches have survived.

The state's subsidy of tuition charges in the state sector deprives the state schools of the invigorating benefits of the tremble factor. In 1988–89, tuition at Boston University is 5.6 times that at the University of Massachusetts. I hardly know which is more marvelous: that independent universities, facing that kind of price competition, manage to survive, or that state universities, thus protected from the tremble factor, can achieve an extraordinary level of quality. They can do this because their faculties, like those of the independent sector, have been accountable to the ideals and standards of the community of scholars. To the extent that this may no longer be true, the problem affects both sectors.

Another common supposition, based more in pseudodemography than in education, has resulted in encouraging mindless expansion in the state sector. It is the foolish belief that additional facilities are needed to meet the requirements of an expanding student population, and that independent colleges have been neglectful or insensitive to the provision of these additional spaces.

Before the mid-1970s, educational planners, noting the high birthrate of the 1950s and 1960s, believed that the population was becoming increasingly younger, and they wondered where we would find all the teachers to handle the hordes of students promised for the 1980s and 1990s. The fact is that the people whose activity is predicted by the fertility rate have played a little joke on those who predict their activity. The birthrate has dropped past the level needed for a stable population, and in 1973 there were only 3.1 million births, compared to 4.3 million in 1961. In more recent years, the number of births has stabilized at the midpoint between the historic high of 1961 and the recent low of 1973—at approximately 3.7 million a year. This means that the total number of students available for the freshman class of 1991 will be at least 31 percent smaller than for that of 1979. Within four years, as enrollments decline, an increasing number of both independent and state institutions will face serious difficulty. In the spring of 1989, colleges and universities began to report the first decline in applications in many years: These declines ranged as high as 12 percent over the preceding year's applicant pool.

By 1995, assuming that Americans continue to go to college at the present rate, both state and independent colleges and universities will be educating nearly 3 million fewer students. Even with extraordinary expansion in continuing education, the deficit cannot be less than 1 million students. The full significance of this number is not obvious so long as it remains merely a number: Think rather that 200 universities of 5000 students each or 500 colleges of 2000 students each will have been annihilated. Many of these abandoned monuments to the folly of overdevelopment will be state institutions.

These are not the linear extrapolations of a Herman Kahn or the futuristic fantasizings of an Alvin Toffler; rather, they describe what must happen as a result of what has already happened. The freshman class of 1991 was born in 1973. It is inconceivable that we shall educate children who have not been conceived. The baby food and toy manufacturers already know this; educators and legislators will eventually find out.

For the next few years, the state colleges and universities can maintain their enrollments at the expense of rapidly declining enrollments in the independent sector. Their advantage is the obvious one of a subsidized and thus artificially lowered price to the students. The time will come, however, when existing classrooms cannot be filled at any price, when both public and private sectors would have extra space even if tuition were free.

We must learn how to balance supply and demand in the context of higher education as a whole. The independent sector cannot ignore the need to provide educational opportunity for all citizens, and the state sector must avoid the wasteful policy of imperialist duplication. If we balance supply and demand in higher education by destroying the independent sector, society will pay a fearful cost in wasted facilities and wasted lives and in loss of educational opportunity and options. Balance must be achieved by some regular and effective plan of state support for independent schools and by a willingness on the part of the state to avoid redundant expansion.

Let no one propose the protectionist expedient of raising tuition in the state sector in order to lower consumption in it.

Tuition increases in the state schools are not an attractive solution—unless they are compensated for in advance by greatly increased scholarship programs. Equal educational opportunity for every citizen of the United States is more important than the survival of any one educational institution. Attaining a balanced system of higher education responsive to the goal of equal opportunity need not require the death of any college, though it does require the abandonment of plans for new colleges that will never be needed. If further redundant expansion is avoided, independent colleges can survive to share in extending equal opportunity.

Independent institutions with small endowments are dependent upon tuition, and their income has no floor to sustain it. Some schools, through imaginative management and good fortune, may be able to survive the coming situation while complaining of nothing more serious than underutilization of facilities. But a great many independent colleges and universities will be forced to close their doors. Small colleges are doing so—235 between 1960 and 1985. Many of these were marginal, but some were not. In 1973, for example, the College of Emporia, a small college in Kansas with almost a century of service, was forced to close. When its facilities were offered to Kansas State Teachers College, they were refused, for enrollment at that institution had already declined 500 below capacity. We have long assumed that the failure of a "private" school represented no great loss because the state would step in, claim the body, and operate a successor on the site. The case of the College of Emporia shows us that such hopes are delusory.

The higher education resources of the United States have been lessened by such closures, and these are but the start. As yet, no large, urban, independent university has gone to the wall. Within five years we shall see either the collapse of more than one large university or an awakening of the taxpayers and politicians to the fact that the survival of these schools is in their own self-interest—that they *must* be willing to provide the requisite support.

Dollar values for the educational services offered to the public by independent schools are not difficult to determine. When an independent school enrolling 6000 students closes, the state has the choice of either assuming this educational cost by further expansion of the state system or denying 6000 of its citizens access to higher education. But the collapse of any large urban university would result in losses of another sort.

Because it has one student for every 100 people in Greater Boston, Boston University makes a major economic contribution to the area. Its payroll in the 1988–89 academic year totaled $235 million, making it as large an employer as Boston Edison or one of the largest banks. The payroll numbered 6700 people, and the institution generated at least 1000 off-campus jobs. The university's total expenditure exceeded $540 million, about one-third the total budget of a state like New Hampshire or Wyoming. Student and visitor spending added another $140 million. Most of this $700 million windfall went to businesses and individuals in Greater Boston. Boston University's students and staff maintained bank accounts totaling $50 million; out-of-state students, parents, and visitors spent $80 million, making the university a major tourist industry and one of the few that operate year-round. The loss of $80 million in tourist money alone would send financial shock waves through any community.

Some argue that universities, by occupying vast tracts of otherwise taxable land, deprive the community of its proper revenues. But in the educationally abundant city of Boston, all the institutions of higher education, independent and state-owned, occupy only 2 percent of the land area. Boston or any other city could tax its educational institutions into bankruptcy without substantially increasing its tax revenue, while damaging and perhaps destroying its local economy.

The average college or university has no less impact on its city than Boston University has on Greater Boston. Indeed, in many metropolitan areas the dominant university enrolls one student for fifty residents, and in many towns a college has one student for every fifteen.

Money spent by the state in support of independent colleges and universities is seed money, for the benefits far exceed the costs. And a growing number of legislators and governors throughout the United States are becoming increasingly sensitive to the importance of developing a comprehensive plan for higher education that encompasses both state and independent sectors.

The Need for Tuition Vouchers

At present, no state has a pattern of aid that will ensure the most economical continuance of a composite system of higher education. All in all, New York has the most developed and elaborated system of state aid. Its direct institutional aid, the Bundy plan, pays $1500 to each independent college or university for each bachelor's degree awarded, $950 for each master's, and $4550 for each doctorate. In 1987–88, these payments totaled nearly $113 million. In the same year, various scholarship awards tenable at independent or state schools amounted to some $434 million. The state also arranges tax-exempt bond issues for construction at independent schools and supports ten chairs (at $100,000 per chair per annum) in the independent sector. Moreover, the tuition assistance program provides direct grants of up to $3650 per year, depending upon parental income. This is comparatively generous, but the student would still be unable to afford the cost of tuition in the independent sector without substantial aid from other sources.

No one in the independent sector is likely to regard any level of state or federal aid with indifference, but no argument for a much larger infusion of state and federal funds has so far been seriously proposed. Suppose that a state estimated the annual operating cost of educating an undergraduate in a state institution and made this amount available to him in the form of a tuition voucher. This sum, nationwide, would now average $6760, although in many states the figure would be much higher. Under such an arrangement, the operating budget for a state school would be the sum of all vouchers brought to it by its resident students plus any tuition paid by them. For an independent school, this sum would be part of its operating tuition income from resident students, and the annual income to a school enrolling 6000 state residents would be about $40.6 million.

Such a program would not call upon the taxpayers for increased operating expense, for the operating cost to them would be the same whether students took their vouchers to the state or the independent sector. A student's choice between the two sectors could not affect capital costs in the state sector, for existing structures must be paid for, used or not. But the taxpayer would be relieved of any need to duplicate facilities already in existence.

By the fall of 1987, the freshman class at Boston University's nationally ranked school of nursing had fallen to *eight*. This was in part a symptom of a national crisis: Very few women now want to become nurses. Notwithstanding the fact that a highly successful school of nursing was finding it almost impossible to recruit students, the University of Massachusetts announced plans to open a nursing program at its Boston campus. Boston University proposed a voucher plan whereby all the students envisioned for the state program could be educated at Boston University at substantially reduced cost to the state. The forces of educational imperialism were not to be denied, and the state went on with its plans and even established graduate programs that provided the *coup de grace* for the Boston University school. It closed in 1988.

The plan sketched here would correct the relationship between the two sectors: Superfluous expansion in the state sector would cease, for taxpayers could never be persuaded to duplicate at their own cost facilities already extant in the independent sector if they were always available, so to speak, on lease. State institutions would acquire the advantage of living with the tremble factor as their operating budgets began to reflect not the number of students who found their tuition an irresistible bargain, but the number of students who preferred their educational offerings. The result would be a competition based, as it should be, on educational quality rather than on price-cutting. The independent schools would gain the income they need to stay alive and would continue to provide a capital subsidy to state education. But the state sector would no longer be parasitic upon the independent, nor would the latter need to sacrifice its autonomy. Its accountability would continue to be assured by the marketplace.

The dominion that superstition can hold over human perception is well illustrated by the remoteness of any such rational scheme for dividing the labor of higher education and sparing the taxpayer needless costs. We are trying to muddle through with something far less than rational, but the public is being educated, and in a steady state we could perhaps struggle along indefinitely. But the situation is not stable, and the independent sector cannot indefinitely prolong its invigorating career at the brink of disaster.

The best we can hope for is that when one or more major independent universities go over that brink, state legislatures and the federal government will make a saving gesture in the tradition of their salvage of Lockheed Aircraft and the Penn Central Railroad. If the government can save corporations too incompetent to survive on their own simply because they are too important to be allowed to die a disorderly death, the government should find no scruple in sustaining institutions that have been operating in a highly competent and socially beneficial way.

The long-range interest of all higher education, and, even more, the public interest, demands that the contribution of the "private" colleges and universities to the education of the public be recognized, and that the independent and the state sectors unite in the cause of rational coordination. The two sectors have precisely the same aim, the education of the public, and it is only through misguided competition for students that they can ever come into conflict.

Paying the Bill for College

BUT EVEN if we do attain rational coordination of higher education, unless comprehensive steps are taken in the financing of higher education—steps comparable in scope to the Morrill Act of 1862 establishing land-grant colleges, or the Servicemen's Readjustment Act of 1944 establishing the GI Bill—increasing numbers of academically qualified students will be denied access and choice in higher education simply because the costs will prove unmanageable.

The crisis in financing higher education has been building quietly but relentlessly over the last decade. Independent colleges and universities have strained their resources to the limit in providing increased financial aid to students. Students in these institutions and their families have gone beyond the limits of prudence in assuming massive debt to finance a college education. Of necessity, independent institutions have balanced their budgets with tuition increases, thus raising tuition beyond the means of middle-class no less than poor families.

Tuition, though a relatively small fraction of the cost of education, has nevertheless been rising substantially in state institutions. In the late 1970s, taxpayers began to resist rising education budgets, forcing regents and administrators to pass on to students the full cost of room and board and a higher percentage of educational costs. In order to hold down the tuition price for state residents, boards of regents raised tuition for out-of-state students to two and three times the price charged in-state residents.

This measure was relatively ineffective, however, as courts tended to grant residency status to anyone who had lived in a state for as little as a single year. As a result, states have had difficulty enforcing differential tuition rates for out-of-state students beyond their freshman year, and taxpayers have found themselves subsidizing the cost of education, not merely for children of their own resident taxpayers, but also for children of nonresidents who had never paid taxes in their state.

Taxpayer associations are pressing state legislatures to force state institutions to charge a tuition that more closely approximates the cost of education. This confronts trustees and administrators in state institutions with a dilemma: Either reduce quality and range of programs or raise tuition. In the former case, students are denied the opportunity for a high-quality education. In the latter, some are denied access to any higher education.

Educational opportunity in both access and choice is even more at risk for students in the independent sector or for parents with two or more children in college, whether state or independent. In either case, many parents face charges for tuition, room, and board that are simply beyond their means. Pell Grants, Supplementary Equal Opportunity Grants, State Student Incentive Grants, Perkins Loans and Guaranteed Student Loans, and College Work–Study programs have proved enormously valuable, but they have not kept pace with the escalating costs of higher education. Moreover, since eligibility for grants is generally limited to lower-income families, many middle-class families find themselves ineligible for assistance under these programs. They have even found themselves excluded from access to subsidized loans. And the increased dependence of parents and students on loans, whether federally subsidized or bank loans, has skyrocketed over the last two decades.

These pressures have become so intense that, as one might have predicted, students and parents have sought to get around the law through fudging. The financial aid officers of every college and university are encountering increasing numbers of parents who falsify their financial reports and an increasing number of students who claim to be independent of their parents and thus without any financial resources. Students using either subterfuge thus compete for financial aid against the genuinely poor.

Without totalitarian powers of investigation into American family life—which no one wants—colleges and universities have no means of accurately assessing the financial resources of middle- and upper-class students who apply for aid. Although many of these claims are fraudulent, the unhappy truth is that the fraudulence is in many cases an expression of a genuine need not yet recognized by the federal government. Most middle-class parents face an intolerable burden in financing higher education for their children; consequently, many engage in a conspiracy with their children to obtain financial aid under present law that, under any reasonable definition of the term, excludes most middle-class families.

Although this practice more often occurs among students applying to independent rather than state colleges and universities, another problem afflicts state and independent institutions alike.

The portion of college costs not covered by federal or state subsidies, by private philanthropy, by student contributions from work, or by parental contributions from savings or current income must be covered by loans. But the present system of loans is in deep trouble. Students who take full advantage of the present federal loan programs graduate with interest-bearing debts as high as $50,000. This is one obvious reason why the default rate on federal loans has soared. The cumulative default rate is 13 percent—a rate that no bank can tolerate without government guarantees.

Even worse, some college graduates have gone into bankruptcy—legally evading their obligation to repay what they have borrowed to finance their education. In doing so, they become morally no less than financially bankrupt. By encouraging loan programs that foster this irresponsibility, American higher education subverts its essential purpose.

Higher education in both sectors—state and independent— desperately needs a method of financing that will cut through these difficulties simply and comprehensively. We need to ensure opportunity of access to higher education and opportunity of choice among various colleges and universities, so that students can pick the school for which they are best qualified and whose programs are most conducive to their own educational development.

A general solution to this national problem cannot be found as long as we leave the major burden of financing higher education on the backs of parents. It is enough to ask that parents pay for their own education and the rearing of their family without adding the unrealistic expectation that they will be able to finance the higher education of their children. We can provide authentic educational opportunity if we introduce the old-fashioned American principle that the person who receives the benefit is the one who pays for it.

Realism dictates that students assume a reasonable share of the cost of their own educations, just as individuals must assume the cost of paying for their own homes. What is lacking is the means to make this reasonable objective possible—that is, a method for spreading the cost of higher education over time.

The Tuition Advance Fund (TAF), which I first proposed in 1977, offers precisely that solution. A comprehensive system for the financing of higher education, TAF gently but firmly transfers the burden of financing higher education from the backs of the parents to the shoulders of the student.

Under the Tuition Advance Fund, any undergraduate degree-candidate in an accredited institution would be advanced money to pay for up to three-quarters of the tuition for as many as four years. At current rates, the upper limit would be about $7,000 a year. After graduation, students would repay their advances through a new payroll withholding tax administered by the IRS.

Repayment rates would be on a sliding scale from 2 percent to 6 percent of adjusted gross income. There would be no repayment on individual income below a minimum level, which at the present time might be set at $15,000. Repayment would continue until one-and-one-half times the advance had been repaid. This excess of repayment over advance would insure the fund against the unemployment, disability, or early death of participants in the program.

Repayment of one-and-one-half times the advance would still

be a bargain for the recipient, who would, on the average, get his or her money back twenty-five times over. In 1988 the U.S. Department of Education estimated that the average college graduate earned over a lifetime $600,000 more than the average high school graduate. The *maximum* TAF repayment obligation—advance plus surcharge—would be no more than 7 percent of this lifetime enhanced income. The *average* would be no more than 3 percent.

The Tuition Advance Fund constitutes an endowment that makes payments to students in college and receives payments from graduates. In fifteen to twenty years, total annual repayments to the fund plus its investment income will equal or surpass the total amount borrowed from the fund each year. Variables such as inflation make it impossible to be more precise, but we can say with certainty that it will not take longer. Then, TAF will be a vast, self-sustaining national endowment for the education of college and university students. In ten to twenty years more, the fund could return to the federal government every cent appropriated out of tax revenues.

It is sometimes argued that TAF would provide a windfall for the very rich by allowing them to take out advances at low interest and invest personal funds thus freed up at higher market rates. This is fallacious: A student with a very high annual income would be obligated to repay at a rate that would impose an effective interest charge well above the market rate. The only windfall, if it could be called that, would be for a student who completed four years of college and then never made an income above the poverty level. Such a student would make no repayment for the advance. Either case will be extremely rare and is taken into account in the construction of the fund.

TAF should be especially attractive to two groups of college students: women and minorities.

Women who incur heavy debt while in college bring negative dowries to their marriages. Those who wish to start and raise families may be deterred from doing so by the need to work and pay off their debt. TAF assumes that the raising of children is work of national importance worthy of some tax subsidy. Accordingly, when two persons with TAF repayment obligations marry and both have income, repayment proceeds precisely as if made by two unrelated individuals. If only one spouse has income, however, repayment begins at an income level of $20,000 and is made for both at a rate that is 75 percent of their combined obligation. If each spouse's repayment obligation were 2 percent, the combined repayment obligation would not be 4 percent but 3 percent.

Although some have argued that TAF, by replacing government grants with advances that must be repaid, is unfair to minorities, the reverse is true. The income gap between college-educated blacks and college-educated whites has narrowed dramatically. The typical black college student comes from a family whose lower income is an artifact of discrimination, but his or her future income is not likely to suffer similarly. TAF allows members of minority groups to pay for higher education out of their own enhanced income rather than out of the income of their parents. And if in later life they suffer from discrimination in the matter of income, their TAF obligation will automatically be reduced accordingly. The Tuition Advance Fund treats minorities in terms of their futures rather than their pasts and makes no expectation of them that is not made of everyone else.

Administering the program would not be complicated. A student admitted to degree candidacy at an accredited college would open a TAF account under her Social Security number. She would pay up to three-quarters of her tuition simply by presenting her account number to the business office, which would bill the fund. When she was employed after graduation, the graduate would check a box on her W-4 form indicating that she had an outstanding obligation to the Tuition Advance Fund. Her employer would withhold the proper amount from her salary and remit the TAF payment to the Treasury along with income and Social Security tax withholdings. Analogous procedures would cover the self-employed.

Many of the advantages to such a system are no doubt obvious. One should be emphasized: It does away with the needs test. The present system for needs assessment is complicated, cumbersome, expensive, intrusive, and highly ineffective: The U.S. Department of Education has estimated that 35 percent of parental income statements contain some element of deception or fraud. There is also a serious problem caused by the existence of the bogus "independent" student. This student says, "Yes, my father does make $200,000 a year, but that's not relevant to my situation; he has cut me off without a penny." Sometimes such claims are true and should be taken into consideration by an equitable system of financial aid. Usually, however, they are false. There is no evidence, for example, of a wave of disinheritance sweeping Fairfield County, Connecticut. Even when there is no element of fraud, a thoroughly equitable system of financial aid would require an invasion of family and individual privacy that no university and no office of education is qualified to make or could make under the Constitution.

The Tuition Advance Fund solves these problems—sparing the U.S. Department of Education the millions of dollars wasted in getting doubtful answers to unnecessary questions—by a fundamental revision of the concept of need. It treats each student as an individual rather than as someone's dependent.

The great majority of students, taken as individuals, are close to indigence. Their need as students is roughly equal to their educational expenses less whatever they may earn part-time and during summers. It makes much better sense to consider them all as paupers for the moment and then exact repayment at a rate automatically indexed to their individual prosperity in later life.

But even if we consider students as dependents, the fact is that 95 percent of the families in America need some help to see one child through college and substantial help to see more than one through at the same time. Perhaps 5 percent of families need no help. Why should we deny aid to 95 percent of American families simply because it may benefit the remaining 5 percent? Given that in an imperfect world we must make imperfect choices, few can be clearer than this one: A small inequity is far outweighed by a widely distributed and badly needed benefit.

In a parallel case, that of the public highways, we decided to dispense with a needs test. We do not require a financial statement from those who want to drive on federal highways, even though a few people can afford helicopters or private planes. Just as we do not delay traffic for everyone on our highways by requiring a means test designed to stop the rich few, neither should we restrict access and choice in higher education for anyone.

The Tuition Advance Fund also offers sorely needed improvements in collection. The present system is no better at collection than at needs assessment. Default on loans in the Guaranteed Student Loan program (GSL) has been running about 13 percent across the board and above 25 percent in some institutions. This is a scandal.

And at least as important as the financial cost of the default is the moral cost. As hundreds of thousands of young people are encouraged, or at least permitted, to begin adult life with a massive renunciation of responsibility, default or bankruptcy becomes a secular rite of passage. The Tuition Advance Fund would solve this problem at a stroke: Collections would be managed by the highly efficient methods of the Internal Revenue Service. This would leave only three means of evasion: unemployment, death, and Leavenworth. None is especially attractive.

Bankruptcy would not be an option. TAF establishes not a conventional debt but, rather, an obligation to pay a tax at specified rates until a specified total has been paid. Bankruptcy might wipe away all debts, but as long as there were income, there would still be an obligation to continue paying TAF until repayment, permanent disability, retirement, or death occurred. To judge from the record of the GSL program, debt repayment is far from certain, but tax payment under the IRS code continues to run death a close second for certainty.

To establish TAF as a fully funded endowment for all undergraduates would cost approximately $13 billion a year. Approximately $5 billion would go to students in state-supported institutions and about $8 billion to students in independent institutions. Increasingly, administrators of state institutions will face the problem of either having to increase their tuition or of having to reduce the quality of their institutions. The need for the Tuition Advance Fund will intensify in the state sector just as it has in the independent sector. The benefits are there for both.

Approximately $7 billion of the $13 billion total could be funded from programs that TAF would replace: Pell Grants, Supplementary Equal Opportunity Grants, State Student Incentive Grants, National Direct Student Loans, and Guaranteed Student Loans (except for graduate students). The existing College Work–Study program, with its emphasis on self-reliance, is thoroughly consistent with the spirit of TAF and ought to be retained.

The remainder of $6 billion can be put into perspective by remembering that it is less than 1 percent of the operating budget of the federal government, and less than one quarter of 1 percent of the gross national product. It may seem anomalous to be discussing a $6 billion addition to the federal budget in an era in which cost containment ought to be of primary concern. But there are in fact many ways by which a $6 billion fund could be established without increasing the overall federal budget. Secretary Carlucci estimated that savings of $10 billion a year in the Department of Defense could be made without any sacrifice of weapons systems simply by shifting from an annual to a five-year procurement cycle.

There are many other ways in which $6 billion could be saved: The important fact is that any cut that allows $6 billion to be added to the Tuition Advance Fund will not consume the $6 billion. Money invested in TAF is not consumption but capital investment.

Americans are well aware of the need for physical capital and financial capital. But we frequently overlook a type of capital essential to all the others and thus the most important of all: intellectual capital. Intellectual capital is fundamental to the wealth of nations in a way that physical and financial capital are not. With few natural resources, Japan, Taiwan, Singapore, and Hong Kong—countries deficient even in arable land—have substituted human capital for physical capital. By substituting trained intelligence and its products for natural resources, they have built the most dynamic economies of our time. If the United States is to continue to compete effectively in world markets, we must understand that our educational expenditures are not consumption but investment in the essential and renewable resource of human intelligence—the one natural resource that is not consumed but rather increased by use.

Funding for TAF should also be considered in light of the fact that, unlike every other federal appropriation, it would have a clear and visible sunset ahead of it. This is because the demographics and hence the economics of the Tuition Advance Fund invert those of Social Security. The financial integrity of TAF will be guaranteed as the number of repayers rapidly increases and as the number of recipients decreases or increases very slowly. It is like a college whose enrollment remains roughly constant but whose alumni—all of whom have signed contracts to repay most of the cost of their education—increase annually.

Within a generation, the fund would no longer require tax support. Moreover, after a further period—ten to twenty years more—the fund would attain a surplus that would allow it to repay to the federal government all the original funding.

In twenty years or less, TAF would end the federal role in financing student aid. It would provide equality of both access and choice more than any program dreamed of by the Democrats, while increasing self-reliance, providing a higher percentage of repayment, and within a few years reducing the federal role in higher education more effectively than anything proposed by the Republicans. The Tuition Advance Fund is a responsible way of funding higher education because those who receive the educational benefit in advance will pay for it during their working lifetime through payroll deductions.

During the preliminaries to the 1988 presidential elections, two proposals deriving from the Tuition Advance Fund were put forward. Each follows TAF by introducing income-contingent repayment and by eliminating the needs test. Each, however, is fatally flawed. The Income Contingent Loan (ICL) program put forward by former Secretary of Education William J. Bennett, enacted in a small pilot version, imposes market interest payments on Draconian repayment schedules, ensuring that some students will fare worse under ICL than in the conventional loan market. Governor Dukakis's program, the Student Tuition Assistance Repayment System (STARS), is flawed by its reliance on existing capital markets for funding, as well as by repayment schedules under which many borrowers would be unable even to remain current on interest charges. These borrowers would sink deeper in debt over their lifetimes and never succeed in paying off their loans.

A third proposal, the Higher Education Loan Program

(HELP), has been advanced by Robert D. Reischauer of the Brookings Institution. HELP would set up a trust fund like TAF, but repayments would be made by increasing the borrower's Social Security tax (FICA). This increase would be proportionate to the amount borrowed and would be paid throughout the borrower's working lifetime. Some borrowers would under-repay, others over-repay. The amount of income subject to the tax would be capped at the same level as FICA (currently, $45,000). Mr. Reischauer estimates that an increase in the FICA rate of 0.24 percent per $1,000 borrowed would be sufficient eventually to make the HELP trust fund self-sustaining. Although this seems a small rate, as Reischauer himself points out, someone who borrowed the GSL maximum of approximately $50,000 would end up paying a combined FICA and HELP tax of over 20 percent of the first $45,000 of his income. The most contro-versial part of HELP is its plan to acquire start-up capital for its trust fund by tapping surpluses expected to accumulate in the Social Security Trust Fund. These would be borrowed by its trust fund at market rates. HELP also differs from TAF in that it would leave existing grant programs in place. The idea of basing repayments on FICA is highly ingenious and worthy of consideration. Mr. Reischauer has put HELP forth with admirable caution, noting that it needs further analysis.

The Tuition Advance Fund offers the potential of a guaran-teed phase-out of a major part of our federal education budget while enhancing our ability to provide higher education to every qualified student. It will also encourage universities and colleges to become more cost-effective than they have to be now.

As long as a substantial part of the tuition charge in the state sector is paid by federal grants, market forces in higher education are attenuated. If, however, instead of spending federal tax dollars or massive subsidies from their parents, students were making a calculated investment in their own future earnings, we should expect them to become more careful consumers, opting for quality and providing a market stimulus for excellence. If there is any level of extravagance in the operation of colleges and universities, we would expect student-generated market forces to demand its reduction and place severe market limits on tuition increases.

The Tuition Advance Fund is a comprehensive and rationally structured program of financial aid that offers responsible cost containment in our dual system of public higher education. If something along these lines is not passed, the long-term costs will be measured in billions of wasted dollars, in the stunted lives of individuals to whom equal opportunity is denied, and in failure to develop our nation's intellectual capital.

III

LESSONS OUT OF SCHOOL

The Pursuit of Fairness

I BELIEVE that philosophy is not merely a polite accomplishment or a jobs program for academics. Even in the field of public policy it is a rational guide to action. For a clear understanding of several crucial issues of public policy, some philosophical groundwork is necessary—particularly as regards the notion of fairness.

Every mother or father who has ever divided a pie in the presence of children knows just how fundamental is the human concern for fairness. Every morally decent person wants to be fair. In fact, fairness is a word that nonphilosophers use much as philosophers use the term "justice."

Justice has been a major concern of all the most comprehensive philosophers. Plato devoted some of his most important dialogues to a discussion of justice, and it was the central focus of his greatest single work, *The Republic*. Polemarchus began the discussion by defining justice as "Give every man his due." But objections immediately arose: Return a deadly weapon to a person who has gone mad? No. Give the cook more food, the cobbler more shoes, the ruler more riches and privileges? No.

To determine the nature of justice, Plato saw, required an understanding of the individual in the context of the society on which he depends for his personal fulfillment. Only in that way can we determine how he and the society can be of the greatest mutual benefit.

Plato held that a fully just society is one in which each

individual is given the opportunity—equal opportunity uninflu-
enced by wealth or family circumstance—to reveal his abilities
and develop them through a system of universal education.
Without detailing Plato's system of education, we can readily
understand his impact on Jefferson and other founding fathers,
who held that each individual has an inalienable right to life,
liberty, and the pursuit of happiness. From Plato came the firm
belief of Jefferson and Adams that these rights can be achieved
only if education is available to each individual.

But we should not misunderstand or misinterpret Plato and
the founding fathers. None of them believed that individuals
were equal in abilities—whether physical or mental—or equal
in the attainment of virtue. In proclaiming that "all men are
created equal," they were asserting the inalienable right to
equality of opportunity.

It deeply troubled Immanuel Kant that inequality was so
prevalent in what he believed to be a just universe. Kant understood that desirable qualities—intelligence, health, physical
strength, artistic ability, and the like—were distributed among
mankind with glaring inequality. But each individual, he
believed, has it within himself to do the best he can with
whatever gifts are his by birth or social circumstances. Kant
found the ultimate foundation of justice in that irreducible
capacity of the individual to exercise his volition in the pursuit
of virtue and self-fulfillment. All men, Kant argued, are on an
equal footing in the pursuit of virtue and in the capacity to be
worthy of happiness.

Unlike Plato, Kant opposed schemes to rebuild society so that
everyone is compelled to participate in a comprehensive system
of education through which each individual is assigned his place
in society according to his character and capacity. Kant rightly
recognized that this would require the creation of a totalitarian
state, destroying individual freedom on which not only morality
but equality of opportunity depends.

From these philosophical foundations derives our national
commitment to fairness: a commitment not to equality of ability,
virtue, health, wealth, or position, but to fairness, to equality of
opportunity. But we live in a world in which equality of opportunity is imperfect, for God has not seen fit to decree that all

individuals shall be born with equal gifts of mind or body. Hence, it would be not only morally wrong but futile for any political party to attempt to legislate equality in all capacities and attainments. The mere legislation of such equality could not have the effect that those born blind shall see, but only that those who see shall be blinded lest they exceed in capacity or attainment those who have been denied sight by birth or accident. Wisconsin has recently promulgated regulations for blind hunters. These include the requirement of a companion, presumably to aim the gun at game rather than other hunters. Thus the blind are made into hunters rather as Queen Victoria was made into a sharpshooter. Invited to test a new army rifle, the queen scored a bull's-eye. The rifle had thoughtfully been clamped in a vise after having been aimed for her.

When we speak of equality of opportunity, we do not mean an equal chance to be an Olympic champion. How I wish I could run as fast and jump as far as Carl Lewis! All of us might wish to have Shakespeare's gift of words. But irreducible inequality is a fact of life—a mystery that no theologian has thus far explained. It has been seen as an aspect of the problem of evil or as a manifestation of grace. It is a simple fact that governments cannot alter irreducible inequalities. Any efforts at amelioration must take this into account.

It is both impious and bootless to take offense at the inescapable inequalities of life. With perspective, humility, and wisdom, we must acknowledge with President Kennedy that "life is not fair." We should devote ourselves to providing for equality of opportunity in the achievable sense—that is, to giving each individual the chance to do the very best with whatever abilities he may have. But no government has the right to limit equality of opportunity by decreeing equality of achievement. That can be achieved only by lowering the performances of the ablest individuals to those of the least able. For example, a law would have to be passed requiring that Carl Lewis shall run no faster than anyone else—a debased notion of equality that has no place in a morally defensible political program; rather, we must do all that lies within our power to advance each individual as far as possible without advancing the interests of one by reducing the opportunities of another.

Every time we try to apply moral principles, we confront the familiar opposition between the absolute moralist and the practicing politician. The moralist insists on acting in accordance with his conscience and says, "Let justice be done, though the heavens fall," whereas the politician says, "I'll compromise my conscience and the ideal of justice to achieve as much actual justice as I can."

This is the ancient conflict between the purist and the meliorist. As a philosopher who has spent his professional life in the study of ethics, I fail to see the morality of the purist position. Persons who consider their consciences the final authority commit the sin of pride, since there is no guarantee of the rightness of an individual conscience. Sincerity is the very least we can expect of a morally decent person. Sincerely following one's conscience is not enough. Everyone's conscience, as conscience, has an equal claim to moral authority. How then do we resolve differences between one conscience and another? How do we resolve the conflict between the conscience of Sheriff Bull Connor and that of Dr. King? No one doubted the sincerity of Connor's racist and segregationist views, but however sincere Connor's conscience, we must reject it, since it reflected a debased moral insight. In humility, we must test the promptings of our conscience against those of others who may be more knowledgeable, wiser, and better than ourselves.

And it is important to note that *compromise* is not a dirty word. The person who refuses to compromise refuses—on principle—to do any good. What is moral about doing justice though the heavens fall and thereby ending the possibility of all justice here on earth? There is something both admirable and morally sound about politicians who go beyond their consciences to find that point of view on which many good and knowledgeable persons agree, and who make every effort to do as much good as possible in the exercise of their political power.

Morally superior politicians are those who are conscientious in testing their consciences. They are sufficiently humble to ask themselves, paraphrasing Oliver Cromwell, whether "in the bowels of Christ, they may be wrong." They work to attain that part of the good that is possible, rather than lose all value in a futile commitment to perfection.

On moral grounds, then, we should reject both the arrogant purists, who deify their own personal consciences, and the cynical opportunists, who sell out their ideals for political expedience. We should prize, instead, those politicians who conscientiously go beyond their individual consciences to do their best.

In fact, there is general agreement on moral principles. Almost everyone, for example, believes in the Golden Rule. If this were all that were needed for a moral world, we would now be living in one. But there are barriers to that happy state: Unfortunately, even when we know the right, we are entirely capable of choosing the wrong.

As we are well aware, the road to hell is paved not only with bad intentions but with good ones. Good intentions may lead to bad actions because the correct application of a moral principle does not automatically follow from an understanding of its abstract formulation. This is true of most principles and their application. Newton stated the principles governing the flight of a baseball in three concise laws. Batters who can apply Newton's principles correctly three times out of ten become millionaires— four times out of ten, and they become legends.

Public policy offers an arena for moral choice in which the problems of application are especially daunting—for instance, the problem of the minimum wage. It is now generally thought to have been established that some wages are unconscionably low, and that by legally mandating a minimum wage, the federal government should assure that all salaries exceed that level. Historically, minimum wages were first introduced to protect white workers from black competition. In 1909, the Georgia Railroad settled a bitter strike by white firemen trying to prevent the employment of black firemen. By agreeing to a substantially higher minimum wage for all workers the railroad eliminated the competitive advantage of black workers. Blacks had been willing to work for less but had been prevented by terms of the settlement from doing so. The Brotherhood of Locomotive Firemen supported this minimum wage with the explicit understanding that it would end employment of blacks in what it regarded as "white-only" jobs. Nor is the use of the minimum wage as a device for racial oppression a matter of historical interest only. Today the white unions of South Africa vigorously support minimum wage laws on the explicit argument that such laws will help keep blacks from entering industries and trades into which they could otherwise move.

When we turn to present-day America, we see that the unintended effect of the minimum wage law has been to assure devastating unemployment among poor teenagers, particularly among black teenagers. The law sets a minimum price for their labor that exceeds its value. The law of supply and demand is inflexible in this regard; there is no economic incentive to hire artificially overpriced labor. This disincentive can be seen in a 1983 national unemployment rate of 16.2 percent for white teenagers and 48.1 percent for black teenagers. This is a social catastrophe.

Charles Murray has suggested an alternative explanation of this phenomenon. He suggests that teenage unemployment is limited less by the minimum wage than by the fact that unemployed teenagers are not looking for work. High unemployment is also explained by the fact that in some black neighborhoods the crime rate has been so high that businesses have not been able to survive.

In an attempt to remedy the problem of teenage unemployment, some members of Congress have proposed a so-called subminimum wage for teenagers that would be set at 75% of the adult minimum. Such legislation would make teenage labor substantially more attractive and possibly reduce teenage unemployment.

The subminimum wage is strongly opposed by organized labor on the ground that if teenagers were hired at $2.50 an hour, an equivalent number of adults earning $3.35 an hour would be laid off. This tacitly assumes that there is a fixed number of jobs, despite evidence to the contrary. But even if we concede that some adult unemployment would result from a subminimum wage, the ethical question remains: Should the federal government protect the jobs of one group of citizens by rendering another group unemployable? The answer is not obvious. The argument might be made that family breadwinners should have first call on available jobs and that teenagers must suffer the consequences of that priority. But are poor teenagers then excluded from our national commitment to equal opportunity?

Fairness is not easily achieved in such a situation, but it is very important that we understand that public policies like the minimum wage may have unintended and devastatingly unfair consequences.

Unintended consequences also abound in government policy toward poor families. The tightly knit and supportive family with two parents devoted to the nurture of children is increasingly rare among the poor. This is no secret, but it is the subject of much misinformation. Some have tried to make this a racial issue. Their argument gains specious plausibility because the traditional family is far rarer among blacks than among whites. The cause, however, is not primarily racial but, rather, reflects the fact that blacks are more likely to be poor than whites. When one looks at families not by race but by income, the percentage of traditional, husband-wife families among blacks above the poverty line is very close to the percentage among whites.

This important but little-publicized truth must be borne in mind when we read in the press that twice as many black as white households are headed by unmarried mothers, and three times as many by a mother who may be married but whose husband is absent. For several decades, white social scientists, seeking to explain this phenomenon, have mistakenly identified it as a legacy of slavery. In fact, the structure of the black family was largely intact through the 1920s and even after the Great Depression. The contemporary precipitous decline in the proportion of two-parent families is statistically associated with the rise of the welfare program known as Aid to Families with Dependent Children. While laudable in its intention, this program has had the effect of encouraging young women, in many cases below the legal age of responsibility, to start families, which neither they nor the fathers of their children do or can support. In many cases, the program compounds the problem by encouraging the young men involved to shirk their new family responsibilities deliberately so that mother and child will be eligible for aid.

The increasing incidence of welfare families headed by very young and usually ill-educated women, families with absentee fathers, represents a government-created social disaster of the first order, perpetuating poverty, inequality, and unfairness.

The phenomenon of the unintended consequence is especially

obvious if we consider the poverty we would have if there were no welfare programs—what poverty economists call latent poverty. Between 1948 and 1968, the rate of latent poverty declined steadily. Then we declared war on poverty, and despite hundreds of billions of dollars spent in that war, latent poverty has sharply increased.

There is no simple solution to the problem of poverty. But it is essential to stop creating poverty through well-meaning but ill-conceived social programs. The Congress and the administration must understand that social policy can have unintended and disastrous consequences. A government concerned with behaving ethically must bear in mind that results are not guaranteed by good intentions.

When President Johnson signed the legislation initiating the War on Poverty, he knew what he was trying to do: "We are not content to accept endless growth of relief or welfare rolls. We want to offer the forgotten fifth of our population opportunity and not doles." Two decades later, welfare policy under both parties has consistently mocked his good intentions.

Inflation should also be seen as a moral issue, especially if we understand that it is not an act of God but the result of inadvertent or deliberate government action. Consider the following case: A provident citizen buys an annuity to provide for his old age. But by the time he is old, inflation has reduced his annuity to a derisory value. Take a person now 84 who, at 35, had planned to provide himself with an annual income of $5000 at age 65. In 1935 this would have meant a very comfortable retirement. But when he reached 65 his $5000 was worth only $2200. And now, at 84, he is destitute—his annuity is worth only $700. The government, whether deliberately or inadvertently, has robbed him of his retirement. Is this fair?

We may disagree on the best way to curb inflation, but can we doubt that a government concerned with fairness will put the restraint of inflation among its highest priorities?

Abortion is a public issue recognized to have a moral component, but the quality of debate on this moral issue is too often appalling. Many who advocate abortion speak of it in terms of a woman's right to do as she sees fit with her own body. What does this have to do with the issue of abortion? No woman gives birth to herself; she gives birth to a child who is a body and personality distinct from herself. Consequently, even if we agree that every woman has a right to do with her own body as she sees fit, we cannot conclude that she therefore has the right to take the life of her child.

If the claim that a woman has a right to do with her own body as she sees fit justified her claim of a right therefore to dispose as she sees fit of the child growing in her body, it could be used to justify the flagrant form of child abuse that occurs when a mother by excessive use of alcohol, tobacco, or drugs gives birth to a deformed and retarded child or a child that shares its mother's drug addiction. Surely this is the *reductio ad absurdum* of this callous argument.

Another argument is based on hedonism. Why, it is asked, should a pregnant woman be compelled to suffer the ordeal of childbirth or the burden of unwanted children? If a woman can justify the termination of a pregnancy following voluntary coition, the same line of reasoning can be used by healthy and able-bodied men to justify abandoning wife and children and refusing to pay child support. In either case, personal convenience and comfort replace moral responsibility.

The Supreme Court holds that the government may not prohibit abortion before the third trimester on the ground that for the first six months the fetus is not viable outside the womb. This is a peculiar use of the term "viable." It ignores the fact that nearly all fetuses that survive until the second trimester would be viable if left in the womb until birth. Moreover, the fetus is not really viable early in the third trimester. If it is born then, doctors must work furiously to save its life, for it is a dangerously premature infant.

In fact, of course, no baby is in any realistic sense viable at birth. It is anything but easy or simple to nurture a newborn child. A human being is not really viable until age four or five— that is, until it has learned enough to cope on its own. If viability is the criterion, infanticide at any age up to four would be justified.

In any event, if potentiality is to be considered, how can an abortion after conception be justified? Who would undertake the burden of caring for a newborn infant if one knew that it would always remain a neonatal creature? A newborn baby, incontinent, speechless, instinctively demanding and gyrating though totally unaware of self or others, would be a creature of abhorrence and terror were it not for the vision of the adult potential in the infant. Imagine that the baby would always be a baby: Such a creature, substantially less satisfactory as a companion than a dog or cat, would be lucky to attract the legal protections now bestowed upon animals.

Without considering potentiality we could in fact justify terminating life at almost any stage. If we recognize the importance of potentiality to the love and appreciation of the newborn infant, why should we deny the importance of potentiality in the assessment of the fetus, whether in the first, second, or third trimester—or at the moment of conception? The ovum unfertilized is not potentially human. The sperm in isolation is not potentially human. The normal fertilized egg is potentially human. It is on its way.

This analysis does not by itself provide a sufficient moral basis for resolving all the legal complications of abortion law. But it does indicate the superficiality of the moral reasoning that has dominated the public debate on this complex question.

My own position on abortion is that the fetus is human and that consequently abortion is homicide. Some homicides are, of course, justifiable. For example, if the continued development of the fetus poses a clear and credible threat to the life of the mother, the doctrine of self-defense clearly justifies killing it. Just as clearly, the mere convenience or preference of the mother does not justify killing the fetus, and on such a rationale abortion is ethically indistinguishable from first-degree murder of a particularly callous sort. But I do not advocate embodying this view in the statute book. In the absence of a consensus that abortion is in most cases tantamount to murder, any law maintaining that position will be unenforceable. It will lead to widespread contempt for the law without improving the moral climate. Given the fact that a substantial proportion of the people in this country regard abortion as murder, it does seem improper to pay for abortions with tax money. And indeed, the pro-choice advocates, by arguing that an abortion is a purely private matter, cannot consistently demand that public funds should be used to carry it out. Our most urgent priority in this area should be developing an understanding of the morally degrading nature of the argument that abortion is simply a case of what women do with their own bodies.

Moral issues arise not only in situations involving the relations of individuals to one another and to society, but in the relations among nations. Frequently this goes unrecognized, however, because in both the theory and practice of foreign policy the relevance of moral principle is itself in question. The problem is so difficult that the advocates of *Realpolitik* sometimes appear to be arguing for an amoral foreign policy as a matter of principle. The other extreme is held by those who would argue that foreign policy is as simple as the Golden Rule.

But moralistic postures and purist expectations are particularly dangerous and inappropriate in foreign policy. We must not fall into the moral trap of opposing the better in anticipation of an unattainable best. The foreign policy of the United States has been bedeviled far too long by the concepts enshrined in James Russell Lowell's famous hymn:

Once to every man and nation comes the moment to decide,
In the strife of Truth with falsehood, for the good or evil
    side . . .

We would all be happier if we lived in a world where there were always clear alternatives between good and evil, right and wrong, innocence and guilt. The determination of foreign policy in the real world cannot be made on such distinctions. Unfortunately, we live in a world that far too often imposes on us choices that are inherently tragic.

The imposition of a tragic limitation on our choices is nowhere better seen than in Central America. If, offended by violations of human rights or defects in the judiciary in a weak, ineffectual, and fledgling democracy such as El Salvador, we abandon that imperfect nation, we may abandon it to an efficient and highly effective totalitarian regime in which human rights or the rule of law will simply disappear. What is more, if we demand— immediately and without time for development—standards of stability and order from Central American governments that lack the human, economic, and social underpinning of developed, democratic societies, we will see them swept away by totalitarian forces.

This is an argument for moral realism, not the advocacy of cynicism. Perfection is impossible. Moral utopianism is a dangerous doctrine that encourages the rejection of the better because it is not the best and thereby aids and abets the worse. Thus, while we keep the moral, legal, and political inadequacies of Central America under our unflinching gaze, we should persist, step by step, in amelioration, supporting those who seek to live in freedom and democracy.

In a famous passage in the *Critique of Practical Reason*, Immanuel Kant wrote: "Two things fill my mind with ever new and increasing awe . . . the starry heavens above me and the moral law within me." Kant identifies in this one short statement the fundamental conditions on which moral action—whether in personal or in public life—depends. One must with good intentions follow the moral law. But to apply the moral law effectively, the person of goodwill must take account of external reality, to which Kant refers as "the starry heavens above." This dual task is difficult: The pursuit of fairness can take unexpected turns. Glib maxims and obvious answers rarely succeed. Fairness is to be found only at the end of an arduous and painful process of analysis constantly tested against experience—a process that requires all our intelligence, all our judgment, and all our goodwill.

America and the Underclass: A House Divided

THE CONCEPT of a fair society is embedded in the inalienable rights to life, liberty, and the pursuit of happiness invoked in the Declaration of Independence. That is, every individual has the right to pursue personal fulfillment. From its origin, America has been committed to developing each individual as a part of our nation's human capital—and by human capital, as opposed to financial or physical capital, I mean intellect, imagination, knowledge, skill, industry, enthusiasm, and willingness to take risks. Developing these qualities in each individual requires that everyone be offered an effective education, on which an equal opportunity to succeed depends.

These qualities are not only essential to each individual's personal fulfillment, they are no less essential to our fulfillment as a nation. Since education and training build human capital, they are, in economic as well as personal terms, investments— wise investments, yielding great returns. This is how the founding fathers understood education, and how our government today should understand it, not as an expenditure but as an investment in human capital.

Today, despite our national commitment to education, every part of our society suffers from underdevelopment of human capital. To people in business this is obvious. We need more entrepreneurs with the intelligence, creativity, and drive to start and develop new companies. We need more people with skills and energy to manage and work in such enterprises. We need inventors of new ideas.

But we also face a more serious problem. Today, for shocking numbers of Americans, the opportunity to achieve personal fulfillment has dwindled. There is no longer a crisis; there is large-scale tragedy.

The American Millstone: An Examination of the Nation's Permanent Underclass, published in 1986 by editors and writers of the *Chicago Tribune,*[1] tells some of the story. Between 5 and 15 million Americans no longer dream the American dream. They do not imagine working hard and moving from where they are to where they would like to be; they do not imagine that each generation will go farther than the last, that children may transcend their parents. They no longer even aspire to move from unemployment and wretched poverty to the working class or the middle class. Since they no longer seek employment, they are no longer even counted among the unemployed.

Why? There will always be those who tell us that the poor want to be poor, that in some mysterious fashion individuals and families, generation after generation, opt for poverty. If such apologists were telling the truth, millions of poor people would simply be exercising their freedom of choice; and while we might not agree with their choice of poverty and despair, we might be justified in respecting their pursuit of this bizarre notion of happiness.

But the reality of the underclass is terribly different. Its basis is not choice, but deprivation—a deprivation that by destroying freedom amounts to slavery. The members of the underclass have been deprived even of the idea that they can escape from their wretched state. These Americans—and their numbers are increasing—have concluded that the game is lost. They no longer look upward to the light, no longer hear the music or see the dream. Each of them lives out an incalculable personal tragedy. Compounding the tragedy, the underclass as a whole can offer the rest of our society only its misery, resentment, and despair. The existence of an underclass threatens the moral integrity of this nation almost as seriously as did the institution of slavery.

Despite hardship, despite cruelty, despite brutal assaults on the institution of the family, slaves in this country kept great reservoirs of resolution, self-discipline, independence, and determination to be free. Many escaped from slavery; many more put their families back together after emancipation. But today the underclass has been robbed even of aspiration: Few try to escape, and often the underclass family, devastated by many forces—welfare programs not least among them—fails to provide even the most basic support, discipline, and education for its children.

Before going further, careful distinctions must be drawn. The term "underclass" is not a code word for blacks and Hispanics. The majority of Hispanics and blacks in America are moving, though not fast enough, toward economic equality. The underclass includes whites and many other ethnic groups. Whatever their ethnic origin, the term is an accurate way of describing the most devastated and oppressed members of our society.

Yet Hispanics and blacks unfortunately constitute most of the underclass—and this is intolerable. To have an underclass at all is a great evil; but to have one that primarily blights the lives and destroys the hopes of certain races, of certain ethnic groups, is a dreadful mockery of everything Americans believe in. If the underclass becomes permanent, we shall have lost the essence of the American dream, and that dream will become a nightmare not only for the underclass but for the rest of us. It is the rest of us, not the underclass, who will be to blame. And therefore we must recognize now the responsibility of this society to emancipate the underclass, just as we earlier recognized our obligation to emancipate the slaves.

For a boy or girl born into the underclass, the right to pursue personal fulfillment—a right claimed for Americans in the Declaration of Independence—is denied. It cannot be otherwise when one out of two children in the underclass is born to an unmarried mother, most often a teenager. Young women lose any opportunity for personal fulfillment if they become parents before they become adults. Removed from school because they are, biologically, mothers, they are forced to take on the often impossible obligation to be cultural and spiritual mothers. When a young girl is deprived of adulthood and of motherhood in any meaningful sense, both she and her children suffer the consequences.

When young fathers are encouraged to evade elementary

responsibility for their children, to brag that they have no intention of marrying the mother or of supporting the family, they are thereby encouraged to be irresponsible in everything else. Unemployment is devastating enough, but these young men, often deprived of families in which to grow up, are further desolated by being deprived of families of their own which would give responsibility and meaning to their lives. Never having known fathers, they will never know daughters and sons. The situation has been aptly described by the columnist William Raspberry as "children having children."

The cause is not far to seek: Our society has reacted to the sexual revolution with such incompetence that we now have an involuntary enslavement of young Americans at a time in life when they are so immature that they lack the knowledge and the insight to protect themselves. Most societies recorded by anthropologists recognize the fundamental need to regulate and formalize the expression of the sexual instinct. Sexuality has been recognized as a natural sacrament in every society that has had any kind of social structure. But we believe we can treat sexuality purely in terms of consumer demand and that this will have no consequences. We believe that we can permit television to portray sex without responsibility—no-fault sex—at frequent intervals, day and night.

Millions of young people are being deprived of the fundamentals of sound human development. Their collective tragedy demonstrates how the disillusionment endemic to the underclass perpetuates poverty and, if not checked, threatens many more millions as far into the future as we can foresee. The people I am talking about are not inhabitants of a third-world nation with fundamental problems of agriculture or distribution. They are Americans; their future shames and threatens all of us.

We must recognize and address this national tragedy. As Lincoln reminded us, a house divided against itself cannot stand. With an underclass perpetually denied the opportunities available to other Americans, we are divided against ourselves, and we shall not stand. No part of our society can be permanently cut off from advancement if we are to retain our moral integrity and our domestic tranquility.

The growing social problems that confront us—the seemingly

ineradicable pockets of poverty, the successive lost generations of children, many of whom become, by the age of twelve, outcasts and enemies of society rather than contributors to it— these unconscionable tragedies in a nation as wealthy, powerful, and developed as ours are not inevitable. They *can* be stopped.

Until they are, we face the terrible contrast between the life of peace and plenty lived by most of us and the life of those for whom all hope is lost. The English critic and prophet John Ruskin's description of this contrast is not likely to be bettered:

> If, suddenly, in the midst of the enjoyments of the palate and the lightnesses of heart of a London dinner-party, the walls of the chamber were parted, and through their gap, the nearest human beings who were famishing and in misery, were borne into the midst of the company—feasting and fancy-free—if, pale with sickness, horrible in destitution, broken by despair, body by body, they were laid upon the soft carpet, one beside the chair of every guest, would only the crumbs of the dainties be cast to them— would only a passing glance, a passing thought be vouchsafed to them? Yet the actual facts, the real relation of each Dives and Lazarus, are not altered by the intervention of the house wall between the table and the sick-bed—by the few feet of ground (how few!) which are indeed all that separate the merriment from the misery.

The difference between America and John Ruskin's London is that we have made great efforts to tear down the walls. It is not through indifference that we have arrived at our tragic situation, but through the failure of well-intentioned—indeed, noble and long-sustained—efforts to improve the plight of the poor and to extend to all American citizens those rights proclaimed in the Declaration of Independence.

Beginning with President Lyndon B. Johnson's War on Poverty and his vision of the Great Society, the amount we have spent on social welfare exceeds, in constant dollars, the amount we spent on World War II and, in fact, the total cost of any single project in any society throughout recorded history. Yet millions of Americans remain below the poverty line, and the programs we have implemented have created problems worse than those we set out to remedy.

It was not the spirit of the War on Poverty that was wrong.

Nor was it the visionary goals of the Great Society. We erred in the selection of the means by which to achieve those ends and, instead of recognizing our mistakes, we compounded them; instead of altering our course, we continued it for a full decade after our mistakes were apparent.

We cannot afford to continue making the same mistakes. If we are going to act as social engineers, we ought to learn from the practice of real engineers. When the first Tacoma Narrows Bridge tore itself apart in a moderate crosswind, the engineers did not rebuild it to the same design. They analyzed the accident, identified its cause, and designed a new bridge. The second Tacoma Narrows Bridge endured; today it still spans the narrows.

Confronting our social problems, we need the same willingness to acknowledge failure, to discover what went wrong, and to produce new designs. Our second attempt to bridge the chasm of poverty and cross over to the great society must not be self-destructive; it must endure, so that future generations may cross. To assure that openness to advancement is maintained for all Americans, to avoid making permanent the growing underclass, we must have new and different programs.

To understand how to develop new programs, we must understand why the old ones failed. Why have we lost the War on Poverty? Why did the bridge to the Great Society destroy itself? What is the new design that we need?

We have lost the War on Poverty because we failed to understand the nature of human motivation and the crucial role of education in bringing about social change. Education, understood in its broadest sense, is the enduring bridge to social improvement. The social programs we have tried have failed because we have ignored this essential insight.

To see this problem clearly, we must first put aside some prejudices. Unfortunately, our efforts to eradicate poverty have resulted in widespread disillusionment, cynicism, and indifference. Since our first bridge destroyed itself, it is all too easy to assume that no bridge can ever be built, that the chasm is uncrossable. Indeed, Charles Murray has argued with great cogency (*Commentary*, August 1988) that American liberals are coming to see the underclass as permanent and therefore to believe that its members should be treated, in effect, as Indians on urban reservations. But we must not be too cynical or too afraid to examine our assumptions and begin again. The key is to think of education not as abetting the cancerous individualism of a "Me Generation," but as contributing to the welfare of society, on which every individual depends.

Once we do this, we find ourselves looking not only at the underclass but at our educational system as a whole—its goals, methods, weaknesses. And what immediately strikes us are the overall changes in the American family—a phenomenon that affects future generations of children from every level of society and all parts of the country. Families in which both parents work are not confined to the underclass. Nearly 48 percent of all American mothers of infants under one year of age work outside the home.

The American family, with two parents or with at least one parent or an adult relative at home to ensure the nurture of the child from birth to the first grade, has been sadly reduced, even where it endures as a formal structure.

We mislead ourselves if we believe that the present day-care system is an adequate replacement for the family. Current private day-care institutions, with a few rare exceptions, do not provide the basic education and nurture that children require. How could they? An average day-care worker in a regulated day-care home earns $4000 a year. In unregulated day-care institutions (about 70 percent of the total) there is a 42 percent turnover of staff each year. This underpaid and transient group, however fine and dedicated some of its members, cannot adequately serve the needs of children in their care.

The crucial, delicate, and time-consuming task of raising children cannot be neglected or left to chance. It is the greatest responsibility of any society. As it stands, day-care often amounts to child neglect and sometimes to child abuse.

Once we acknowledge the inadequacy of current day-care programs and the decline of the family, we have made a start toward identifying the problem. But too many people today stop just at this point: They are critical of day-care; they bemoan and document the decline of the American family but offer no alternatives. This only deflects our attention from the solution of the problem. To offset the decline of the traditional American family, we must create alternative institutions to provide for the essential nurture of children from birth through at least the elementary grades. These problems have been discussed with learning and common sense by Lisbeth B. Schorr in *Within Our Reach* (Doubleday, 1988), written with Daniel Schorr.

There is nothing new in the idea that a society must care for children when parental care has ceased or is deficient. In times when the family was often disrupted by the premature death of one or both parents, our society provided an alternative in the form of orphanages. If today we want to build a more just nation in which the potential of future generations is developed rather than destroyed, we must provide alternative institutions that can supply at least some of the supports once provided by the family.

What programs, what alternative institutions should we provide? For children of the underclass, we must provide for the very earliest years. How early? Most of the brain cells develop in the first few months and years of life. A fetus malnourished in the womb will be born with significantly fewer brain cells than a healthy fetus. Sound nutrition is educationally essential for carrying mothers and for children from conception to the age of six or eight. Privation suffered later in life can usually be overcome, but privation that occurs at the very beginning of life and in the first two years may be beyond redemption. When a carrying mother consumes a diet of junk food, when she smokes, drinks, or uses drugs, her child will probably come into the world mentally and perhaps physically defective. We must prevent this gratuitous retardation, a cruel denial of the equality of opportunity of which our founders spoke.

This is one of a number of areas in which the programs I am proposing differ from those of President Johnson's Great Society. The War on Poverty was an attempt to solve all our problems at one stroke, but it failed to attack the origins of the problem with sufficient intensity. The Women, Infants and Children Nutrition Program now in operation is only a start: After more than ten years, it reaches only one-half of the young mothers-to-be who need it. The Reagan administration, ignoring its proclaimed commitment to capital formation, proposed to cut the program, thereby further wasting our nation's human capital. One of the most important criteria by which we can judge political candidates is their understanding of the moral and social necessity of expanding programs such as the Women, Infants, and Children Nutrition Program. Perhaps even more important, we must ask which candidates understand that money spent intelligently on education is not wasteful expenditure but profitable investment in our nation's future.

Nourishment and education work together. Inevitably, malnourished and miseducated children have difficulty becoming responsible adults. The problem will not be solved by looking for a cure. Some remediation is possible for those retarded by malnutrition and miseducation, but for most, a cure is impossible. The solution to the problem is to be found rather in prevention, which requires a sustained effort over a long period of time. The public support required for a comprehensive preventive program will not easily be marshaled, for the benefits will not be apparent for a decade or more—well beyond the temporal horizon of the Congress.

Our children should begin developing skills essential to their further education no later than age three, either in a well-organized and caring home or in a surrogate institution. These basic skills, more fundamental than reading, writing, and arithmetic, are best elicited by caring adults who encourage the development of hand-eye coordination, the development of aural acuity, and the acquisition of language. These once took place normally in a middle-class family without anyone realizing that education was going on. Today it is clear that the many children of all classes, but especially the underclass, are denied these formative experiences. All such children are at risk.

The institution best equipped to provide adequate nurture for children in the absence of families is a national educational day-care system to care for and educate otherwise neglected children from age three to six on every workday throughout the year. The current Head Start program not only fails to provide this extended care, it also fails to reach its constituency. Only 18 percent of eligible preschoolers are now enrolled.

Children would not be required to attend a properly staffed educational day-care center if their parents can and do take care of them. But with these centers in place, children whose parents failed to take care of them would not be neglected. In extreme cases truancy laws would guarantee this provision of care for neglected children. No parent should have the right to engage in child neglect.

Educational day-care should be available to children aged three to twelve on all working days when school is not in session. With such a program established, parents—including single parents and unwed adolescent parents—would no longer face the alternative of accepting welfare while trying to nurture their children or seeking gainful employment while neglecting them. Indeed, the eligibility of mothers for welfare payments would be contingent either on their arranging proper care for their children or on their placing their children in these day-care programs while they attend programs preparing them for gainful employment. Families in which both parents are at work during the day could also make use of this program, but tuition would be charged for parents with adequate financial means.

Such a program would benefit not only single parents on welfare or working parents. It would benefit children most of all. This is crucial. If we properly nourish and educate the next generation of children, we can break the cycle of poverty that builds the underclass; we can begin to ensure sound preparation for children from families across the social spectrum. If we cannot help all, it is imperative that we at least help the children. In this way, for the least cost, we can provide the greatest personal and social benefit.

In addition, if there is to be any hope of gradually recovering family structure among the underclass, parents and potential parents must be educated. Most important, perhaps, are unmarried mothers, many of them no more than teenagers, caught in a culture of hopelessness and ignorance. These young women, who may have not one but two or three children by the time they are 18 or 19, must be given the opportunity for education.

This requires that someone care for their children while they gain the education that will release them from permanent bondage in welfare. It requires that they know not merely how to avoid pregnancy when they have no means of taking care of their children, but that they put such knowledge into practice. The idea that we can be a free people without being capable of self-control and self-discipline is absurd.

If we continue the practice of offering a welfare check to any teenager on the occasion of her first pregnancy, we will obviously continue to encourage teenage pregnancy. While we should neglect neither the child nor the mother when such pregnancies occur, financial support should be contingent on the mother's placing her child in a preschool nursery program and enrolling in a school to qualify her for employment. Such a careful and compassionate program of reform, while assuring proper care for the child, would minimize economic incentives for teenage pregnancy and encourage self-control and responsibility in teenagers.

The need for awareness and self-discipline among teenagers applies, as does the need for educational day-care, to all strata of our society. Everywhere, school programs dealing with teenage sexuality must emphasize the dignity and self-esteem of individual teenagers and their capacity to make responsible decisions about their lives. Pregnancy and drug addiction, for example, do not just *happen* to teenagers. Adolescents have the capacity and the obligation to shape their lives. It is the responsibility not only of their parents but also of the schools to awaken, deepen, and strengthen their sense of responsibility for themselves, their capacity for moral choice. Then they, not the blind forces of appetite and circumstance, will shape the course of their lives. And nowhere is the need for the influence of vital religious instruction more apparent.

An incompetent educational system leads many of our young people today to believe that their lives are not worth the effort of trying to make them better. They see themselves as flotsam and jetsam to which things *happen*. They accept the idea that they are driven by passions over which they have no control. Our schools today fail to pass on a most basic but profound truth expressed by Kierkegaard. Individuals, he observed, are to be judged not on the basis of what happens to them but on the basis of what they do. Many children today fail to realize that they *do* things—that they are *actors* and not passive respondents to outside forces.

To become active and not passive, to make decisions about our lives, we all need the help of moral principles and values, not because they sound good, but because they are as real as any laws of science. Religious principles and values are also helpful, though it is not the province of society or government to provide them.

There is no area of contemporary life in which misunderstanding is greater than in the area of moral education. Values are treated today as if they were merely matters of taste. This is a thorough perversion of the nature of true values. Well-poisoning is wrong because well-poisoning is incompatible with human life. It is not wrong because I place a low value on well-poisoning and decline to award it my seal of approval. And well-poisoning is not right because someone says: "I like well-poisoning. It's fun. You ought to try it sometime."

The disastrous values of hedonism promulgated by television, the drug culture, and other influences must be rejected—and of necessity this has become a major burden on the school system. Schools today are compelled to assume responsibilities that have been abandoned by parents. Yet even as they do this, it is essential that they not undermine the serious moral teaching that takes place in sound families. Along with the rejection of false values, it is the task of the school system to support the principles and values we learn from sound families, from religion, and from the best examples in the society around us—values that are not whims but the accumulated wisdom of centuries of human experience. These values must be taught throughout the school system, but particularly in the formative years of a child's life, years of crucial importance morally no less than physically and intellectually. If we ignore these formative years, we will forfeit quality in primary and secondary education, and eventually quality in higher education, and quality of life for all Americans.

I have tried to identify the problems we face and to suggest a logical and desirable solution. Now the question must be faced: Is the solution workable? Do we have the resources for its implementation?

The answer is yes—but we must begin once again by distinguishing between expenditure and investment. In proposing a comprehensive program of nutrition and day-care, I am not proposing a giveaway. Indeed, those with a vested interest in the current giveaway programs will be the most vociferous opponents of my proposal, for besides perpetuating an underclass, we are perpetuating a welfare industry of bureaucrats, administrators, and social workers. Some are generous and well-intentioned, but all depend for their livelihood on the abject dependency of others.

Far from proposing to expand our current welfare bureaucracy, I propose to reduce it within ten years and replace it within twenty. I do not propose adding to expenditures that have already outstripped anything known in human history. I propose, rather, transforming expenditure on welfare into investment in human capital.

Within less than a generation, the cost of a nationwide educational program of the sort I have sketched will be more than paid for in two ways: first, by increased productivity and income tax payments; second, by a decline in the cost of welfare, delinquency, crime, and drugs. For instance, it is estimated that for each $100 million spent on building a prison, another $1.5 billion is spent to operate that prison for one generation—for only twenty-five years. I do not propose another generation of more prisons, but many generations of liberated Americans. Within two decades this will cost the government and the taxpayers not more money but a good deal less. If done right, it will not increase but decrease the size of government.

Most important, only through such a program will we meet our constitutional obligation to provide life, liberty, and the pursuit of happiness for all our people. This program would not be a dole or a handout to welfare recipients, hoodlums, and junkies; it would be a hand *up* for the poorest of our people and a helping hand for many others.

Only through such a program can we break the vicious cycle of poverty and degeneration that afflicts millions of our citizens. Only through such a program can we begin to restore to all citizens the use and enjoyment of their cities, parks, playgrounds, subways, and buses without the risk of being attacked and brutalized by other citizens—who in a real sense exist not in a state of civil society but in a state of war against that society.

If we succeed in restoring these gradually eroded civil rights to all our citizens, the greatest beneficiaries will be the underclass since the victims of underclass crime are all too often fellow members of the underclass. Worse yet, one of the starkest reminders of the extent to which our society is still segregated is the fact that within the underclass most black crime and Hispanic crime is directed against blacks and Hispanics. It is therefore the underclass that will benefit most from a reduction in crime.

Only with such a program can we begin the successful rebuilding of our primary and secondary schools. Once we have developed institutions to compensate for the decline of the family, we can set about making a career of teaching attractive once again to that large number of men and women who find their satisfaction in the education and development of young people. When all children are prepared for the first grade, primary school will no longer need to be remedial. It will then make sense—it will then be possible—to put an end to the fraudulent high school diploma, and to begin to restore, on a nationwide basis, the meaning of a college degree.

In addition, fully developed human capital depends on our ensuring equal opportunity for higher education in both the independent and state sectors of public education. I have proposed the Tuition Advance Fund by which students, on admission to the accredited college or university of their choice, could receive an advance from the federal government of up to 75 percent of the tuition cost.

The programs I have sketched are investments in the intellectual capital of our nation. On such investments our economic future absolutely depends. They must not be confused with a recommendation to spend our national treasure on something that will be consumed or will deteriorate over a short period of time.

Only if these programs are introduced—a preschool program that includes nutrition for mothers and infants, a national educational day-care program, the education of young mothers, teenage education, the restoration of intellectual standards and of the attractiveness of the vocation of teaching, and the Tuition Advance Fund to ensure that educational opportunity continues to the end of the undergraduate period—only with these programs will we be able to restore America to her true destiny of equal opportunity for all.

That the slavery of the underclass is not legally mandated makes no difference to the people who endure it—especially to the children born into it. An initiative to abolish it is a legitimate and proper function of government, because government is the only agency capable of creating local institutions to step in for the family.

Our moral integrity is at stake, but even more fundamental, our national survival is at stake. Abraham Lincoln was referring to both when he said, "We cannot live half slave and half free."

The Litigious Society

T HE PURSUIT of fairness, one would think, can be best supported by an institution whose *raison d'être* is justice. Unfortunately, our legal system not only supports the aims of justice and fairness but also imposes real obstacles to the achievement of those objectives. For the law is a human instrument. Although it is our glory and embodies our commitment to public order and the rational settling of disputes among citizens, it also— simply because it is a human instrument—embodies our folly. I agree with Sir William Gilbert's Lord Chancellor that "the law is the true embodiment of everything that's excellent." On the other hand, I cannot agree with his view that, in addition to embodying everything that's excellent, the law has no visible fault or flaw. The faults and flaws in the American legal system have become all too visible—though we have only begun to understand the staggering costs involved.

Since the mid-1970s, inconclusive studies of the American legal system have been billowing and spreading over the landscape.[1] But since the academy rejects the principle of *res judicata*, the data-gathering is forever preliminary, the findings are provisional, and any attempt to seek remedies is premature.

However, these studies are the smoke that proves there is a fire, and their authors are nearly unanimous in taking note of the explosive growth in the number of lawyers in the United States, an increase far out of proportion to the increase in the population. Varying estimates suggest that there are now some

650,000 lawyers. All studies agree that, between 1967 and 1983, the number of lawyers in the United States more than doubled; that is a rate of increase seven times that of the population. Connoisseurs of linear extrapolation should note that if we project the average rates of growth over this eighteen-year period for both lawyers and the general population, by the year 2074 every man, woman, and child in the United States will be a lawyer. The court calendar in that year does not bear thinking on.

The proliferation of lawyers in the United States is often compared to the situation in Japan, where the total number of lawyers is smaller than the number we graduate from law school each year. The population of Japan is, of course, smaller than that of the United States, and its culture places severe sanctions on almost all private litigation. Japan is a country in which it is presumed that differences among citizens are to be solved without legal process. But the figures are also drastically different for European countries culturally much closer to ours. In the United States there are 365 people for each lawyer—that is, we have reserved for each lawyer a human sacrifice of one citizen for each day of the year—whereas the western European countries have on average 1500 people per lawyer, and are thus about 3½ times less dense with lawyers than the United States. England, with 1250 people for each lawyer, is 3 times less thick with lawyers.

It has been projected that we will have 1 million lawyers in the year 2000, which means that for every 267 people there will be one lawyer, thus allowing each lawyer a well-earned two months' vacation from the daily round of sacrifice. Chief Justice Warren Burger may have sounded hyperbolic in 1978, when he warned: "We may well be on our way to a society overrun by hordes of lawyers, hungry as locusts, and brigades of judges in numbers never before contemplated." But on the basis of current statistics, we can expect the hordes.

This growth in the lawyer population and the accompanying growth in litigation are often said to be an inevitable result of the American character: We are, the argument goes, an individualistic, competitive, and therefore litigious people, and the growth of the legal profession is no more than a response to an increased demand for legal services. Whatever truth this argument may contain, it ignores the most obvious and probably the most important cause of the problem: The legal profession in America has become not only a self-perpetuating but a self-expanding organism driven by professional imperialism, under the motto, "The client works 'til set of sun, our meter's work is never done."

Since 1980, American law schools have graduated more than 35,000 new lawyers each year. In 1954, about 8,000 were graduated, and in 1965, around 12,000, so the number graduated each year has more than doubled since the 1960s and quadrupled since the 1950s. Like any skilled worker coming into the job market, these new lawyers need employment. Their product is legal services, and the market demand is directly related to the amount of litigation in the United States. Anyone blessed with a normal amount of common sense can see this, and anyone blessed with normal enterprise will attempt to expand and indeed create markets for his or her product.

In this regard we cannot accuse lawyers of lacking either common sense or enterprise; nor should we doubt the ability of law students to identify their market. Recently the *New York Times* quoted an intelligent and practical young woman, a law student, who noted that "if government [were to] cut down on environmental regulations, it would be harder . . . to find a job."[2]

The trend, of course, has been not to reduce regulation, but to expand it endlessly. To use a term developed by W. W. Rostow in describing economic development, a "takeoff" point was reached during the early 1970s. When the *Code of Federal Regulations* was first issued in 1938, it contained 18,000 pages. By 1970 it had reached 54,000 pages—in other words, it was growing at an average rate of about 1,125 pages per year. From 1970 to 1974, moreover, it grew an additional 15,000 pages—an average in excess of 3,000 pages per year. By 1984 it had reached 100,000 pages in 177 books, maintaining an average annual growth from 1974 through 1984 of about 3,100 pages each year. The 1987 edition had some 110,600 pages. The growth rate held steady despite the Reagan administration's stated objective of deregulation. The *Federal Register* contained 2,411 pages when first issued in 1936. In the next thirty-four years, it increased by an average of about 500 pages per year and by 1970 contained 20,036 pages. Just four years later it had doubled to 42,422 pages, an average increase in excess of 5,000 pages a year. At the close of 1984 it contained 50,997 pages—an average increase, over ten years, of more than 850 pages per year.

These numbers measure what Professor John Wettergreen of San Jose State University has called the "regulatory revolution" of the 1970s. "During the whole twenty years of the New Deal and the Fair Deal," Professor Wettergreen writes, "the federal regulatory apparatus did not change as much as in the four years between 1970 and 1974."[3] Sixteen of the 70-odd currently existing regulatory agencies were created during this period and 35 others overhauled. But this change, Professor Wettergreen points out, was not only one of quantity but of quality. The takeoff in the number of federal regulations and regulatory agencies was a symptom of a qualitative change in the role, indeed in the very nature of the federal government:

> Prior to 1970, agencies were typically established to regulate a single industry for a single purpose. [But] during the regulatory revolution, Congress and the President cooperated to produce a large number of agencies with extraordinarily broad and vaguely defined purview. . . . Ten agencies were established which have authority over every kind of economic activity. Some agencies' authority extends beyond commerce to the activities of state and local governments, including school boards and sewer and water districts, and in some cases over individual citizens.[4]

The huge areas of concern and the broad authority of these agencies go hand in hand with a lack of definition or restriction of their purposes. The Environmental Protection Agency, for instance, was established to protect the environment—without any legal definition of "the environment." The Consumer Products Safety Commission was established without a definition of consumer products. In addition, the powers of these agencies were immeasurably strengthened by radical changes in the Administrative Procedures Act of 1946—changes that weakened the powers of private individuals to appeal to the courts against these agencies.

In consequence, members of Congress acquired substantial

new patronage as providers of regulatory relief. Constituents turned to their senator or representative for assistance in navigating the shallows and rapids of the regulatory process those very legislators had helped to create; and at the agencies themselves, regulation writing and enforcement, both lawyer-intensive activities, multiplied. The need for the public to turn to Congress for regulatory relief has given members of Congress increasing occasions for patronage. This may explain the recent decline in successful challenges to incumbents. In the 1988 elections, 95 percent of all House incumbents who ran were reelected; there were only about ten serious challenges to incumbents.

It is safe to say that the overwhelming majority of the 57,000 new pages added to the *Code of Federal Regulations* between 1970 and 1987 were drafted by lawyers. Ask members of Congress about a new regulation, and they will refer you to lawyers on their staffs. It is also safe to say that only lawyers understand many of the regulations, which are the product neither of public consensus nor of our elected representatives, but of lawyers in the agencies and on congressional staffs and committees.

It is sobering to realize that in 1789 the First Congress had a staff of zero. Not until the eve of the Civil War, in 1856, were the first House committee staffs appointed, and senators had to wait twenty years more before acquiring staff. The executive branch was even more abstemious. President Lincoln entered office with a White House staff of *one*, a man named John Nicolay. When increased paperflow generated by the Civil War overwhelmed Nicolay, John Hay was appointed to assist him. Hay's salary had to be funded through budgetary manipulation. The staff of the Executive Office of the President now numbers 2,500. In recent years it has increased along with that of the Congress. As late as 1935, members of the House were limited to two staff members each and senators were allowed only three staff workers. In that year, the total staff of the two houses of Congress numbered 1,588; by 1976 it numbered 12,808; and in 1985 it numbered about 19,000. The numbers have more than tripled in three decades.

Some part of this growth is attributable to the increase in the number of constituents represented by each member of Congress.

But if we make a generous allowance for this factor, and note that secretaries have become far more productive through modern technology, we will understand that the growth in congressional staff reflects the increasing number of lawyers and clerks for whom the regulatory revolution has become a source of income and power. The vastly increased staff commanded by each senator and representative has vastly increased their ability to make laws, and in consequence, as we have seen, they make more laws. If increased production were the only criterion for the quality of the legislative process, we would have to call this progress. But a more voluminous code is not necessarily a better one. In fact, the increased arcaneness of the code and the inconsistencies, ambiguities, and confusions arising through the proliferation of rules certainly make it worse—except, of course, for the lawyers who must adjudicate the conflicts arising from the contradictions and confusions of the code.

We should also note that this system permits members of the congressional staff, who have never stood for election, to write into law provisions about which no more than a handful of members of Congress are informed. The legal profession—the most powerful professional interest group in Washington—does not really need a lobby, since its members are either employed by the legislature or the government, belong to the legislature or the government, or have returned to private life from the legislature or the government. More than half the members of Congress are lawyers, and at times the number is closer to two-thirds. Many career paths lead from private practice through government agencies or the Congress and back into business, private practice, or special interest groups in Washington. An indication of the role of lawyers in the federal government is the quadrupling, between 1972 and 1984, of the membership of the District of Columbia bar.

With the growth of the regulatory revolution, our government became, in Professor Wettergreen's striking phrase, not a government "but another special interest group." Historically, private lawyers have been prevented from soliciting business or creating causes for litigation. There was a word for this, *barratry*, which might be described as a lawyer's saying "Let's you and him fight and I'll represent you." I remember, during my year at the law school of The University of Texas, talking with one of my professors, now a distinguished appeals judge. I told him that in the course of my work as an enumerator with the U.S. Census I had become aware of massive and flagrant violations of sanitation and housing codes. I asked him how, when I became a lawyer, I could help the victims of these violations. He explained to me that there was little I could do because to go to the victims and propose litigation would constitute barratry. Now the papers and television are rife with advertisements from lawyers telling parents to check their children for abnormalities and, should they find any, to come in for a free consultation on their legal rights and pecuniary opportunities. Not only is ambulance chasing now consistent with legal ethics, but lawyers can call the ambulance.

This, however, is a rather modest opportunity for barratry when we compare it to those offered the lawyers of a regulatory agency. Their *raison d'être* is to bring lawsuits on their own initiative on behalf of a client who is never consulted on the matter—the citizen. If a regulatory staff decided that the legislation under their purview was being adequately complied with, they would, by acting honestly on that perception, render themselves unemployed. Their work is, accordingly, fraught with a serious conflict of interest. This may well explain the increased role of the federal government as plaintiff. Between 1975 and 1983 there was a massive increase in the number of federal cases initiated by the federal government itself. In the earlier year, the number was 12,742; in the latter, 59,222.[5] This rate of increase is even more striking if expressed as an index: If we take the number of cases in which the United States was a plaintiff in 1975 as 100, in 1983—only eight years later—the index had risen to 464.8. In contrast, the 1983 index of all other cases begun, again taking 1975 as 100, was only 174.6. At the state level, the situation is unfortunately quite similar. Many states have enthusiastically proceeded to enact additional layers of regulation. In cases where state regulatory law conflicts with federal rules— New Jersey's occupational health and safety standards, for example—businesses face added litigation and other costs because of the uncertainty caused by this conflict between state and federal guidelines. In other cases, for example, California's

Proposition 65 law, businesses are required to notify workers and consumers of potentially hazardous chemicals on the site. This adds to administrative costs for business that get passed on to consumers, and yet it is debatable whether these regulations contribute to the public welfare. It is time we developed reasonable alternatives to excessive federal and state regulation.

It is important that we realize that the federal government is a plaintiff unlike any other. By this I do not refer to the fact that it is suing in its own courts, since the very independence of the federal judiciary is sufficient to prevent this from becoming a problem. The important differences between the federal government and all other plaintiffs is that all other plaintiffs are ultimately restrained by limitations on their purse and time. The only imaginable private plaintiff as unrestrained as the federal government would be one with literally infinite wealth and bound by no constraints of reasonableness. This may seem a harsh characterization of the U.S. Department of Justice, but a close look at its practice in the past decade suggests that the judgment is not hyperbolic. When an official in the department initiates an action, he or she differs from a private plaintiff in not having to put a cent of his or her own money at risk; and the litigation, far from being a time-consuming distraction, is the official's job. And because it is likely that by the time the case is finally disposed of, there will be another president, another attorney general, and another staff of antitrust lawyers, he or she does not risk his or her job even in the event of failure.

This fact is abundantly illustrated in the government's failed attempt to break up IBM.[6] Three days after Ramsey Clark filed the action, the man who might have fired him for failure was no longer president and Ramsey Clark had retired to private life. Clark was followed by a succession of attorneys general who continued the case and left office before its conclusion, therefore avoiding any risk of being removed for failure.

But I fantasize. I cannot believe that any federal attorney has ever been removed from office for initiating pointless and unsuccessful litigation. Clearly, the federal attorney deserves well of the legal profession. He is a philonomist, one who creates work for fellow lawyers. Ramsey Clark and his successors employed hundreds of attorneys on the IBM case without exposing them to the financial risks of an unfavorable verdict.

Among hundreds of government-initiated cases, *U. S.* v. *IBM* is merely the most flagrant. Another is the one by which the federal government successfully broke up Ma Bell. Looking at the telephone case, a practical philosopher—let us say, an intelligent longshoreman who had recently gone on a package tour to Europe—might have observed that since Ma Bell gave us the best telephone service in the world at the lowest cost, the purposes for which the Sherman and Clayton Acts had been passed had been abundantly served. We had a telephone company that worked, and it was therefore not necessary to fix it. A practical philosopher might have gone further and observed that since it was not necessary to fix it, it was necessary not to fix it.

Whether or not it was a public benefit to murder Ma Bell is a question perhaps best left to the historians. We need not wait, however, for a decision on the wisdom of the IBM case. IBM was accused of gaining a monopoly during a period when its share of the market actually declined. A practical philosopher might observe that whatever its intentions, IBM had clearly failed to make them good. It is difficult to avoid the conclusion that IBM was prosecuted, not for having a monopoly, but only for being big. It is certainly that; it is nearly as gigantic as the astonishing proceeding to which it was subjected. The suit was filed in the last hours of the Johnson administration, ground on through the Nixon, Ford, and Carter administrations, and was finally dropped in the second year of the Reagan administration.

Discovery and pretrial proceedings occupied six years. The trial lasted another six years, generating a transcript of 104,400 pages. *U. S.* v. *IBM* and related litigation have been estimated to have consumed 66 million sheets of paper. All during *U. S.* v. *IBM*, the courts were hearing a number of private suits against IBM involving many of the same issues.[7] IBM won each of these, and six months was the most that it took to dispose of any one of them. All in all, *U. S.* v. *IBM* would have been more accurately docketed as *Jarndyce* v. *Jarndyce*, the legendary case in Charles Dickens's *Bleak House* that ran on over decades, grinding to a halt only after the lawyers realized that they had consumed the entire estate.[8]

The difference is obvious. The private plaintiffs, confronting the increasingly clear evidence of IBM's declining share of the market, were forced into a responsible assessment of their claims. They were not backed by the inexhaustible resources of the U.S. Treasury. The government estimated its costs at $13.4 million. Anyone who believes that figure also believes that the federal budget is in balance. IBM is not talking, but outside estimates for the entire litigation have ranged as high as $250 million.

While it is conceivable that history may judge the breakup of Ma Bell to have been wise and the legal costs well spent, every cent of the hundreds of millions of dollars spent on the IBM case was wasted. IBM's share of the costs represented an indirect tax on the corporation and its stockholders, only part of it recovered by higher prices on its products and by income tax deductions supported by the federal taxpayers. At the high, but reasonable, estimate, it amounts to a head tax of nearly fifty cents on each American.

Another cost, perhaps even more serious, is a distortion of the priorities of the U.S. Department of Justice. How many serious violations of the law and the public interest went unprosecuted because the staff of the department was diverted for more than a decade by its preoccupation with IBM from fighting organized crime and other more socially useful work?

Next consider a case that by its ridiculousness makes *U. S. v. IBM* seem almost sublime. This was a rule-making case before the Food and Drug Administration (FDA). Like the IBM case, it consumed twelve years. It was less profligate of paper than the IBM case, but the lawyers did their best: The transcript of proceedings was 24,000 pages long and the documents in the case totaled more than 75,000 pages. The issue was how to define peanut butter.[9]

A modest grant of $25,000 from the National Endowment for the Humanities would have set a philosopher to work on an exhaustive definition of peanut butter, clarifying its essence, its form, its accidents, and its causes both formal and efficient. At the completion of the philosopher's work, we would have come to know peanut butter not only metaphysically and ontologically, but phenomenologically, for no more than $25,000. For an additional $10,000, we could have developed guidelines for its use—when its application is morally justified and when it is prohibited by the rights of man. For a paltry $1 million, the government could have endowed the George Washington Carver Chair, whose occupants would provide an ongoing source of enlightenment that would still be refining the nation's understanding of peanut butter when all of us are dust.

All that the federal government achieved by the expenditure of many millions of dollars of federal and private funds was the dubious knowledge that if substance X is 87 percent peanuts, it is not peanut butter, and that when the peanut content hits 90 percent, metamorphosis occurs and peanut butter ensues.

But the FDA ignored the really serious policy issues. What about the butter in peanut butter? Suppose a careless housewife, preparing dinner for her husband's boss on the eve of his expected promotion, were to use peanut butter to make hollandaise for the asparagus? Suppose a promotion were to be lost and a marriage were to fail in consequence? Would Peter Pan be held to strict liability? And should not OSHA promulgate stickiness standards for peanut butter issued to workers with false teeth?

The 1938 legislation establishing the FDA charged it to "promote honesty and fair dealing in the interest of customers." Not content to remain within the modest mandate of their charge, the bureaucrats of the FDA have gone beyond it in an attempt to guarantee that for which churches, families, and schools have proved inadequate—not to promote virtue, but to make men good. The vagueness of the charge indicates that the federal government had learned the value of indefinition long before the regulatory revolution identified by Professor Wettergreen. Ironically, the attorney for Procter & Gamble, makers of Jif, and therefore an interested, and, considering its costs, aggrieved party, was the same man who had in 1938 suggested the "honesty and fair dealing" standard. This, it should be noted, is a particularly farsighted use of regulation as a cash cow: As a young man one earns a fee for urging the government into mindless regulation; then, in one's sunset years, one earns another for defending one's victim.

We must realize that before and after this preposterous regulatory boondoggle, the American people were able, with regard to semiviscous crushed peanut products, to choose among them from traditional, natural, sticky peanut butter, the latest high-tech slick peanut butter, or no peanut butter at all. It does not appear, however, that the regulators gave them credit for this much taste or intelligence.

Many examples of the role of the federal government as an unreasonable and profoundly deep-pocketed plaintiff never make the newspapers and may not even attract the attention of legal scholars. But their comparative obscurity is no consolation to those who have been crushed or bruised by Leviathan. I have in mind a recent labor relations case involving Boston University.

Before 1972, the National Labor Relations Board (NLRB) did not extend its jurisdiction to colleges and universities. In that year, in a case involving Cornell University, the NLRB was invited and moved with alacrity into this area. Shortly thereafter, in 1974, a labor organization petitioned for an election to represent a portion of the Boston University faculty. The bargaining unit established by the NLRB had many anomalies, the most extraordinary perhaps being that it included department heads. This meant that the department heads were labor while their administrative assistants, whom they hired, fired, and supervised, were management. Boston University pointed out this and other anomalies, but the NLRB allowed the election. After an appeal to the Circuit Court had failed, the university recognized the union and bargained with it, while continuing its appeal to the Supreme Court.[10] In 1980 the Supreme Court held that the faculty of Yeshiva University were management— a position Boston University also held with regard to its faculty— and remanded Boston University's case to the Circuit Court, which remanded it to the NLRB, which ordered new representation hearings. These ran over two and a half years, occupied 157 days, and generated 21,000 pages of transcript and 1,190 separate exhibits. In June 1984, a decade after the case originated, an administrative law judge held that the NLRB had erred in including *any* member of the Boston University faculty in the bargaining unit because all members of the faculty were clearly both managers and supervisors.[11] The First Circuit Court of Appeals confirmed the judgment and awarded the university costs and fees for its appeal. The union waived its appeal to the Supreme Court, on condition that the university not enforce its judgment for $4,238 in costs. The entire process was no more than a massive multimillion dollar distraction—costly not only in money, but in the colossal waste of time and attention.

Consider another example. The costs of medical malpractice suits, in money and in less efficient health care, are beginning to be documented. A recent American Medical Association report says that one out of every five physicians practicing today can expect a claim or suit to be entered against him or her. In California, the average award to a plaintiff in a medical malpractice suit has increased 224 percent over the last decade and is now $650,000. Malpractice insurance costs in Florida have risen 300 percent, with premiums in the range of $20,000 to $30,000 a year, and $70,000 and up for high-risk specialties. In New York, 60 percent of the practicing obstetricians have been sued—and as a result, malpractice insurance for obstetricians had risen 52 percent by 1987. Despite this increase in premiums, insurance losses in the medical malpractice field outstripped payments by $500 million, which could spell the end of business for a number of insurance companies. A professional liability insurance firm sponsored by the Florida Medical Association went into receivership in 1985.

The monetary cost, great as it is, is outweighed by the effects of this uncontrolled litigation on doctors and those responsible for health care. In Florida, 25 percent of the state's obstetricians have abandoned their specialty. Thirty percent more report that they are considering doing so. As a result of malpractice awards, so many doctors have abandoned gynecology and obstetrics that some areas lack these essential specialties. For example, in rural areas around Austin, Texas, pregnant women who can afford to do so move to Austin before delivery. Hospital physicians find themselves squeezed between cost-cutting measures and the necessity to protect themselves by prescribing numerous expensive and unnecessary medical tests and consultations. A recent estimate put the total cost of what the study called "defensive medicine" at $100 billion a year.[12]

While numbers are not available, many doctors report that colleagues who have achieved financial stability are more inclined to retire early to get themselves off the firing line. I use the term "firing line" advisedly. The situation can be described as the war of the lawyers and the doctors. The difficulty is that the costs of the defensive measures taken by the doctors fall entirely on their patients and the general public, whose role is as hapless as that of civilians during the Thirty Years' War.

The extraordinary growth of the malpractice industry does not follow from any growth of malpractice, but from the increased success of lawyers at converting "malresult" into malpractice. Increasingly, when an operation is not fully successful, lawyers are able to convince juries that the cause was negligence or ignorance on the part of the surgeon. The implied axiom is that a competent surgeon can correct or cure anything; this axiom, if baldly stated, would be rejected by anyone of sense.

If lawyers were treated similarly, lawyers who lose a case or get a lower settlement than their clients anticipated would be seeing their clients in court again. If this salutary practice were initiated, court calendars would be temporarily even more clogged than they are now, as every piece of litigation inevitably spawned another, but eventually lawyers would begin to consider whether malpractice may be a mixed blessing after all.

There is also a growing war between business and the legal profession, as manufacturers large and small find themselves the target for product liability suits in ever-increasing numbers, and with ever-increasing awards to the plaintiffs. And of course some lawyers who *defend* businesses from product liability suits might well grieve as much as lawyers on the other side if product liability law were to be substantially reformed.

Predictably, the cost of product liability insurance has sky-rocketed. A pharmaceutical firm that might, in 1984, have paid $72,000 for $100 million in liability insurance, by 1986 faced costs of $1.8 million for $15 million in coverage. Piper Aircraft estimates that product liability premiums average $75,000 for every plane built—an amount greater, in some cases, than the manufacturing cost of the aircraft.

In 1986, liability premiums reached the peak of the five- to seven-year cycle typical of the insurance industry and have declined slightly since then. The shallowness of the decline is very bad news indeed: Premiums still exceed any previous peak of the cycle, and claims and losses have continued to increase, driven in large part by ever-increasing litigation and huge awards. This makes inevitable another escalation of premiums—almost certainly to unprecedented heights. The general public will ultimately bear these increased costs, while lawyers reap the benefits.

In addition, the high costs of defending against a product liability suit—costs often measurable in millions of dollars and hundreds of man-years—force many companies to succumb to legalized extortion. Though clearly in the right, a company may offer a plaintiff a large out-of-court settlement—choosing to make the legalized payoff rather than face the staggering costs of winning its case.

In such a situation, the art of the plaintiff's lawyer has little to do with interpreting the law or determining the veracity of the client; rather, the lawyer's attention and skills are brought to bear on discovering the highest possible figure at which the defendant will think it better to settle than to fight.

Skillful lawyers will also devote their energies to selecting their targets. They will choose, not the defendant who may be responsible for an alleged injury, but the defendant who, however innocent of responsibility, has the deepest pockets. A case in point is an extraordinary 1983 decision by the Supreme Court of California. One Charles Bigbee was injured when a telephone booth in which he was standing was struck by an automobile that had jumped the curb. Mr. Bigbee reached a quick settlement with the driver of the car—who was drunk—and with the companies responsible for serving her alcoholic beverages. But then, in a classic application of the deep-pockets theory, his lawyer entered an additional lawsuit against Pacific Telephone and Telegraph and associated companies, on the grounds that the telephone booth in which Mr. Bigbee had been standing was deficient in design and manufacture. Bigbee's injuries demonstrated without trial that the telephone booth did not sufficiently protect him against an automobile that had jumped the curb with an inebriate at the wheel. A lower court's judgment in favor of the telephone company was reversed by the California Supreme Court, which, though not insisting that the telephone booth meet the specifications of a concrete bunker, nevertheless ruled that a jury should decide whether the phone booth, located well off the street, was removed a prudent distance. The case was finally settled out of court, and the public has been denied access to the terms of the settlement. This almost certainly means that the plaintiff reduced his demands on the deep-pocketed defendant to the point that the latter was willing to pay, even if blameless. The defendant had to consider that the delight of juries in extorting massive sums from corporations, which can in turn be indemnified by thousands of customers, is increasingly commonplace.[13]

As in a play by Aristophanes, the situation was farcical, but its implications remain devastating. The economic effects of product liability—this latest loophole for professional and amateur greed—are severe. Some small industries—the piston aircraft industry, for instance—have essentially been destroyed. In many industries, large and small, development of new products has been severely slowed, or halted altogether. In contrast, many of our strongest international competitors are protected in their own country by severe legal limits placed on product liability. Many of them—the Japanese in particular—have resisted becoming lawyer-driven societies like our own. American firms, burdened with the increasing costs of product liability, are finding it more and more difficult to compete effectively in the international marketplace.

Beyond the direct costs imposed by litigation there are the equally direct costs to businesses of coping with outrageously complex and unpredictable networks of regulations. A 1977 report noted that the steel industry was subject to 5,000 separate federal regulations from 29 separate agencies administering 57 distinct programs.[14] The costs to all industries in opportunities forgone, inventions uninvented, labors frustrated, investments not made, and new products not produced can only be guessed at. In 1978, it was estimated that it cost Americans 3.6 percent of the gross national product simply to comply with federal regulations.[15] It is certainly higher now.

The tendency of those in power to regulate the affairs of a nation to the maximum extent possible is inevitable. Once again, Lord Acton's concise formulation applies: All power tends to corrupt, and absolute power tends to corrupt absolutely. Writing in *The Federalist*, Alexander Hamilton was prophetic in seeing the legal consequences of excessive and confusing legislation:

It will be of little avail to the people that the laws are made by men of their choice if the laws be so voluminous that they cannot be read, or so incoherent that they cannot be understood; if they be repealed or revised before they are promulgated, or undergo such incessant change that no man, who knows what the law is today, can guess what it will be tomorrow.

Alexander Hamilton only sketches the consequences of voluminous law. Alexis de Tocqueville, in a powerful chapter entitled "What Sort of Despotism Democratic Nations Have to Fear," spells it out:

Over society [will stand] an immense, tutelary power providing for security, providing men's necessities, facilitating their pleasures, directing their industry. It will cover the whole society with a network of petty, complicated rules from which men of the greatest ingenuity and enterprise could barely escape. It would not destroy anything, but prohibit much from being born. It would not be at all tyrannical, but would burden, restrain, enervate, stifle, and stultify.

The largest cost of such a system cannot be measured only in loss of wealth, loss of business activity, loss of inventiveness, or the distraction of government. It must be measured in many additional losses, for instance, in the decline of the moral character of the people. If average citizens cannot be expected to choose a safe toy for their children or to use tools or medicines safely, how can they be expected to choose the men and women who will govern them? If parents cannot be held accountable for toys—or even peanut butter—they buy their children, for what can they be held accountable? The ultimate cost of a government that, assuming the role formerly reserved to the deity, seeks to balance, regulate, facilitate, protect, and guide all aspects of life—the ultimate cost of a providential government is the loss not only of freedom but of the capacity to be free. Social reformers frequently become so preoccupied with their worthy goals that they lose sight of the totalitarian nature of the programs by which they hope to reach them.

There is a still further, and again unmeasurable, cost of attempting to control every detail of behavior by means of legislation. This is the inevitable weakening of the social fabric as government and the legal system are perceived not only as the remedy for all wrongs but as the most appropriate intermediaries between organizations, individuals, families, and relatives. Still more costly is the unavoidable perception that it may well be to one's economic advantage and personal well-being to be fired from one's job, deserted by one's spouse, injured at the job through one's own carelessness, or given bad advice by one's pastor—if one can only find the right lawyer. The proper injury, the proper helplessness, can become a source of income both for the individual and his or her lawyer. If only one is willing to forfeit self-respect as a free and responsible person, the world opens up. The Grand Inquisitor, in our generation no less than in Dostoyevsky's, still offers to exchange freedom for happiness— or what one thinks is happiness—until freedom is lost.

One of the most serious costs is the extent to which the regulatory revolution and the rising tide of litigation condition us to be a nation averse to risks. This has no part in our tradition. Much of the western United States was settled by comparatively prosperous Ohio and Illinois farmers who turned their backs on security in the search of a still better and more fulfilling life. Contemporary American entrepreneurship is no less fueled by intelligent risk-taking. But now the regulatory process increasingly seeks to deny Americans the right to take calculated risks, while untrammeled private litigation imposes serious and indeterminate risks that intelligent people may well hesitate to take. The society that wishes by law to eliminate the contingencies and risks that are a normal part of human life will be a pale and sterile substitute for a free society.

Indeed, it will be, in essence, unfree. Tocqueville was wrong in saying that a regulatory society "would not be at all tyrannical." Perhaps unable to imagine a tyranny without a tyrant, Tocqueville failed to realize that, though its purposes may be benevolent, the effects of the Risk-Free Society will be worse than tyrannical—a totalitarian state in which everyone, from the president to each private citizen, is caught in a net of regulations that "burden, restrain, enervate, stifle, and stultify." If Big Brother comes to America, he will not come in jackboots but in the three-piece suit of a regulatory lawyer.

As we have seen, we cannot measure precisely the total drain on our system caused by misguided attempts to create a utopia through regulation. Nevertheless, the consequences that can be measured are horrifying enough. We can begin by noting that between 1972 and 1983 the GNP increased by 179 percent, while in the same period the value of legal services—that is, of private attorneys' fees—increased by 253 percent. In other words, attorneys' fees are being collected at a rate that grew 1.4 times faster than that of the GNP. Lawyers are not yet doing as well as John Gay claimed for them in *The Beggar's Opera:*

> A fox may steal your hens, sir,
> A whore your health and pence, sir,
> Your daughter rob your chest, sir,
> Your wife may steal your rest, sir,
> A thief your goods and plate.
> But this is all but picking,
> With rest, pence, chest and chicken;
> It ever was decreed sir,
> If lawyer's hand is fee'd, sir,
> He steals your whole estate.

But at present rates of increase, they will do so by 2073. That is the year in which, if present trends continue, lawyers' fees will exceed the GNP. But this will be quite all right because, as I observed earlier, only one year later, in 2074, everyone will be a lawyer—and the firm of Gingham, Dogs, and Associates, locked in legal combat with Calico, Cats, and Associates, will devour each other, freeing the North American continent to absorb the excess population of the third world.

In 1983, legal receipts were $38.5 billion, about 1 percent of the total GNP—but this only begins to measure the full cost, since it only measures attorneys' fees while failing to count the costs of providing a courtroom, judges' salaries, the salaries of bailiffs and stenographers, and so on. A recent study by the RAND corporation suggests that it costs taxpayers $564.60 for each hour that a U.S. District Court judge spends on a case.[16] Nor does this reckoning count the millions of dollars and man-years lost by all the others caught in the toils of our legal system: battalions of clerks and secretaries, divisions of managers and executives, and armies of accountants.

Although no adequate study has been made of the total cost of our current legal system, such a study would have to include not only direct costs but also the costs to other professions, to institutions, to industry and to government in opportunities forgone, initiative lost, time wasted, enterprise destroyed. And it would be folly to assume that this crippling hidden tax on our economy could be less than $200–$300 billion a year.

"A lawsuit," the Italians wisely say, "is a fruit tree planted in a lawyer's garden." One measure of the actual benefits produced by litigation was provided by a 1982 study which showed that, if a plaintiff won a judgment worth $10,000, and his lawyer was billing him on an hourly basis, he could expect to receive about $8,200—the rest going for attorneys' fees. Adding together the plaintiff's and the defendant's attorneys' fees, the average outlay in fees was $5,130—to recover, if the plaintiff was successful, $8,200.[17]

One does not need an expert in cost-benefit ratios to interpret these figures. Elementary notions of equity and justice will lead to the conclusion that being in the right should cost nothing. When a system in effect imposes a tax on just men, it has taken a large step toward totalitarianism—that system in which it is the whims of the state, not one's personal merits, that determine one's treatment.

If we take as a premise that neither human nature nor the tendencies of government are going to change, and if we accept the equally relevant premise that endless studies of phenomena will not give us a clue as to how to proceed toward something better, where then do we turn?

When Solon, the great Athenian lawgiver, was writing his laws, a certain Anacharsis tried to discourage the whole enterprise. According to him, "Written laws are like spiders' webs, and will, like them, only entangle the poor and weak; while the rich and powerful will easily break through them." Here in a nutshell is one of the essential themes of the development of American justice, and Solon's reply is instructive. He does not suggest free legal services, government sponsorship of certain types of cases, contingency fees, amassing of data, or a strengthening of the web by adding new strands. Solon in fact rejects the notion that the law is a spiderweb, and invokes instead a principle that is fundamental to Athenian law and also to American life: enlightened self-interest. As he replied to Anacharsis, "Men keep their engagements to the law, when it is to the advantage of both parties not to break them."

There is another principle that can guide our thinking, one that has received many formulations. The best formulation in English is that of Thomas Hobbes: "Unnecessary laws are but traps for money." The corollary to this insight is that only necessary laws should be enacted. This is not likely to happen soon, but there may be a way of discouraging unnecessary lawsuits.

Hobbes was echoing a wisdom as old as ancient China, where Lao-Tzu, around 500 B.C., said, "The more mandates and laws there are enacted, the more there will be thieves and robbers." It is not recorded whether Lao-Tzu was talking about lawyers or their clients or both. Tacitus, the Roman historian, made perhaps the most chilling formulation of this principle: *Corruptissima re publica, plurimae leges,* he wrote—the more corrupt the state, the more laws it has.

Keeping in mind both Hobbes's implied minimalism—there should be only as much law as necessary—and Solon's recognition that men will seek their advantage rather than justice, we may acknowledge that the advantage today is with the lawyers, and with the proliferation of law.

The fulcrum of advantage needs to be placed differently. The issue, finally, is who pays and who benefits, and the answer must not be swept under the rug. Society, that is, each of us, pays— in money, in loss of productivity, in loss of invention, in loss of the fruits of invention, in the loss of advantages that come from living in a society where the law is respected, in loss of time, equanimity, dignity, freedom—the list could be indefinitely extended. Only the lawyers and those associated with them benefit.

A legal mechanism that distributes benefit and advantage in a way that encourages less, not more, law is needed. There is one well-known, relatively simple mechanism historically tested and sound in principle. This is the English rule of costs, which in America is often referred to as "fee-shifting." Its general formulation, that "costs follow the event," says nothing about the good faith or bad faith of either party.[18] It merely says that the winner of the case benefits, and the loser pays. The plaintiff's lawyer may have told him he had the best case in the world. The plaintiff may have thoroughly believed him. But if he loses, he is liable not only for court costs and his own attorney's fees, but for the fees of the defendant's attorney. If a defendant, seeking complete vindication, presses a case in which a settlement has been offered and subsequently loses it, he too is liable for court costs and the attorneys' fees of both parties.

The practical advantages of such a system seem to me indisputable. For the defendant who is being wrongly sued, the probable outcome of his case under the English rule would encourage him even if his resources were limited. A plaintiff tempted to bring suit because of its nuisance value or because of a potential big payoff would have to weigh the odds of winning and losing. Fee-shifting would cancel at least some of the advantage of the rich man who is in the wrong over the poor man who is in the right, since the rich man, if he loses the case, will pay the poor man's costs. It would focus attention, not on the motives of either plaintiff or defendant, and not on the various strategies by which each may annoy, delay, and harass the other, but on the interpretation of the law: Is one going to win or lose? If there is a good chance of losing, there is a good chance of receiving the bill not only for all one's own tactical maneuvers but for the opposition's reaction to them.

There would be no increased burden of decision on the judge. In fact, there would be less. The judge would not be required to see into the hearts of the antagonists, but only to interpret the law properly—and this in fact follows the wisdom of another ancient rule of Aristotle, who said, "Laws should be constructed so as to leave as little as possible to the decision of those who judge."

The mechanism of fee-shifting is the most effective application of Solon's principle yet devised. The development of the American rule, under which each party pays his own legal costs, has not been clearly traced. But one strand in the weave is certainly the desire of lawyers for deregulation of fees; and the effect of the American rule has been to put the fulcrum in the least efficient place.

There is evidence that various lawmakers are becoming aware

of the costs of the American rule and the desirability of the English rule. There are now some 150 federal statutes, for instance, and close to 2,000 state statutes that authorize some form of attorney fee-shifting.[19] However, as the numbers suggest, the approach has been piecemeal, inconsistent and limited, and thus ineffective. Each of the statutes now in existence, federal and state, is limited to some certain class of cases; and the majority of the statutes do not bring into play the principle behind the English rule, since they provide that victorious plaintiffs can recover attorneys' fees with ease, while victorious defendants are either *de jure* totally barred from recovering attorneys' fees or have their chances reduced *de facto*, since they must meet more stringent conditions than victorious plaintiffs.

A precedent-setting case in this regard is the 1978 decision of the Supreme Court in *Christianburg Garment Company* v. *The Equal Employment Opportunity Commission.*[20] Christianburg Garment Company was the defendant in a suit brought by the EEOC. When the suit was dismissed on procedural grounds, Christianburg Garment petitioned for an allowance of attorney's fees on the basis of Section 706 of Title VII of the Civil Rights Act of 1964, which authorizes the court "in its discretion, [to] allow the prevailing party . . . a reasonable attorney's fee."[21] This language does not limit itself to plaintiffs, nor does it require that the suit must be shown to be frivolous or malicious.

Yet the District Court disallowed Christianburg Garment's claim on the grounds that the EEOC suit could not be shown to be unreasonable, frivolous, or meritless, since "the basis upon which [Christianburg Garment] prevailed was an issue of first impression requiring judicial resolution" and because the EEOC's interpretation of the rule under which suit could have been brought was not, in and of itself, frivolous.[22] Other lower courts had divided on the issue of requiring that a suit must be frivolous before a defendant can recover costs.

The Supreme Court, citing an earlier decision that emphasized that in civil rights cases "the plaintiff is the chosen instrument of Congress to vindicate a policy . . . considered of the highest priority"[23] agreed that Christianburg Garment could only recover defendant's costs if the suit were shown to be frivolous or unreasonable, and that in this case, such grounds could not be shown.[24] Justice Potter Stewart, who wrote the opinion, spent considerable time dealing with the delicate and controversial interpretations that lower courts were called on to make in this situation, and in distinguishing "subjective bad faith" from frivolity, vexatiousness, and meritlessness.

These issues would disappear under the English rule, and while, in this case, the cost of the EEOC's carelessness might have simply been passed on to the taxpayer, the overall effect might well be a decrease in ill-founded litigation undertaken by government agencies.

The majority of subsequent decisions, however, have followed the precedent set in *Christianburg*, in effect penalizing the defendant even when the action brought against him is unsuccessful. As numerous corporations, universities, and other institutions can testify, this makes them a target of opportunity for the whims, greed, or injured feelings of former employees—and also for the greed of attorneys, especially underemployed attorneys who take their cases on contingency.

This has given rise to a practice that can hardly be distinguished from legalized blackmail or extortion. The employer is told, "If you want to spend the money, you can almost certainly win your case. But settle this meritless claim now and it will cost you less." Many defendants have found this an offer they cannot refuse. Too often the institution, though clearly in the right, must pay dearly for a vindication that should never have been required in the first place and should cost nothing.

There are, within the English rule of costs, numerous recognized exceptions, and special provisions for handling suits that are clearly frivolous or vexatious. But the judge is not, as a rule, required to decide upon the motives of either party when costs are assigned. This general principle needs to be incorporated into American legal procedures, and the place to begin is in the Federal courts. However, it is extremely unlikely that any wholesale change will be made.

As a specific focus for action, let me mention a proposal put forward in 1983 to amend Rule 68 of the Federal Rules of Civil Procedure.[25] Rule 68 provides a mechanism that encourages the early settlement of cases and functions in a manner similar to the English rule under which either party in a case may, by "paying into court" an amount equal to a proposed settlement, make the other party vulnerable to all further costs should he reject the settlement. Rule 68 provides for a pretrial offer by a defendant, which must be accepted or rejected by the plaintiff within ten days. If the plaintiff rejects the offer, and subsequently wins the case, but "the judgment obtained is not more favorable than the offer, the [plaintiff] must pay the costs incurred after the making of the offer."

The proposal to amend Rule 68 that was put before the Judicial Conference of the United States would have made it applicable not only to offers of judgment but also to offers of settlement. The rule would have been further amended to cover not only costs but attorneys' fees from the date of the offer, and to make clear that the sanction was triggered either by a loss on the merits or by a failure to recover more than the amount of the offer. The amendment would also have provided that either plaintiff or defendant could utilize the rule.

The primary argument advanced against the proposed amendment to Rule 68 was that it would be effective, that it would tend to discourage litigation rather than encourage it, and that it might introduce the chilling effect that Congress, in passing Title VII, was trying to avoid.

But it is clear that the flood of litigation itself has a chilling effect on the entire society: Doctors practice defensive medicine, obstetricians leave their specialty, employers receive only favorable letters of recommendation because those providing references fear legal action should their honest but negative judgments become known to the candidate. A greatly strengthened Rule 68, by lowering the cost of being proved right, would have removed some of this chill.

As it stands, Rule 68 offers only a tentative step toward the English rule of costs. But it provides a mechanism by which we could gradually, with ample opportunity to observe the effects, get from here to there.

Certainly it is the lawmakers, not the judiciary, who must ultimately change. But I think it most likely that increased use of Rule 68 would discourage primarily those suits that should never have been undertaken in the first place and reduce the exposure of citizens and institutions to capricious litigation. In the event, the Judicial Conference failed to recommend the amendment to the Congress. Rule 68 remains unchanged, a not surprising result considering that judges are lawyers.

No application of the English rule will of itself cancel the effects of the regulatory explosion, or society's increasing reliance on the law to solve every problem, ameliorate every ill—and, of course, provide income. But by bringing the costs of legal action home to those who engage in the action, it will make Americans more aware of those costs and less likely to abuse the legal system. It will encourage each citizen to learn that "great art" of which John Milton speaks in his *Areopagitica:* "To discern in which things the law is to bid restraint and punishment, and in what things persuasion only is to work."

I would propose a second reform: that in cases involving triple damages, punitive damages should never be collected by the plaintiff but, rather, collected by the court. There is no intrinsic reason why punitive damages, whose purpose is to penalize a defendant, must or should enrich a plaintiff. This reform would, if implemented, be of double benefit to society. While maintaining the deterrent effect of punitive damages, it would not encourage greed. In accomplishing this, it would provide a fund that could be used to compensate persons who have been sued unreasonably, to compensate victims of crime, or to provide legal aid to persons who cannot afford a lawyer.

I would also propose a limitation on the role of the U.S. government as a plaintiff, especially in arbitrary antitrust action aimed at corporations whose sole sin is bigness, like IBM, and a limitation on its ability at bureaucratic whim to stand at the side of selected citizens in essentially private litigation.

An example of private pleading at government cost is provided by another recent case at Boston University. A member of the faculty was denied tenure. Her department was one in which two men had also recently been denied tenure and one woman had gained it. The process by which the tenure decision was made was elaborate and in accordance with an agreement with the faculty, as was the internal process of appeal. Notwithstanding, she filed a sex discrimination suit against the university in which she was joined by the Equal Employment Opportunity Commission. She was thus absolved of paying for her litigation;

nor did the EEOC pay her fees. They were paid by the federal taxpayer, and thus neither plaintiff nor the attorneys at EEOC faced any risk. At the end of the discovery stage, the university offered a settlement to avoid the costs of further litigation. Both plaintiffs refused it. When the case came to trial, the university won on all counts. It cost the University $500,000 in legal fees to achieve vindication. The EEOC's costs are not known. But the cost to the taxpayers and to institutions of all similar cases must be calculated in the billions.

Boston University applied for attorney's fees under the Equal Access to Justice Act. The application was denied. It is hard to see how anyone benefited from government intervention except for the government lawyers who were thereby employed. Boston University was in effect fined $500,000 for being in full compliance with the law.

And at what additional cost! It is not only the individual or institution that is damaged—it is justice itself. When a vindicated party can be deprived of large amounts of money and time simply in order to mount a defense, there is, in effect, an assessment of punitive damages for being in the right. The innocent are thus at the mercy of the spiteful and the greedy. It should not cost any defendant a penny for being in the right, and it should cost a plaintiff dearly for bringing an irresponsible action.

If the principle of fee-shifting is to be effective in reducing unwarranted litigation, it must be applied to lawyers as well as to their clients. Otherwise, the practice of taking cases on contingency—regarded as unethical in the English and other legal systems—will continue to lead to abuses. An underemployed lawyer has every reason to pursue a case, for he puts at risk only his time, which by virtue of his underemployment has no commercial value. That is a risk insufficient to ensure sound judgment. To discourage this abuse, we might assign to an attorney who has served on contingency a share—perhaps 15 percent to 20 percent—of the costs and attorney's fees assessed against his or her client.

The argument is made—most often by the legal profession—that contingency fees are designed to help those who would otherwise be unable to afford the services of a lawyer. For the most part, however, the beneficiaries are not the needy but the lawyers and the greedy. I can suggest a policy that preserves the putative benefits of contingent fees while making such fees unnecessary: In an era in which $250 an hour for legal services is commonplace, lawyers with compassion or a sense of civic duty can well afford to do occasional pro bono work. Their profits are more than sufficient to permit them to shut their meter off for a few hours in order to take the case of a client in need.

In urging the adoption of the English rule of costs and the assignment of risk to lawyers serving on contingency, I may already have committed a capital offense. But following the ancient English wisdom that one may as well be hanged for stealing a pound as a penny, I will go further and propose that the English rule be made to apply to the government as plaintiff. The Equal Access to Justice Act of 1980 (EAJA) made a small step in this direction, but this bill was limited in scope. Under it the government could be sued for attorneys' fees, but only by individuals and small businesses, and only when it could be shown that the government was not "substantially justified" in bringing suit. In addition, civil rights actions were construed as being exempted from coverage under the EAJA. A later version of the EAJA promised to provide some relief for small businesses and not-for-profit organizations, but clearly did not go far toward curbing government litigation. Perhaps due as much to its limitations as to its possible effectiveness, this new version of the Equal Access to Justice Act became law in August of 1985.

To apply the English rule properly, governments should be required to budget for the costs of lost cases. At present there is nothing to deter the directors of the EEOC, for instance, from conduct through which, without risk to themselves, they in effect fine an innocent party. This is what happened to Boston University in the tenure case discussed earlier. By forcing a defendant to engage in costly and unnecessary legal self-defense, the EEOC engages, under the color of due process of law, in an unjust taking of property.

The principle of fee-shifting suggests a remedy: the cutting of the EEOC's budget by the defendant's costs—in the case of Boston University, by $500,000—if the defendant prevails. This would have three salutary effects. First, it would impose an automatic reduction in the cost of operating the federal government. Second, it would reduce the EEOC's predilection for bringing ill-conceived lawsuits. Third, it would save innocent citizens and institutions from an unjust taking of their assets.

Such a policy can and should be general. If the government were required to plan its activities as a plaintiff on the same cost-benefit ratios that would govern private litigation—that is, to hold in reserve in operating budgets the funds necessary to cover the costs of litigation—the IBMs and the peanut butter makers of the world would gain new protection from its deleterious attentions. If an outgoing administration of the U.S. Department of Justice filed torrents of meritless litigation that might gut the budget of its successor, the incoming administration could avoid such consequences simply by withdrawing the actions. If this approach were undermined because the Congress or state legislatures supplemented the operating budgets of agencies to cover the costs of litigation, at the very least the waste following from the capricious judgment of administrators would be manifest to the taxpayers and become an issue in subsequent elections.

Some years ago at a banquet for lawyers and doctors, the distinguished Texas attorney Warren Burnett reminded those present that when the professional forebears of the physicians were applying leeches to George Washington, Burnett's professional forebears were writing the Constitution. In this century, physicians have redeemed their profession by the development of scientific medicine. To the extent that nature will cooperate, they may be said to be making a good-faith effort to put themselves out of business. Lawyers, in contrast, through their dominant role in legislatures and regulatory commissions, are engaged in creating new rules, torts, and crimes, new occasions for litigation. That is, they are busily engaged in the equivalent of creating new diseases and in applying themselves as leeches to the body politic.

Rather than limit the number of lawyers or place arbitrary restrictions on their energy and ingenuity, I would propose a simple solution for the problem of excessive regulatory legislation and excessive regulations written thereunder: the sunset. No regulatory act should have effect for more than ten years unless it is renewed. Every ten years, such laws should be reenacted or allowed to lapse. Similarly, existing federal regulations could be given sunset dates on a staggered schedule so that each year one-tenth of them would either be reaffirmed or die. This would introduce a review of regulation with some of the force of the medical practice of "grand rounds," whereby experts assess the diagnosis made and treatment employed by members of a hospital staff. No regulatory agency should be allowed to adopt a regulation until a social impact analysis has been completed. This would at long last force the regulators—who have never run for office or been selected for office by the people—to meet those whose lives they attempt to regulate. Although it might require the employment of a few additional lawyers to make these studies, by delaying the promulgation of new rules, they would delay the proliferation of litigation that follows from them.

I am a realist. I do not expect any of these measures to be adopted. Short of a major political upheaval, the situation is not likely to be corrected. Why should the lawyers who make the law throw away a good thing? We already expect them to be more intelligent than the average, and it would clearly be unreasonable to expect them to be more virtuous.

Instead, in the tradition of Jonathan Swift, I wish to offer a modest proposal. It is a simple constitutional amendment, and it reads as follows:

> Admission to the bar of any court of the United States, or to any bar of any of the several states, shall be an absolute disqualification for candidacy for election to either branch of the legislature of the United States, or to either branch of the legislature of any of the several states, provided, that no sitting member of any of the several legislatures when this amendment shall be ratified shall be removed from office or prohibited from standing for reelection. In addition, no lawyer shall be the director of any regulatory agency.

Similar in intent to the restriction that forbids any general from serving as secretary of defense, this provision would establish civilian control of the regulatory.

Those who find this proposal extreme should remember that it is no more extreme and far more benign than the legal reform proposed by Dick the Butcher in Shakespeare's *Henry VI:* "First thing we do, let's kill all the lawyers." Given present trends, the time cannot be indefinitely deferred when some genuine extremists take up Dick's remedy and act on it.

The Ethics of the Sword

THE KINDS of questions I have raised about the legal profession have been raised about many professions. Not only the law, but medicine and business have increasingly found it necessary to develop specialized codes of ethics. Of late, the profession of arms has joined this trend, and there is now a field called military ethics.

The first and the most important thing we can say about military ethics—or any so-called professional ethics—is that there is no such thing. To speak of the ethics of the professional military is as misleading as to talk of the physics of civil engineering or the physics of electronics. We might as well speak of the physics of airmen or the physics of soldiers. Most people recognize that there is only one physics, which has different applications in different fields.

Ethics and physics are fundamental disciplines. Seen at the most basic level, they are the application of logic, one logic, to different human purposes. All human effort to think clearly is dependent upon logic, for logic is the science of sound thinking. There is not one logic for scientists, a second for bookmakers, a third for physicians, a fourth for artists, and a fifth for politicians. Those who want to think clearly and rigorously must subordinate themselves to the laws of thought, those canons of rigorous thinking by which one moves by valid reasoning from true assumptions to true conclusions. All ethical and scientific thinking makes use of and exemplifies logic that applies in all areas in which mankind strives to think clearly.

Ethics is that branch of philosophy devoted to the examination of universal principles of conduct. It is a normative science dealing with the principles and procedures in accordance with which individuals and society should act, just as logic describes the principles and procedures according to which individuals should think. Neither attempts to describe the ways in which individuals and groups actually think or act.

Correctly understood, there is one ethics, one set of principles for the guidance of human conduct. And it is wholly consistent with the objectivity and universality of ethical principles that they are applied differently in a variety of fields. The moral obligations of doctors, soldiers, scientists, and other professionals may differ from the moral obligations of farmers, bankers, bureaucrats, bus drivers, chimney sweeps, and homemakers, but the ethical principles by which their conduct is guided and judged in these various contexts are the same.

This distinction may be made more clearly in the context of physics. What a faddist might call the physics of field artillery is, correctly understood, no more than the correct application of Newtonian physics to short-range trajectories. The application of Newtonian physics is made easy for artillery by the provision of range tables that indicate the proper elevation of the artillery piece for the myriad possible ranges, projectile weights, and propellant charges. This situation is not altered by the introduction of computerized weapons. Newton and his laws are alive and well inside the computer. The equations on which the range tables are based are all derived from the law of gravity and the laws of motion, which Newton was the first to formulate accurately. None of these need be modified because they are used by soldiers rather than bridge builders, the clergy, organ-grinders, or small boys throwing stones. If you ask a child of ten to throw a one-half pound stone twenty feet and then ask him to throw the same stone forty feet he will, without knowing anything about Newton or physics, put greater force behind his second throw. And if one could accurately calibrate the force of each of his throws, one could develop a range table for rock-throwing small boys.

What holds for physics holds also for ethics. The currently popular courses and books on business ethics, medical ethics, legal ethics, and the like are frequently grounded on a fundamental mistake—namely, that there are different ethical principles for doctors, merchants, ministers, or soldiers. There is one ethical or categorical imperative that must be applied in all walks of life—the responsibility to act according to principle.

It is interesting to note that when we speak at the level of principles we can use ethics and morals interchangeably, although ethics is the study of principles, whereas morals may also refer to practices normative in a given community or group. It may also be of interest to note that there are communities in which it is said that there are neither ethics nor morals. It is frequently said, for example, that Bostonians have no morals, only manners. (Indeed, some say that Bostonians have no manners, only customs.) But if we move beyond the world of professional philosophy, we find that there is general confusion between ethics on the one hand and morals on the other. Laypeople use the terms interchangeably. More precisely, however, the term "morals" describes generally the normative practices of communities: what is done and what is not done. Cannibalism, thus considered, can be moral or immoral, depending on the practices of the community. Any student of comparative anthropology or the history of normative practices in his own culture will find apparent relativity in morals. But this does not prove that cannibalism is ethically justified. If cannibalism can ever be ethically justified, its justification must depend upon a very unusual set of circumstances, and on carefully taking into account all relevant ethical issues.

Some of the relativity in moral practices is only apparent, since it merely reflects sound applications in different contexts of objective and universal ethical principles. Other instances of apparent relativity may reveal a genuine relativity deriving from ignorance or error in the determination of the relevant ethical maxim—that is, an error in the application of the ethical principle in a specific context. Additional instances of relativity may reflect nothing more than deliberate failure on the part of some individuals and communities to live up to what they recognize as their moral, that is, ethical obligation. (In this context, "ethics" and "morals" are used interchangeably.)

No one has formulated the principles of ethics or morality more rigorously than Immanuel Kant. This does not mean that Kant invented ethics or morality—any more than Newton invented gravity. Rather, Kant described ethical principles in formulations that met strict philosophical standards. He recognized that Confucius's statement, "Do not do unto others as you would not have them do unto you," and Jesus's statement, "Do unto others as you would have them do unto you," were first steps toward the formulation of the fundamental principle of morality. These partially expressed a sound ethical point of view, but unfortunately they were inadequate as formulations of the principle of ethics. As George Bernard Shaw observed in *Man and Superman*, "Do not do unto others as you would that they should do unto you. Their tastes may not be the same." In his humorous comment Shaw identified a problem that Kant had corrected a century before. The principle "your moral obligation is to do unto others as you would have them do unto you" can be faithfully carried out by two heroin addicts. One is pleased to give the other a heroin shot, provided his good deed is reciprocated. As each of the addicts gives and receives a shot, each does unto the other as each would be done by.

This is obviously a grotesque misapplication of the intent of the Golden Rule; nevertheless, it is a perfectly consistent and reasonable application based on the literal formulation of the Golden Rule. Kant recognized that the true nature of the moral principle was disfigured in the formulation of the Golden Rule, and he tried to formulate that principle without distortion.

He began by examining the nature of the person, to discern those characteristics an entity must possess if the personal pronoun is to apply. No one, Kant showed, is a person unless capable of acting in accordance with his own idea of law. If one's only ability as an individual is to act according to the stimuli that impose themselves, then he lives the life of a thermostat. He is nothing more than a mechanical device responding to heat. Such a life would not justify using personal pronouns or names. We do not name our thermostats—"This is Paul, who works in the living room; John here works in the bathroom." We apply personal pronouns and names to beings who can act independently of forces impinging upon them. To express him- or herself as a person in genuine action, as initiator of a sequence of events for which he or she is responsible, a genuine person must have the capacity to transcend those influences.

The human capacity to conceive of acting and to act independently of forces, whether external or internal to the individual, is what Kant meant when he said that the will is free. This freedom can be expressed negatively as the person's immunity from determination by all such influences. But freedom in this negative sense is incomplete, because the person would still lack the capacity for individual, personal action. To be genuinely or fully free, the individual must also be free in a positive sense—that is, individuals must have the positive capacity to act, while preserving personal transcendence of influences upon them. The only way an individual can achieve this transcendence is by acting according to a principle that—because it is universal—transcends any and all particular motivations, stimuli, or influences.

This, in very short form, is the analysis and argument behind Kant's derivation of the categorical imperative. "So act that the maxim [that is, the applied principle] of your act can be a universal law"; or, "so act that the maxim of your act can, through your will, become a universal law of nature"; or, "so act that you treat other persons never as means merely but always as ends in themselves"; or, "so act that you become a law-giver in a kingdom of ends of which you are also a member." (By a kingdom of ends Kant meant a community of rational beings who, by virtue of their capacity to establish rules and objectives and to make free decisions, are in themselves centers of moral value.) Kant provided these various formulations of the single categorical imperative simply in order to clarify its meaning and thus to offer guidance in applying this abstract principle in daily life.

To explain the meaning of that single imperative, Kant offered a variety of formulations. The formulations were not different imperatives but simply alternative ways of expressing the meaning of that single imperative. Kant's alternative formulations parallel his formulation of his three basic procedures of sound thinking: first, to think for oneself; second, to put oneself in thought in the place and point of view of others; and third, always to think consistently or coherently. These three logical formulations were, Kant held, the guides to sound thinking. The various formulations of the categorical imperative are similarly guides to sound volition.

The rule to think for oneself requires the universalization of the principles of thought, just as the categorical imperative requires the universalization of the maxim of action. The rule of thinking oneself into the viewpoint of others describes the procedure by which one comes to know what he must do in order to treat others as ends in themselves. The rule to think consistently requires that the ruler in the kingdom of ends assess his laws from the perspective of one who must also obey them.

In order to think and act soundly, one must think and act for oneself. But in addition, nothing is more important than the ability, by means of imagination, to put oneself in the place or point of view of others. By this means one comes closest to achieving that universality which is the hallmark of moral action.

By placing oneself in the point of view of others, one comes to know the nature and consequence of his or her acts from the point of view of others. This enlargement of understanding is of fundamental importance in all aspects of life, including the ethical fulfillment of one's professional responsibilities.

Disciplining oneself to think and examine policy by this procedure is of obvious importance to the military. In thinking through a problem in tactics, a military commander must examine the situation not only from his own standpoint, but also from the standpoint of subordinates down to the smallest military unit and the rawest recruit. In addition, he must examine the situation from the enemy's perspective and his likely response. Every relevant point of view must be taken into account and incorporated into a coherent plan of action.

If, when mounted at the head of the Light Brigade, Lord Cardigan had known his Kant, he would have asked himself what the Russians at the other end of the valley were going to think of the charge he was about to lead. As we know, the Russian commanders thought the only explanation for the Charge of the Light Brigade was extreme drunkenness on the part of those who had ordered it and made it. When they interrogated English prisoners, the Russians were astonished to discover that their captives were perfectly sober. Had Lord Cardigan been a competent ethicist, Balaclava would have been a different affair, and the principal casualty of the day would have been a famous poem.

I have not here turned from applied ethics to merely professional considerations—in this case military considerations of strategy and tactics. When writing about the application of ethics to a profession, it is a common mistake to suppose that what individuals do professionally is separate and distinct from their ethical responsibility. On the contrary, the professional's paramount ethical obligation is to be professionally competent. The moral assessment of active professionals must be based on the quality of their professional performance.

The ethical surgeon is not the one who does not overcharge or who is unfailingly polite. He is the one who performs his operations effectively, thereby restoring the patient's health. The ethical internist is not the one with the irresistible bedside manner, but the one whose diagnosis is correct.

If we assume that a correct diagnosis can be made and proper surgical conditions are available, an internist who misdiagnoses and a surgeon who butchers the patient are not merely incompetent. They are moral failures. And so is a general who, like Lord Cardigan, commits his forces to an operation that is tactically or strategically stupid. He fails morally because he fails professionally. He and he alone must assume the moral responsibility for the pointless deaths of hundreds of men. And a general like George A. Custer who allows his egotism to replace professional analysis must bear posthumously the moral, no less than the military, responsibility for the loss of his entire command. It is the military man's professional responsibility to review the situation not only from his own vantage point but from that of his enemy, and to anticipate the enemy's response to his initiatives.

There is, however, no way in which the individual alone can provide all the knowledge on which sound application of the categorical imperative finally depends. Even if one applied the categorical imperative conscientiously and in accordance with the most enlightened views of the time, one's act might be wrong. But it would not be wrong from the point of view of moral assessment, since the individual's actual moral responsibility can never exceed the limits of enlightenment available at the time. If ignorance is not due to personal negligence, it cannot be held to one's moral account. Perhaps at a later time, from a perspective of greater enlightenment, one might find that the decision of a morally good person was nevertheless wrong. This subsequent assessment would in no way diminish the moral worth of the individual denied that additional insight. Kant, and everyone else who has thought seriously about the subject, has recognized that we are all creatures of our time, limited to a significant degree by the scientific, artistic, and social milieu of the day.

There are ideas we know to be ridiculous that were not known to be so at some earlier time. Cotton Mather, for example, was perhaps the best educated and most thoughtful American intellectual of his day, and recognized as such in England by his election to the Royal Society. Nevertheless, Mather could quite seriously and conscientiously put himself in the place and point of view of the villagers of Salem convicted of witchcraft. And he could, after a most conscientious and intense examination of the ends and the issues involved, hang the witches. From all the evidence and knowledge available to him, Mather believed them to be possessed by devils; as a Christian of his day he believed that the possibility of saving their souls was more important than saving their bodies, and he tried to achieve that greater end by hanging those bodies. In his Preface to *St. Joan*, George Bernard Shaw detailed the conscientious procedures followed by officers of the Inquisition in determining the guilt of those accused of heresy and demonstrated that these clerics were not insensitive men who cared nothing for justice or truth. They had acted in accordance with the best knowledge available to them in their time, from a profound concern for the eternal well-being of those who became victims of their judgment. It is sobering, humiliating, and tragic to realize that in all we do we all suffer the limitations of the knowledge of our time. Our posterity, no doubt, will have their favorite examples of our profound ignorance.

It seems to me, for example, that a century from now, or perhaps far sooner, our posterity will judge today's nuclear freeze movement as ill-advised as the appeasement movement of the 1930s. Each reader will have a favorite example, and we must all realize that even in our prediction of what posterity will judge to have been our follies, we may well be wrong.

All of us are trapped by the limited enlightenment of our time, and we are thus limited in our ability to apply without error the universal ethical principles. We can only try to transcend our times by thoughtful, considerate, and scientific examination of what we are about. But despite our best and most honest efforts we can be influenced and misled by those general ideas of our time that are so pervasive that we are unaware of them and therefore fail to examine them.

One attempts to do one's duty not in isolation but in conformity to moral law within a social context. Kant differentiated on the basis of their motivation and intention between people who are merely legal in their behavior and people who are truly moral. He taught that an individual who acts according to universalizable maxims—that is, rules of conduct that make sense, not only from the point of view of the actor, but also from the perspective of all those affected by his actions—acts in accordance with moral law. Kant called this action legal. When the motive for such action is solely the individual's respect for the moral law, that is, their respect for themselves as persons capable of transcending their desires and inclinations in free action in accordance with reason, then they have moral worth. Their action is not only legal but also moral. If, however, their motive for lawful action is not respect for the law but, rather, fear of punishment or hope of gain, they achieve only legal rather than moral worth.

There is another dimension to lawful behavior, of course, and that is the obligation of morally responsible persons to obey the laws of their society. Kant considered conformity to the laws of one's society a moral obligation. Those who observe the law of their society *because* it is the law—that is, the expression of the full freedom of the moral individual—exhibit moral worth. Those who conform to the laws of their society merely for fear of punishment or hope of gain exhibit mere legality in their conduct.

In his "Letter from a Birmingham Jail," Martin Luther King

gave one of the most readily accessible explanations of Kant's intent when he said that an unjust law is one "that a majority inflicts on a minority that is not binding on itself. . . . A just law is a code that a majority compels a minority to follow that it is willing to follow itself." An individual who is acting in accordance with the moral law must be acting in accordance with a principle that not only others but he would be prepared to obey. As a lawgiver and member of a kingdom of ends, he is proposing to do something that would be just not only for himself but for all other individuals in comparable situations. He would feel himself obligated to accept the reasonableness of such action on the part of another if he were the one being affected by that action.

Those who act only legally are, in Kant's view, morally inferior to those who act morally as well. Still, those who fail to achieve this moral distinction but nevertheless abide by the law for nonmoral motives are, in Kant's view, substantially superior to those who fail to act in accordance with the moral law at all. Those who violate the moral law or the laws of society are, in Kant's view, morally inferior to those who, even from improper motives, conform to the dictates of law.

In this, Kant takes a quite different view from T. S. Eliot, who said it was "the greatest treason/To do the right deed for the wrong reason." Kant clearly recognized that it was far better to do the right thing for the wrong reason than to do the wrong thing for whatever reason.

Thus far I have considered ethics as applied to the individual. While Kant was fully aware that individuals cannot exist in isolation, he did not engage in an extended discussion of the dependence of individuals upon society. That had already been done by Plato, who, if there were Nobel prizes in philosophy, would take most of them posthumously. In *The Republic*, Socrates argued that no individual is self-sufficient, a position he successfully maintained against all those who argued to the contrary. It is impossible successfully to challenge this position, since no one gives birth to oneself. The most conceited individual must acknowledge some dependence on his parents.

Granted at least this dependency, is it still the case that no individual is self-sufficient? It is not merely that we do not sustain ourselves in the first four or five years of our lives, but require sustenance by others, by those who know the foods that will nourish us, that we require water, personal hygiene, and, when ill, to be treated. There is not only physical dependence but something much greater—cultural dependence.

Simply try to find an example of the independent, self-sufficient person. There is the example of Daniel Boone, the wilderness man, who spent years alone in the forest and survived. And how independent was Boone? Under one arm he carried a long rifle, and under the other a Bible. But the Bible is a repository of at least 100,000 years of human experience; the long rifle is a repository of at least 40,000 years of human technology. Imagine Daniel Boone, bereft of his entire cultural heritage, trying to produce his rifle. He would first have to discover iron ore and invent the process of smelting, then learn how to carbonize iron into steel; then to work his way through an understanding of catapults to the principle of the projectile, and invent gunpowder and understand its application to projectiles. Once he had achieved a sound understanding of all these principles, he would need to recapitulate centuries of the history of craftsmanship in order to apply them. When Boone set off into the wilderness, he was accompanied and sustained by millions of ancestral ghosts. And so are we all as we proceed through life, no more self-sufficient than Daniel Boone.

No individuals are self-sufficient. And if not self-sufficient, then they are dependent upon others—on society. The individuals who depend for their fulfillment on the sustenance of a society owe that society the conditions of its sustenance. There is no right of parasitism. This may be called the principle of nonparasitism, or the duty of symbiosis.

Several years ago I received a number of letters criticizing Boston University for its support of the Solomon Amendment, which makes registration for the draft a prerequisite for federal financial aid. Several of the writers defiantly claimed they "owed nothing whatever to society." Such ignorance of one's origins and the conditions of one's fulfillment is possible only in a society as gravely deracinated, as ignorant of history, as the one in which we live.

Those of us who like to live in houses without too much

concern for their being burned to the ground are clearly dependent on and therefore obligated to our local fire department. Those of us who enjoy the safety of our homes and do not have to worry at night lest we be subject to abuse by intruders are obligated to the police who provide that security. Those of us who enjoy fresh food should be grateful to those who provide it, not only to the farmers who grow it, but to those who distribute it. Thoughtful and responsible individuals in any society, from ancient Athens to New York, must clearly recognize the symbiotic relationship of the human being and society and the obligations that each one owes to others in order for that society—and thereby its individual members—to flourish, or even to survive.

To know the obligations of physicians, Plato argued, we must know what they do and whom they serve. Physicians should serve the interests of the patient, not their own. The shipwright, whose craft ensures that the ship is safe and secure, serves the interests of the people who sail it. All professions require the subordination of the interests of the professionals to the interests of those they serve. In arguing in this fashion, I am making a point about the ethics of professionals. I am not offering a sociological description of professional conduct, which is often unprofessional.

What, then, are the professional obligations of the soldier? Just as the police officer protects society from criminals within, so the soldier protects it from enemies without. Now, while we justify the maintenance of our armed forces primarily on the notion that they help us preserve the peace, this justification does not reveal the way in which the military is used to preserve the peace. Although the military is used as a means for preserving the peace, peace is not its primary function.

Preserving the peace is the highest obligation of the president of the United States. The military provides the means by which the president is able to maintain peace. How does he do this? He cannot preserve the peace by telling our opponents: "Let me assure you that you have nothing to fear from our military. They are peace-loving soldiers. They hold human life in the highest esteem, and under no circumstances would they dream of taking it. They make Ferdinand the Bull look like Attila the Hun. It can be truly said of them, that peace is their profession." The president who truthfully said that about his army would be the laughingstock of the world.

The president of the United States maintains the peace by saying in effect: "We can call on a dedicated group of professional killers. They have been trained to kill professionally, effectively, economically, and systematically. They are so effective in their profession, which is to send their enemies down to the underworld, that any nation on earth would be making a serious mistake in threatening the security of the United States."

The ability of the United States to maintain peace depends upon the power of our military to prevail in war. Only if our armed forces can prevail in war can they provide the means whereby the president can preserve the peace. The president has peace as his business, and he can succeed at it only because there are, at the ready, fighters who are good at their job.

I was once asked by a friend to recommend his son for the U.S. Naval Academy. I asked in response, "Does your son want to be a professional killer?" And he said, "Well, no, of course not. He wants to be a peacemaker." I replied, "Well then, tell him to enter a seminary."

A person not prepared to use his skill, knowledge, techniques, and all the weapons at his disposal for the purpose of killing on behalf of the United States of America when ordered to do so has no business in the military. That is the military's ultimate business. That is the profession of the military. Cadets at West Point, Annapolis, or Colorado Springs who find themselves ashamed of their profession should make a rapid midcourse career correction.

But of course no one should be ashamed to defend this country. There is no reason why police should be ashamed to use their revolvers when necessary to prevent a murder. Nor should soldiers be ashamed to use their military skills in defense of their country.

There are many, of course, who preach that soldiers and weapons cause war and that we can have peace simply by getting rid of them. This fallacy is matched by the claim that the police cause crime. In truth, the professional soldier stands on the highest and firmest moral ground. The soldier's commitment to the life of the sword is justified by much more than gut-level feelings of patriotism; it can stand up to the most rigorous philosophical analysis.

There are, of course, costs and penalties in the life of the professional military man. They have never been expressed better than by Homer in the *Iliad*. Achilles says, "My goddess mother Thetis of the silver feet tells me I bear two fates with me on my way to the grave." This will come as no surprise to those who have learned from Socrates that the problem of living is the problem of learning how to die. We are all on our way to the grave. Life is a chronic disease that is always fatal. As Achilles said: "If I stay here and fight the Trojans I will never return to my home but men will remember my glory forever. But if I go back to the precious land of my fathers no glory at all will be mine but no early death shall ever come over me." Achilles' choice is the choice of the professional soldier in a worst case.

In most ways, the history of war is the history of mass movements—and by *mass* I mean aggregations as small as a squad or as large as an army group. But much of the art of war turns on the individual within the mass. Consider what went on in the mind of a foot soldier in the Civil War. More often than not he was still in his teens, hundreds of miles from his home, indifferently fed and clothed if he wore blue, inadequately clothed and fed if he wore gray, facing the risk of death not merely from a bullet through the head but from dysentery and infected scratches that today would not rate the Purple Heart. A boy who enlisted in April 1861 and survived to be a man at Appomattox would have seen a horrifying number of his comrades die or be mutilated. If he was a Confederate, he would have spent at least half the war with a growing suspicion that the cause he fought for was doomed. And for the last six months, he must have known it.

Yet he honorably completed the job he was sent to do. His peace of mind depended upon being starkly aware that he was probably on his way to an early grave. And what he got out of it was the recognition that he served his country. That was his reward: the glory of that recognition! *Mutatis mutandis,* we could say the same for a soldier in the Revolution or a grunt in Vietnam.

A name that holds a special place of honor in the consciousness of my generation is that of a West Point graduate of the class of 1937, Captain Colin Kelly, a pilot in the Army Air Force. One week after Pearl Harbor he attacked and crippled the Japanese battleship *Haruna* and lost his life in the encounter. What thoughts were in his mind? Surely, thoughts very similar to those of Achilles.

The goddesses in the *Iliad* are not mysterious figures: They personify the forces in our lives. To say that one is possessed by Aphrodite is, in contemporary speech, to say that one is overwhelmed with a sexual passion. Thetis says that on the way to the grave there are two choices. One may be as prudential and as careful as possible and live to an obscure, ripe old age. Or one may be a patriot and a hero, and run the risk of a very short life. In this she merely voices thoughts that must come to any professional soldier. A professional soldier is capable of considering these options and deciding that he is capable of living up to that profession—that he is willing to pursue his obligations even though the price may often be a short life.

I count among my friends a fairly large number of military people: enlisted men, noncommissioned officers, and officers of all grades. As I have come to know more of them, I have been impressed by the extraordinary qualifications of those who have risen to the top. Many soldiers who might have ended with high rank have their lives cut short in battle. Others survive and as flag officers come to positions of great authority, power, and prestige. Their influence often extends even beyond retirement.

In reflecting on such individuals, particularly in recent years, I have also recognized that courage, the particular virtue of the soldier, is required not only when one is very young but also in middle life and to the last day of one's active duty.

Courage is a strange virtue that has often been misunderstood. Some think of courage as the capacity to overcome the jitters, to quell fear, to conquer the desire to run. That, of course, is a very superficial notion of courage. Properly understood, as Plato understood it and explained it, courage is the knowledge of what is and is not to be feared. An infantryman going over the top must not be hampered by the fear that, like the young man in the film *Gallipoli*, he may be struck down a few paces from his trench. He is prepared for this outcome. A soldier in battle should fear disgracing himself by running. He should not fear losing his life, but his honor. He may not be able to preserve his life, but he can always preserve his honor. It was in this spirit that Francis I of France wrote to his mother from the field of Pavia: "All is lost except for honor."

To be straight on the path, to fear disgrace but not death, to fear not duty but dereliction of duty—this is courage. The truly courageous do not live in anxiety from morning to night. They are calm because they *know* who they are, what their profession is, and its duties. In that knowledge, they do their duty with equanimity.

Courage of this sort—true courage—is not limited to young men on the battlefield. A four-star general headed for the chairmanship of the Joint Chiefs of Staff may be asked by the commander-in-chief for his best advice on a professional issue with serious political ramifications. The general may suspect that the commander-in-chief wants advice that is contrary to the general's best professional judgment, and that to state his true opinion may lead to premature retirement. The history of Vietnam records examples of presidential importuning of just this sort. But the general should not fear the termination of his career; rather, he should fear the dishonor of denying the commander-in-chief his best professional judgment. Morally, such a failure would be indistinguishable from abandoning one's post under fire. The soldier should be prepared not only to die for his country, but to be fired for it.

From the knowledge of what is to be feared follow most of the moral decisions facing the soldier. Not to do one's utmost in the face of the enemy; to inflict or to suffer more casualties than necessary to attain a military objective with speed and efficiency; to fail to support one's comrades; to fail in any way to give of one's best—this is how a soldier fails to live up to the ethics of the sword. When and if he does, he fails on one level as a soldier, but on a deeper one as a human being. His obligation is to develop and possess knowledge and to use his intelligence and judgment. No one has ever put this obligation better than a Victorian soldier, General Sir William Butler, who observed, "The nation that will insist on drawing a broad line of demarcation between the fighting man and the thinking man is liable to find its fighting done by fools and its thinking done by cowards."

We live in an age in which commitment and honor often have been given a bad name, and in which a devotion to first principles is all too often regarded as eccentric. The curriculum of our public schools has been largely stripped of moral content, and at all too many colleges and universities the curriculum has been reduced to a salad bar where the students may, if they wish, avoid ethics entirely.

The cadets at the service academies have an important advantage over most other college students today. At an early stage in their lives they have chosen a career that, ethically pursued, is sometimes challenging, frequently dangerous, and always noble. During their four years, they have the additional advantage of a curriculum and a way of life designed to deepen, strengthen, and confirm that commitment. And, not least important, they are provided with watchwords—the Marine Corps' *Semper Fidelis*, or the U.S. Military Academy's Duty, Honor, Country—that can see them through the hell of battle and even beyond, to the minefield of a Senate hearing room. By this I mean, not Oliver North testifying before an investigative committee, but rather the Chiefs of Staff making their regular and routine appearances on the Hill.

The students at our military academies have already chosen their careers. But it is important that they use their years at the academies to ensure that they have made a truly ethical choice. More than most students, they must seek self-knowledge before committing themselves to their profession. For if they are to graduate as officers capable of doing their duty, it is essential that they come to a clear understanding of who they really are, what their true nature is. At the end of that self-examination, they must be able to say that they prefer the importance, the dignity, and the glory of the profession of the sword—even if it may mean a shorter life than they might have had in a less noble and a less demanding profession. If they cannot say this, their first obligation to themselves and their country will be to admit that the uniform—Army, Navy, Air Force, Marines—is not for them. Those who decide that they can be professional soldiers take an oath and thereby pass a point of no return.

As I write this, I recall the occasions on which I have visited Annapolis, Colorado Springs, or, most recently, West Point. Whenever I am at these places, I find myself immediately inspirited, but not merely by the settings and the memories of glory that grace them. Certainly, at West Point, for instance, the ghosts that walk the Plain are many and magnificent—Lee, Jackson, Grant, Marshall, Patton, Bradley, MacArthur. Neither I nor any citizen could miss their presence. But I am most deeply moved by the splendor of the Corps. We live in a world that is in many ways dangerous and debased. At West Point, at Annapolis, at Colorado Springs, however, it is possible even for a pessimist to take heart from the commitment of our young men and women to Duty, Honor, Country. Their commitment comprehends the ethics of the sword.

The Kennedy Doctrine: Principles for a Settlement in Central America

In the 1962 Cuban missile crisis, President John F. Kennedy, as commander-in-chief, faced a crucial test of the ethics of the sword. Although he was able to resolve the crisis peacefully, his role as the nation's military leader was essential to his success as its diplomatic leader.

President Kennedy reached an understanding with the Soviet Union involving certain ground rules of Soviet and Cuban behavior in return for an American pledge not to invade Cuba. The crisis that confronts the United States in Central America today is the culmination of a methodical Soviet, and Cuban, effort over the intervening years to transgress and circumvent the understanding with a large-scale buildup of military power in Cuba and the projection of that power, along with the export of revolution, into the hemisphere. The key to resolving the crisis lies in a two-sided U.S. approach: to reinvoke the principles of the Kennedy Doctrine and hold the Soviet Union and Cuba to the terms of the 1962 understanding, and to give full encouragement to the revolution for democracy that is sweeping Central America.

On May 9, 1984, addressing the nation on the situation in El Salvador, President Reagan cited President Kennedy's words on communist penetration of the Western Hemisphere: "I want it clearly understood that this Government will not hesitate in meeting its primary obligations, which are to the security of our nation."

John F. Kennedy, President Reagan noted, had referred to the "long twilight struggle" to defend freedom in the world. As a matter of fact, President Kennedy was far more than a phrase-maker with regard to Soviet ambitions in Latin America. Indeed, if there is today a single key to the situation in Central America—and to U.S. policy in that region—it lies in the 1962 exchange of letters between Kennedy and Nikita S. Khrushchev, and more generally in the set of principles that can be characterized as the Kennedy Doctrine.

The Kennedy Doctrine

The goals Kennedy pursued in the 1962 crisis were consistent with his inaugural statement that the United States under his leadership was prepared to "go anywhere and pay any price in the defense of freedom." Perhaps that promise was overly ambitious in global terms; surely it applied, however, to the defense of freedom in the American hemisphere. Kennedy pledged in 1962 that Cuba would not be invaded so long as it did not threaten the peace or the freedom of the United States or the other nations of the hemisphere. He thus recommitted the nation to a set of principles that are as relevant today as they were at the time they were enunciated.

The position John F. Kennedy adopted in 1962 represented, in fact, a reaffirmation of the principles of the Truman Doctrine and their application to the Western Hemisphere, as well as a responsible extension of the Monroe Doctrine into our own era. Fundamental to the Truman Doctrine was the principle that U.S. interests require the protection and preservation of democracy. As President Truman declared in 1946, when communist insurgency was threatening the fragile postwar foundations of democracy in Greece: "It must be the policy of the United States to support free peoples who are resisting attempted subjugation by armed minorities or outside pressure."

The Monroe Doctrine, when it was proclaimed in 1823, was cast in a form appropriate to nineteenth-century colonialism. It addressed itself principally to the direct acquisition of territories abroad. It did not address, nor could it anticipate, the indirect methods of Soviet imperialism in the latter part of the twentieth century: the use of satellite and surrogate forces, directed from and subservient to Moscow, trading on the instruments of subversion, terror, and insurrection against third-world targets in the guise of a "liberation struggle." In these circumstances, the principles that President Kennedy set forth in 1962 constituted a restatement of the Monroe Doctrine appropriate to the contemporary situation, combined with the U.S. commitment, under the Truman Doctrine, to the defense of democratic societies.

From the beginning of the Cuban missile crisis, it was the goal of the U.S. government not merely to compel the removal of Soviet intermediate-range ballistic missiles from Cuba, but to prevent the Soviet Union and Cuba from threatening Central and Latin America with the export of totalitarian revolution. In his proclamation of October 23, 1962, implementing the quarantine on arms shipments to Cuba, President Kennedy declared:

> The United States is determined to prevent by whatever means may be necessary, including the use of arms, the Marxist-Leninist regime in Cuba from extending, by force or the threat of force, its aggressive or subversive activities to any part of this hemisphere, and to prevent in Cuba the creation or use of an externally supported military capability endangering the security of the United States.

In this sense, the historical label that has been placed on the events of October 1962—the Cuban missile crisis—is misleading. That crisis was not merely about Soviet missiles in Cuba; it was about the transformation of Cuba into a forward base of Soviet military power and into an aggressive and destabilizing force in the hemisphere.

Even in the brief letter that President Kennedy sent to Nikita Khrushchev enclosing his speech of October 22, 1962, he noted that the United States objected not only to Soviet IRBMs but also to "other offensive weapons systems in Cuba." That his demand was fully understood—and accepted—by the Kremlin was clearly demonstrated by subsequent events. In the months following the missile crisis, the Soviets withdrew from Cuba far more than just their IRBMs. They also pulled out some 10,000 to 15,000 Soviet combat and support troops and all nuclear weapons of whatever description, as well as the IL–28 bombers stationed there.

Even so, the Kennedy administration was never satisfied that the terms of the understanding had been fully carried out by the Soviet Union. President Kennedy's letter to Khrushchev of October 28, 1962, unequivocally stated that the U.S. pledge not to invade Cuba would be in force only *after* the Soviets had lived up to their side of the bargain. At his news conference on November 20, 1962, the president repeated this condition and observed:

> Nevertheless, important parts of the understanding of October 27th and 28th remain to be carried out. The Cuban Government has not yet permitted the United Nations to verify whether all offensive weapons have been removed, and no lasting safeguards have yet been established against the future introduction of offensive weapons back in Cuba.

And he went on to warn that there would be peace in the Caribbean only "if all offensive weapons systems are removed from Cuba and kept out of the hemisphere in the future, and if Cuba is not used for the export of aggressive communist purposes."

Breaches of the 1962 Understanding

What might have transpired if John F. Kennedy had lived to serve two full terms is one of history's moot questions. But it is a fact that in the intervening years the Soviets have systematically transgressed, circumvented, and otherwise flouted the principles of the 1962 understanding. They have done so methodically and patiently, making small and ostensibly "marginal" moves and measures that, if undiscovered and/or unchallenged, have been followed by new incremental moves. This has led to a steady buildup of power on the island of Cuba and to the projection of that power into other parts of the hemisphere.

I do not mean here—nor would it serve a useful purpose— to point an accusing finger at successive U.S. administrations for permitting this buildup in contravention of the 1962 understanding. Forcing the Soviet Union to fulfill its international obligations has required, under the best of circumstances, unwavering vigilance, determination, and large measures of political courage on the part of the leaders of democratic governments. The formal deficiencies of the 1962 understanding further tended to inhibit U.S. challenges to Soviet and Cuban violations of the agreed-upon ground rules. Moreover, the attention of U.S. governments in the 1960s and 1970s was diverted elsewhere, in particular to Vietnam, and later to Watergate.

In any event, the legacy of the intervening years is the crisis that now confronts us in Central America. Cuba, supplied, trained and supported by the Soviet Union, has been allowed to grow into a power with major offensive capability. It has built a standing army of 230,000 men—by far the largest in Latin America except for Brazil (the population of which is nearly thirteen times larger than that of Cuba). On a per capita basis, the Cuban armed forces are ten times the average for all of the Caribbean basin; thanks to Soviet support, they are also by far the best equipped. Cuba has the capability to deliver massive military forces by air anywhere in the world. It has extensive combat experience on foreign soil, sophisticated weaponry, and a high level of training. It is rated, by the International Institute for Strategic Studies in London, as second in this hemisphere only to the United States in military capability. In addition, Cuba has paramilitary and reserve formations totaling some 780,000.

Propped up economically and militarily by the Soviet Union, Cuba has been able to finance, train, advise, and participate in insurgent movements in Guatemala, Nicaragua, Honduras, El Salvador, Bolivia, Colombia, Venezuela, and elsewhere in the hemisphere. It has, with Soviet aid, erected a powerful radio communications facility that is being used to relay the orders of insurgent leaders based in Nicaragua to their troops in the field in El Salvador and Honduras.

Moreover, the Soviets have constructed in the port of Cienfuegos a base capable of tending and repairing nuclear submarines. Such a facility is crucial to supporting the Soviet submarine fleet now prowling the waters of the South Atlantic and the Caribbean—a force already twice the size of the German fleet that sank 50 percent of U.S. shipping during the first six months of 1942. In the event of war, this fleet could effectively block the needed U.S. supplies and reinforcements from reaching NATO battlefields.

In 1979 the Carter administration discovered that a fully equipped Soviet combat brigade was based in Cuba. Despite protest, that brigade of some 2,600 men is still there, still combat-ready, still supported by at least 500 additional Soviet military personnel.

The patient, methodical effort by the Soviet Union since 1962 to undermine, circumvent, and erode the Kennedy Doctrine is seen most clearly in air power. First, the Soviets introduced into Cuba the Bear (Tu-95C), a reconnaissance plane. These were then replaced by the modernized Tu-95F, which can be used not only for reconnaissance but also in antisubmarine, or anti-antisubmarine, warfare. Now airfields have been built in Cuba that can accommodate the supersonic Backfire, a bomber equipped to deliver nuclear weapons and capable of flying from the Soviet Union across the United States to bases in Cuba.

In fighter aircraft the pattern is the same. To the MiG-21 was added the MiG-23. Because it is virtually impossible, short of inspecting the cockpit, to distinguish the MiG-23 from the MiG-27, the Soviets may well have supplanted the MiG-23 with this newer and improved aircraft, which is capable of supersonic delivery of nuclear weapons.

Reactivating the Kennedy Doctrine

Thus the clear plan that President Kennedy projected in 1962 has given way to the very situation that the Kennedy Doctrine sought to prevent. In 1962 it appeared that Cuba, through an exercise of American will and projection of American strength, would be neutralized as the springboard for Soviet military power and as a threat to the developing countries of Central and Latin America. Now the threat is being reasserted in forms far more dangerous to the stability of the region than was signified by the Soviet IRBMs of the 1960s.

If the United States seriously intends to stop the threat posed by the Soviet Union and its regional surrogates to the Caribbean basin and Central America, it must act to hold both the Soviet Union and Cuba to the understandings reached in 1962. But it must be recalled that the principles of the Kennedy Doctrine expressed a bipartisan consensus that freedom should be preserved and defended, and that both the Executive Branch and the Congress were in agreement that U.S. power should be used, if necessary, in support of those principles.

In implementing the Kennedy Doctrine, the United States must first and foremost use diplomacy and economic incentives rather than military force. Yet there is little doubt that the projection of U.S. military power in some form will be essential in preserving the interests of the United States and those of other free nations in the region. Diplomacy can be effective only if it is understood that there are circumstances in which, as a last resort, the commitment of military power—by the United States or by others—may become necessary in order to protect valid national interests.

A political strategy designed to protect our interests must be based upon healthy economies and strong economic relations within Central America, coupled with our own willingness to commit significant resources to the betterment of the region. For example: The Kissinger Commission recommended that 10,000 college scholarships for study in the United States be provided to young Central Americans. In 1983, 7,500 Central American youths were given scholarships in the Soviet Union and the Communist bloc, while fewer than 30 were thus educated in the United States. If this trend were to continue, virtually all politicians and government officials in Central America would, within the next fifteen years, have received their education in Soviet schools.

U.S. Policy in El Salvador

Let us now look at the two countries that are at the focus of the Central American crisis: El Salvador and Nicaragua. What are the choices available to American policymakers?

In El Salvador, we can try to maintain basically the present situation and the present methods for dealing with it. Unfortunately, this means continuing a debilitating stalemate in which insurgents destroy electric power systems, blow up bridges, raze crops, engage in urban and rural terrorism, and so destabilize the economy that eventually the people of the region, and the American electorate as well, will call for peace at any price. And because the Salvadoran insurgents are organized and supplied from outside the country, they can be sustained in the absence of strong popular support within the country.

El Salvador historically has little tradition of strong and effective government. The judiciary has not been independent, the military has been divided, and what is left of the oligarchy wants to preserve the past and to protect itself from what it perceives as the threat of confiscation of its property. Initially, the election of the Duarte government in 1984 gave grounds for qualified optimism. We could be reasonably sure, since he was freely elected, that José Napoleón Duarte had the general support of a large majority of his fellow citizens. Some 70 percent of those eligible participated in the election that returned Duarte to the presidency that was stolen from him after the election of 1972. Working in harmony with General Vides Casanova, commander of the armed forces, President Duarte sent the former head of the Treasury Police, General Carranza, into virtual exile abroad and disbanded the intelligence unit of the Treasury Police. That organization was turned into a nonuniformed service on the model of the Internal Revenue Service in the United States. Official involvement in the so-called death squads came to an end and personal involvement on the part of those in authority dropped sharply.

As Duarte's reforms took hold, the rebels began to face serious problems in recruitment and resorted to kidnapping recruits and shooting deserters. Losing the support of the people, they could no longer confront the army in the field and were reduced to operating purely as terrorists. They increased their assassinations of mayors of villages. They remained a disruptive and destabilizing force, but no longer posed a strong, direct threat to the government.

If the Duarte government had remained strong, and if U.S. support had been more steadfast, the rebels might well have been defeated. They certainly came close to defeat. Among the lingering myths of the Vietnam War in the United States is a belief in the invincibility of Marxist insurgencies; yet the true measure of their vulnerability can be found in their defeat in such countries as Greece, Malaya, and Venezuela.

Unfortunately, the Duarte government was seriously weakened, both from within by corruption and by shortsighted and counterproductive policies, such as nationalizing the Salvadoran banks, and from without by the failure of Congress and the Reagan administration to implement the recommendations of the Kissinger Commission.

Among the most important measures recommended by the commission but ignored by Congress was the following: "We recommend that the financial underpinnings of the efforts to broaden land ownership be strengthened and reformed."[1] Such an effort would have been particularly beneficial in El Salvador. The deep internal divisions there are caused in large part by the violent reaction of the former ruling classes to the potentially confiscatory consequences of land reform. Although this reaction is not justified, it is comprehensible. In El Salvador, a comparatively weak central government threatens the economic interests of the large landowners, and it would be naïve to expect them to view this threat with complacency.

In considering the problem of land reform in El Salvador, we in the United States tend to forget a tragic chapter in our own history. In 1860 and afterward, the southern slaveholders, protecting their property rights in slaves—an interest that was morally compromised as property rights in land are not—defied a powerful central government and required it to spend four years fighting the first modern war, which reduced the South to desolation before it capitulated. In 1862 Abraham Lincoln had proposed that the federal government buy all the slaves in the country from their owners and free them. His proposal died in the Congress because the abolitionists argued successfully that to purchase the slaves, even for the purpose of freeing them, was to recognize a property right in slaves and therefore represented an unacceptable compromise with the South. Others argued that the cost—approximately $15 billion in current dollars—was too high. And so the war went on, at a cost of $150 billion and nearly a million lives in a nation of only 30 million people.

No such considerations of moral compromise or cost would arise in the case of El Salvador. Far from being morally compromising, both the end and the means would have been highly moral if the United States had, for the sake of the future of El Salvador, underwritten genuine compensation for those Salvadorans whose land was to be taken and distributed under the land reform programs. To those who were prepared to remain and invest their money in building the infrastructure and in financing El Salvador's economic development, we should have offered 80 or 90 cents on the dollar. This investment should have taken the form of municipal and utility bonds to build bridges, roads, power networks, waterworks, sewage systems, schools, and the like. The bonds themselves, bearing a dividend of perhaps 10 percent for as long as twenty years, should have been guaranteed by the government of the United States.

Such a program would have removed one of the strong motivations to resist land reform and to support right-wing terrorism. The acceptance of a U.S.-backed bond would have constituted a quitclaim to the land being distributed and would have cleared the way for prompt issuance of valid title to the farmer or cooperative receiving the land.

Such arrangements would also have played a decisive role in ensuring that land reform, so essential to building popular support in El Salvador, was consolidated. In the absence of our underwriting, the land reform movement was a program of land confiscation. Understandably, it lacked the political backing that would have carried it through. Whether or not land reform is to go further than its present stage, the plan still offers a practical means both of reducing violence by disgruntled landowners and of providing development funds to improve the lot of the poor.

In the absence of U.S. backing of a land reform that can be in any way successful with the landowners, we must confront the unpleasant fact that, even if all U.S. military aid were to be withdrawn from El Salvador, the landowners would have the motive and the power to frustrate land reform and deny any hope of freedom and prosperity for the majority of the people of that country. We must ensure that land reform, which is in the interest of the *campesinos*, is also in the interest of the landowners. Even if the decision of the Salvadoran National Assembly to suspend the later stages of land reform is not rescinded, the proposed approach can be used retroactively in order to solidify the land reform already completed.

If we assume that half the landowners left the country and half stayed and reinvested their compensation, the total cost would be about $166 million, plus accumulated interest over twenty years of $332 million. The total cost of all land reform programs would be less than $1 billion—the cost, in current dollars, of fighting the Vietnam War for just ten days, and less than we have spent on El Salvador up to now.

The United States also failed El Salvador by not following the Kissinger Commission's recommendations on military aid. In its report issued in 1984, the commission said:

> There might be an argument for doing nothing to help the govern-ment of El Salvador. There might be an argument for doing a great deal more. There is, however, no logical argument for giving some aid but not enough. The worst possible policy for El Salvador is to provide just enough aid to keep the war going, but too little to wage it successfully. . . . While an insurgency can sustain itself over time if it has access to sanctuaries and external sources of support, there is nothing to suggest that a government, especially a weak one, can endure the cumulative toll of protracted conflict. . . . In the Commission's view it is imperative to settle on a level of aid related to the operational requirements of a humane anti-guerrilla strategy and to stick with it for the requisite period of time.[2]

Far from reducing military aid to El Salvador, the United States should have, and still should, substantially increase it. Continuing only the present level of outlays provided by the Congress—approximately one-third to one-fifth of the funds deemed necessary by the U.S. Department of Defense for the effective defeat of the insurgents—has worn down the Salva-doran people in a protracted civil war, undermined the morale of the democratic center, and may lead eventually to the loss of democracy altogether. Our present policy, regardless of our intentions, allows the insurgents to administer the death of a thousand cuts to the nascent Salvadoran democracy.

Moreover, U.S. military assistance to El Salvador has not been spent to the best advantage. American advisers, rather than being assigned on a long-term basis, are being rotated in the same mindless way that characterized U.S. personnel policies in Vietnam. A former commanding officer of the U.S. advisers in El Salvador, Colonel Joseph Stringham, was reassigned after only ten months, just when he had acquired the experience essential to his demanding task. Larger numbers of U.S. officers acquire the El Salvador ribbon, but the mission in El Salvador suffers. The Kissinger Commission repeatedly requested that the Defense Department provide it with the rosters of the American mission so that the turnover could be evaluated. The request was never granted.

Additionally, the commission determined that the Defense Department had failed to adapt the material sent to El Salvador to the needs of its army. The American trucks that were supplied were too large for many of the roads, bridges, and Salvadoran drivers. A sophisticated communications set costing $3,000 was sent when 100 inexpensive walkie-talkies could have vastly extended the communications capability for the same price. These are some examples of our failure to adjust to the realities of counterinsurgency warfare in El Salvador.

If we are to support the legitimate government in El Salvador at all, we must do so at a level sufficient to permit that government to accomplish a prompt and decisive military victory over the insurgents. The key to such a victory, as the quotation from the Kissinger Commission implies, lies in cutting the insurgents' supplies and communications. Aid should be targeted to stop the insurgents' access to bases in Nicaragua and Honduras, to block their reinforcements, and eventually to achieve their effective dispersal. With adequate support, this should take no more than one year.

It should be noted that the Salvadoran military, for all its defects, strongly supported the free elections held in the spring of 1984 and supported the constitutionally mandated elections of March 1989. It was also the Salvadoran military that originated the land reform that accounted for much of the early popularity of the Duarte government. The behavior of the Salvadoran army refutes the stereotyped notion that the military in all Latin American countries automatically favor and support right-wing dictatorships.

If land reform could be consolidated and made more effective, popular support for the Salvadoran government would rise. Some of the Kissinger Commission's recommendations on economics, education, and health—designed to help rebuild the country—could then proceed. The other reforms could follow immediately upon the restoration of peace.

The Salvadoran government's negotiating position is, and should be, to guarantee the insurgents' safe participation in future elections as mandated by the Salvadoran Constitution. It is one thing to invite insurgents to participate in free elections and to allow them access to the media; it would be quite another to permit them to join the government without having been elected and then to expect that they will allow the peaceful observance of due process and free elections. The history of communist takeovers, from Czechoslovakia and Hungary in 1948 to the present, attests to the futility of that hope. Power-sharing would give the Salvadoran insurgents a legitimacy unwarranted by their small base of popular support; it would simply present them and their external suppliers with the opportunity to defeat the ends of democratic politics. Wielding a monopoly in military power, the insurgents, with the full support of Nicaragua and Cuba, would seize control in El Salvador.

One cannot blame Duarte for the failure of the United States to support him, nor can one criticize him for the increasingly terrorist nature of the rebels' attacks and their kidnapping of his daughter in 1985. The kidnapping, the earthquake in and around San Salvador in October of 1986, and finally Duarte's increasing ill health all contributed to the weakening of his administration.

During Duarte's years as president the rebels, continually supplied from without by Cuba and Nicaragua, expanded their terrorist activities, and then in early 1989 they suddenly offered a cease-fire and agreed to participate in elections—provided the scheduled elections were postponed for six months from the date specified by the Salvadoran Constitution. The insurgents, of course, had had the opportunity to participate in three free elections but consistently refused. One of their spokesmen, communist leader Jorge Shafik Handal, expressed his contempt for the wishes of the Salvadoran people, saying that the Salvadoran revolutionaries "will be victorious by the armed road. . . . There is no other way."[3]

At any time in the six years of Duarte's administration the insurgents could have changed their minds and offered a cease-fire and participation in the elections scheduled for the spring of 1989. Instead, they withheld their offer until its acceptance would have required the suspension of the Salvadoran Constitution. Thus they made the Duarte government an offer it could not accept without itself expressing its contempt for a democratically established constitution. The timing of the insurgents' offer revealed its bad faith and its purpose, which was to disrupt and if possible destroy democracy in El Salvador. Only the forgetfulness of democratic leaders in Central America and the United States with regard to Handal's clear pronouncement and the historic practice of communist insurgents can explain the initial enthusiasm for their offer.

Once their offer was rejected, the communist insurgents immediately abandoned not only their pretended interest in democracy but also their own longtime allies, Guillermo Ungo and his left-wing Democratic Convergence (CD). Invited into the political process by Duarte, the CD had been campaigning throughout the country and expected to receive at least 10 percent of the March 1989 vote. When Duarte and the Salvadoran National Assembly refused to violate their Constitution by postponing the elections, the insurgents threatened all Salvadorans with violence and death if they tried to vote. The insurgents' radio broadcasts told Salvadorans that if they tried to vote they would become targets for bombs, land mines, rifles, or machetes, whether they supported the right-wing ARENA party, the Christian Democrats, the CD, or some other party.

The guerrillas' threats of violence undermined the strength of the leftist party and increased the appeal of ARENA, which pledged to bring the insurgency to an end.

The future will reveal whether ARENA will be dominated by Roberto D'Aubuisson, representing the extreme right wing of the party, or the more moderate elements supporting President Alfredo Cristiani. There is hope that Cristiani and his followers, committed to small business and free enterprise, can strengthen the Salvadoran economy and, by avoiding the terrorist activities of the party when D'Aubuisson was in charge, gain broad-based support both in urban and rural areas. This, together with support from the democratic countries of Central America and the United States, will be necessary to end the insurgency. Cristiani proposes to negotiate—from a position of strength— with the guerrillas. But as long as Cuba and Nicaragua continue to supply the insurgents, there is little reason to believe that the war can be ended by nonmilitary means.

Alternatives Vis-à-Vis Nicaragua

Let us now consider U.S. policy toward Nicaragua. In dealing with that troubled nation, the United States basically is confronted with three choices. The first is a continuation of the present situation, which in all probability will lead to the collapse and "Cubanization" of independent governments in El Salvador, Costa Rica, Panama, and then Honduras and Guatemala, with the eventual subversion of Mexico. No one should dismiss this probable pattern with glib references to a "discredited domino theory." Developments after the collapse of the U.S. commitment in Vietnam have vividly demonstrated that the domino theory should more accurately be described as an empirically tested and confirmed law of contemporary international relations. The fall of Cambodia and Laos followed precisely as had been predicted by the domino theorists. Thailand was left standing only because Communist China moved to block the Vietnamese, and thereby the Soviet, expansionist drive in Southeast Asia.

If a diminutive country like Nicaragua is allowed to develop a fully equipped armed force in excess of 100,000 men, buttressed by an excellent structure of command, control, communications, and intelligence, those forces—which exceed by far any conceivable defensive needs of Managua—will most certainly be used (along with Cuban forces) in military operations in the region.

A second alternative is a solution similar to that which the United States contrived at the close of the Korean War to contain North Korean aggression. This would involve the containment of Nicaragua through the militarization of all countries in the region with the possible exception of Costa Rica. The overwhelming disadvantage of this course is immediately obvious: It would entail the expenditure of billions of dollars in an effort to match the military buildup of Nicaragua without any real prospect of substantially reducing the dangers in the area.

Indeed, massive diversions of funds from the economic, social, medical, and educational development of the region into military channels would exacerbate the problem of poverty and otherwise burden the fragile economies and social structures of the countries involved. Not only would the creation of a congeries of garrison states virtually guarantee the elevation of their armies into permanent ruling classes, but the very amassing of those armies, amid mounting stockpiles of arms, would also heighten the risks of regional conflict and thus sharpen the instabilities that U.S. policy is striving to dampen. In the process, the road of a true democratic revolution for the nations of Central America would be blocked indefinitely and perhaps forever.

Encouragement of the Democratic Revolution

The revolution for genuine democracy is the only effective way for the societies of Central America to escape their oligarchic and quasi-feudal backwardness in order to join the community of modern democratic nations. It is the democratic revolution that inspired the rising against Somoza in Nicaragua, but that was betrayed by the Sandinistas and perverted into their instrument for totalitarian power. And it is the presence of Soviet-financed and Cuban insurgents that hampers the United States in the encouragement of democratization in other countries in the region—for example, Guatemala—lest the temporary instabilities caused by that process open the doors to new Marxist takeovers.

Fortunately, developments in Guatemala suggest that democratization in that country may be gaining a momentum of its own. Perhaps warned by the developments in Nicaragua, the Guatemalan junta held an election for a constituent assembly that gained the massive participation (70 percent) of the Guatemalan people. President Cerezo was elected with a similar turnout in 1985. Though his presidency has been a difficult one, Guatemala appears to be on the path toward representative democracy. If we were to try to prod this process beyond the internal tempo of Guatemalan society, we might not only jeopardize the process but also intensify the instabilities that will be inevitably exploited by the totalitarians of the left.

As long as a Soviet-Cuban threat persists in the region, we

shall be compelled to support governments not subject to the influence of the Soviet Union or Cuba, even though they do not measure up fully to our expectations of democracy or protection of human rights. We face the tragic limitation on our moral choice in that we do not always have the option of choosing between good and evil. It is perfectly moral to support the lesser of two evils. It is utterly immoral to abandon an inadequate democracy struggling to become an effective one, leaving it an easy prey to forces that are effectively totalitarian.

It is obvious, then, that a regional policy of containment is unlikely to be successful for the reasons cited. Moreover, such a policy would stand little chance of blocking Nicaraguan ambitions simply because it would need to be sustained over many years through annual congressional budgets, through changes in administrations, and against a background of probably enhanced instability in the region.

A Policy for Nicaragua

There is, however, a third alternative for U.S. policy: to impose direct pressure on Nicaragua in order to compel the Sandinista regime to divest itself of the means of regional destabilization and to conform to its own solemn pledges. In tangible terms, this would mean a reduction of the Nicaraguan armed forces to the levels that obtained in 1979, the departure of all foreign advisers, and the dismantling of its massive intelligence and command and control centers. Nicaragua would be required also to observe the commitment it made to the Organization of American States in July 1979 to hold genuinely free and competitive elections and to abide by the results. This requirement cannot be met by an empty propaganda exercise of the sort familiar under Marxist-Leninist regimes.

Such U.S. pressure on Managua should include open and effective support of the betrayed leaders of the anti-Somoza revolution who were combatting the Sandinistas—the "contras" or "counter-revolutionaries" as they were labeled by the Sandinistas and fellow Marxists. The term is a perverse bit of propaganda contrived by the totalitarians because the men thus labeled—Pastora, Robelo, Chamorro, Cruz, and others—were and are the true leaders of the democratic revolution against Somoza and the true freedom fighters, as they properly call themselves. They were striving to redeem the revolution and to attain its democratic objectives, including a free and democratic Nicaragua with a free labor movement, a free-market economy, a free press, independent judiciary, free and contested elections, and the other requisites of a democratic society.

The United States can fully justify direct and open pressure on the Sandinista government on the basis of the principles enunciated by President Kennedy in 1962. We respect the right of the people of Nicaragua to be free of both the tyranny of a Somoza and the yoke of a Castro. We respect the right of the Nicaraguan people to true democracy, and we oppose in the Western Hemisphere the imposition of a totalitarian rule and the occupation of a hemispheric country by the minions of foreign powers that have clearly proclaimed their objective of subverting the continent to their own imperialist aims. We rightly oppose the perversion of education in Nicaragua into a vehicle of mass indoctrination. In accordance with the Kennedy Doctrine, we also oppose Cuba's callous use of Nicaragua as a massive staging area for the further extension of totalitarian coups that would ultimately pose a tangible threat to the security and economic stability of the United States itself.

It is impossible to understand why, in negotiating the INF Treaty, the Reagan administration did not insist on the cessation of Soviet-supplied arms, equipment, and ammunition to Nicaragua and the withdrawal of Soviet and Cuban forces as a condition for our signing the treaty. It is quite clear that Gorbachev desired to have the world believe in the peaceful intentions of the Soviet Union. As Jeane Kirkpatrick has pointed out, this perception in the rest of the world is necessary to achieve a prime Soviet objective: the neutralization of Germany and thus the impairment of NATO. The hope of achieving this objective may well have persuaded Gorbachev to withdraw Soviet troops from Afghanistan. It is impossible to believe that if Gorbachev were willing to abandon Soviet objectives in Afghanistan for the sake of undermining NATO, he would not also have been willing to abandon Nicaragua, so far removed from the Soviet homeland, in order to encourage economic and trade advantages with the United States.

The alternative of bringing pressure to bear on Nicaragua requires effective support of the contras. If we are now to abandon them, it will eventually entail, as a last resort, direct military action by the United States or consolidated economic pressure by all democratic nations on Nicaragua in order to push it toward meaningful negotiations and genuinely free elections.

Unfortunately, the failure of the Arias peace plan—a failure foreseen by many observers—left the democratic resistance facing extinction. The effect of the Arias plan was to grant the Sandinistas what they most wanted—time further to develop their military forces and consolidate their regime. By offering the illusion of constructive action, it fatally undermined congressional support for President Reagan's commitment to the contras.

The hiatus between the Reagan and the Bush administrations left the United States unprepared when in February 1989 the five Central American presidents met and reached an agreement making it nearly impossible for the Nicaraguan democrats to continue their fight. It is ironic that this agreement came in the same week in which the troops of the Soviet Union were leaving Afghanistan. Our bipartisan commitment to the Mujihadeen contributed to the Soviet withdrawal. The absence of bipartisan support for the contras explains in large part the continued presence of Soviet and Cuban forces in Nicaragua to prop up the Sandinista regime. The decision of Congress and the administration to provide only $4.5 million per month in nonmilitary aid to the contras is no match for the $1 billion a year—$500 million for the military—of Soviet aid to the Sandinistas. There is no pressure on Cuba and the Soviet Union to withdraw from Nicaragua, and there is no pressure on the Sandinistas to abide by the terms of the Arias peace plan. It would appear, then, that the U.S. government, both the administration and Congress, may have abandoned the Kennedy Doctrine.

With continued and unopposed support from Cuba and the Soviet Union, the Sandinistas have no reason to hold genuinely free elections as called for by the Arias plan. In December 1984 they demonstrated their ability to hold bogus elections in which only one outcome was possible. Arturo Cruz, the only viable opposition candidate, was not allowed to campaign effectively. His meetings, and other meetings of the Coordinadora Democratica, the four parties united behind him, were broken up by *turbas*—Sandinista mobs. Anyone who came to hear speeches by Cruz or other members of the Coordinadora knew there would be thugs waiting for them. Cruz was unable to procure anything close to equal time on television or radio. Finally, convinced that fair and free elections were impossible, Cruz withdrew.

Foreign observers, citing the fact that there was little evidence of vote fraud, called the election fair. Of course, with only Daniel Ortega truly in the race, and the Sandinista surveillance system in place, there was no need to steal the election.

In addition, all the Sandinistas offered for election was the title of president. Ortega took up a presidency whose duties had not yet been defined, since the constitution governing them had not yet been ratified. As soon as it was ratified, he used his powers as president to suspend all civil rights. Real power remained where it had always been—with the Sandinista party and the commandantes who control economic policy, the secret police, and the military. The election was really over whether to cosmetize Commandante Ortega into President Ortega; shortly after the election, the Nicaraguan foreign minister, Miguel d'Escoto, appeared on U.S. television and repeatedly referred to "Commandante" Ortega, correcting himself each time to "President." He was right the first time: To call Daniel Ortega a president is an insult to all democratically elected presidents.

With this record of open contempt for democratic elections, what reason has anyone to believe that the Sandinistas will now live up to the promises they have made to the other Central American presidents? In fact, it is almost certain that the Sandinistas will continue as long as they can on their course of not only oppressing their own people but also directing insurgency and military threats against their neighbors. They have said repeatedly and with pride that they are a Marxist-Leninist regime. That is, their policies and actions cannot and will not be guided by free elections and the rule of law. Elections are, as Commandante Bayardo Arce once told his party in secret, "a nuisance," something necessary to "make us presentable in the international context," useful only as long as they are "manageable from the revolutionary viewpoint." A Marxist–Leninist regime cannot be elected, nor can it be removed by unarmed voters. For the Sandinistas, democracy is an illusion to be "managed," as Arce says, in order to "disarm the international bourgeoisie." While the Sandinistas may simulate free elections, in the absence of pressure they will continue to consolidate their hold on Nicaragua.

In Nicaragua, the Soviets have acquired an extremely useful puppet state. Although neither has been fully developed, and work on both has been suspended since 1986, the Soviets have constructed two facilities of great strategic potential. One is an airfield far to the northeast of Managua built to accommodate the heaviest bombers, a capacity far exceeding any commercial need. The other is a major harbor on the Pacific coast, superfluous as a commercial facility given a concomitant expansion of the Atlantic port at Bluefields and Nicaragua's proximity to the Panama Canal, but a prime site for a Soviet naval base. Both of these could eventually threaten the vital interests of the United States.

President Kennedy, recognizing a threat to our vital interests in the Cuban crisis, secured the removal of the threat by reaching an understanding with Khrushchev that embodied what I have called the Kennedy Doctrine. As we have pointed out, the explicit alternative of U.S. military action was a keystone of the Kennedy Doctrine and the main incentive behind the U.S.–Soviet understanding that brought about a peaceful settlement of the crisis. Today, when the challenge that triggered that crisis has reappeared in much broader and more ominous form, the Kennedy Doctrine offers a proven design for meeting it. But applying the Kennedy Doctrine effectively will require a revitalized political bipartisanship, an element that is essential to purposeful U.S. policy.

The Kennedy Doctrine is one side of such a purposeful U.S. policy design toward Central America. The other side must be a vigorous U.S. commitment to the revolution for democracy that is stirring in Central America. We must actively support the striving of the peoples of the region to erect free-market economies and thus allow for the development of the middle classes on which democratic institutions depend. Above all, we must give full and active support to their quest for those democratic institutions, including independent judiciaries and free and open elections contested by unfettered political parties. And we must continue to champion the advancement of human rights, including the right to be free of terrorism and of subversion from both the right and the left.

The Illusion of Peace

As INTELLECTUALS of the Middle Ages groped slowly toward what we today know as science, they developed highly ingenious fields of inquiry long since gone out of fashion. One of these was that quaint conflation of moral philosophy and natural history known as the bestiary. The author of a bestiary, known professionally as a bestiarist, would devote considerable detail to describing an animal and its habits, either of which might or might not exist, and then explain their moral significance. God, in the world view of the bestiarist, would not be so wasteful as to place animals on earth merely for themselves, or even as food for other animals. The animal kingdom was provided to man as a moral key to the universe. In describing the whale, for example, the bestiarist would note that sailors, finding a whale floating on the surface, might mistake it for a small island and land upon it. Suddenly, the supposed island would dive into the depths, drowning all those who had thought it terra firma. The whale's behavior, the bestiarist would tell his readers, "signifieth that of Satan." All those who mistake his works for the works of God are liable without notice to be cast down into the depths.

The difficulties and illusions of mankind's long search for international peace have led me to revive this medieval practice. Consider one of the smaller rodents: the lemming. Except to naturalists, lemmings rank in general interest just ahead of newts. What claim they have to the public's attention derives from the widespread belief that they periodically herd together and make a mad dash for the sea and self-destruction. Even this basis for notoriety is dubious. In fact, three of the four species of lemmings pursue the even tenor of their lives in unblemished if undistinguished rodentry. It is only the Norway lemming whose behavior on occasion justifies the popular view. Every three years or so, groups of Norway lemmings foregather and begin to migrate with great earnestness.

They do not lack all circumspection; they avoid, for example, such obvious hazards as large bodies of water or burning forests. But occasionally, in their enthusiasm for getting from where they are to where they aren't, they run beyond the terra firma before them and fall over cliffs to their destruction. This outcome does not seem deliberate, however, and some, like Spinoza's rock falling through space, may think, "I'm free." We may even assume that as they tumble through the air, the more thoughtful among them sense that something has gone wrong with what had seemed a good idea at the time.

Now, the lemming signifieth, as the bestiarist would have put it, massive, mindless, and speciously purposive behavior that leads to disaster. When we examine contemporary culture, we will be tempted to believe that the Norway lemming is, despite its name, a citizen of the world. It is certainly as American as apple pie.

The prevalence of lemming behavior is nowhere better seen than in the chase after peace. The recurrence of peace movements, from their fictive treatment in Aristophanes's *Lysistrata* to the present day, bears more than a similarity to the behavior of lemmings: The *mot juste* for the relationship is identity. In these movements we find the same sudden and inexplicable rush of mass behavior, the same joyful charge toward an unknown destination, the same cliff waiting unseen. Few issues are as capable of sending the lemmings down to the sea as an illusory vision of peace. It is an old will o' the wisp. Isaiah looked forward with anticipation to the day when the lion would lie down with the lamb. This is a wonderful image for the millennium, but no one would run a zoo on this expectation. Except, of course, as part of a research project on lion nutrition.

Isaiah looked forward to a time after the coming of the Messiah, when it would be possible to beat swords into plowshares. Those in the peace movement, on the other hand, propose to beat our swords into plowshares *now*, as if this might hasten the Messiah's coming. But hoping alone does not make possible what is hoped for. The difference between what is hoped for and what is possible is the difference between wish and fact.

It is one of the most vicious and dangerous myths of our time and place that we are divided into those who wish peace and those who wish war. The fact is that no one wishes war, and that the disagreements which divide Americans are not as to whether peace is preferable to war but as to how war may best be avoided. The myth is perpetuated by the use of the term "peace movement" to describe a group of organizations that work for peace through methods that have been amply proven to make war more likely.

A brief review of peace movements demonstrates this point. Between the two world wars, peace was vigorously pursued. The first step was of course the Treaty of Versailles, which ensured that Germany would never again be a military threat. Under Versailles, Germany was forbidden to build warships in excess of 10,000 tons—and thus denied battleships. (Within the 10,000-ton limit, Weimar built a class of powerful cruisers with an exceptional cruising range. The press tagged these "pocket battle-ships," but the term was oxymoronic.) Confident that Germany had been disarmed, the Harding administration in 1920, under the leadership of Secretary of State Charles Evans Hughes, tried to bring a measure of arms control to the victorious allies. At the Washington Naval Conference of 1921–22, the great powers ended what they perceived as the dangerous arms race in battleships.

In compliance with the treaty, the signatories scrapped many existing vessels, canceled many capital ships already under construction, and converted a number of dangerous battle cruisers into harmless and peaceable aircraft carriers. A British observer at the conference, Colonel Repington, astutely observed that Secretary Hughes had sent more warships to the bottom than all the admirals of past centuries.

Once the great powers had determined to reduce and then freeze their strategic arsenals, they moved with increasing enthu-siasm into the process of making peace rather than war. In 1925,

Great Britain, France, Germany, Italy, and Belgium signed the Locarno Pact. Nations that until the late nineteenth century had made a cockpit of Europe publicly and formally agreed not to use force to alter the existing boundaries between Germany, Belgium, and France. The Locarno Pact set the stage for the Kellogg-Briand Pact of 1928, ultimately signed by 63 sovereign states, all of which agreed to renounce war as an instrument of national policy.

The Oxford Peace Resolution of 1934 was another major development. The Oxford Union—a debating society numbering among its members the flower of young England, many of them the grandsons of those who had died fighting Queen Victoria's wars and the sons of fathers lost in the Great War—voted, "Resolved, this House will not fight for King and Country." It seemed to all but the most cynical that peace had scored another triumph.

On the fiftieth anniversary of this debate, the Oxford Union debated the question again, and this time the motion failed. One of those who had earlier voted that he would not fight for king and country, Lord Beloff, rose to say that he believed that the 1934 vote helped convince Hitler that England would never fight. Lord Beloff acknowledged a deeply felt personal guilt over the deaths of many friends who had gone in 1939 to fight bravely for their king and country and who had not come back.

In 1935 the League of Nations, which opposed rearmament, conducted a house-to-house poll in the United Kingdom to which over 11.5 million responded. More than 10 million still favored disarmament, answering yes to questions that called for an "all-around reduction of armaments," an "all-around abolition of military and naval aircraft," and the prohibition by international agreement of the manufacture and sale of armaments for profit. This poll, the so-called Peace Ballot, was an impressive show of good intentions that, by providing additional evidence that England would not fight, helped pave the road to a hell more literal than that to which good intentions are usually said to lead.

Responsive to the peaceable intentions of their people, in June of 1935 the British concluded the Anglo-German Naval Pact. Because the pact sanctioned Germany's clear violation of the

Versailles provisions against rearmament, France condemned it. But Britain maintained that it was better to have Germany voluntarily limit herself to a reasonable level of armaments than to adopt a high moral attitude toward treaty violation. The 1935 agreement gave Hitler the first international sanction of his rearmament policy and the opportunity to make reassuring but false promises about armament levels. Though hailed at the time as a compromise that produced a step toward peace, it was in fact a decisive step toward war, encouraging Hitler to test the resolve of England and France by remilitarizing the Rhineland.

Peace continued to make impressive gains as the decade moved to its end. During 1938 and 1939, the European community acquiesced in Hitler's annexation of Austria and the Sudetenland. National conflicts that would once have led to war were peaceably resolved at the conference table. Neville Chamberlain believed he had achieved "peace in our time." Instead he had achieved peace for a year.

Ignoring (or perhaps ignorant of) this historical precedent, the United States has been slow to confront the Soviets on their violations of the ABM and SALT II treaties. The immense Soviet phased-array radar at Krasnoyarsk in eastern Siberia, for example, is in clear violation of the ABM Treaty. The Soviets have tested ground-to-air missiles and laser weapons usable against ICBMs. Although the U.S. government has repeatedly pointed out these violations, it has refused formally to declare the Soviets in violation of the ABM treaty. The United States has responded almost apologetically to the Soviets' objection to our development of SDI, even though the Soviets have been developing a similar system for more than a decade. The Soviets are likely to treat these tokens of goodwill precisely as Hitler treated the earlier behavior of the democracies: as proof of naïveté and weakness.

We now know the true and terrible cost of the beggar's crust that Chamberlain brought back from the table at Munich. In his definitive account of the German resistance, Peter Hoffmann tells us that the German General Staff was convinced that if France honored its treaty with Czechoslovakia and went to war over the Sudetenland, the Wehrmacht would be quickly and devastatingly defeated. Under the leadership of General Halder, the General Staff prepared the best-laid of all the plots to remove Hitler. An assault party had been selected to invade the Reich Chancellery and seize Hitler should he order the invasion of Czechoslovakia, but at the last moment Chamberlain spared Hitler by agreeing to attend the Munich Conference.

Churchill noted at the time of Munich that some denounced the agreement because it avoided war at the price of dishonor. They were wrong, Churchill said: They had the dishonor now, and they would get the war later.

Looking back with hindsight at the rise of Nazi Germany and the outbreak of World War II, it is evident that the nations of Europe, exhausted from the war to end all wars, were reluctant to face the implications of disarming themselves and of allowing Germany to rearm. They wanted to believe that weakening themselves and strengthening their former foe would lead to peace. They were immeasurably aided in this belief by the genius of Hitler as a politician and shaper of public opinion.

Today, looking back on the devastation Hitler caused, we may find it hard to understand how he was seen at the time. We find it easy to dismiss him as a rabid madman who inexplicably managed to inflict the immeasurable evil of his being upon the world. But Hitler was an astute manipulator of image and intellectual cliché. He would invite groups of French war veterans to Germany and assure them that he and all of his principal associates had fought in the Great War and in consequence, acquainted with the horrors of war, were men of peace. When Lloyd George visited him in 1936, Hitler utterly charmed that shrewd and cynical Welshman by telling him that it had been no shame for Germany to be defeated by a coalition led by so great a statesman as Mr. Lloyd George. Lloyd George went back to England describing Hitler as a man of peace and the George Washington of his country. The foreign statesmen who experienced Hitler in his bullying mood, such as President Hacha of Czechoslovakia and Chancellor Schussnigg of Austria, met him when he was about to devour their countries and had no reason to be charming or even to mask his purposes. By and large, those he wanted to fool, he fooled with great success.

Between 1920 and 1939, the nations of Europe were faced with decisions similar to those that confront Americans today:

decisions about arms reduction, disarmament, the intentions of allies and opponents, and the likely consequences of each nation's foreign policy. The debate was dominated by Lemmings for Peace who rushed toward their goal with great energy, shouting their peaceful battle cries. And on September 1, 1939, they suddenly found themselves clawing at thin air, still murmuring, "All we were saying, was 'Give peace a chance' " as they tumbled over the cliff. Regrettably, they took millions of nonlemmings with them. The fact that their intentions were excellent does not absolve them of having helped to bring on the war.

Among the decisions that confront us today, decisions that will have the most far-reaching consequences for our future and the future of all democratic societies, is the question of General Secretary Gorbachev's new programs of *glasnost* and *perestroika*. In assessing these we must take account of the historical context, which might illuminate the present.

This is what Alexandr Solzhenitsyn, the great Russian writer now living in exile in America, attempted a decade ago. He was concerned with the antecedent to *glasnost*—détente. When détente and the Helsinki accords were the headlines of the day, Solzhenitsyn warned us not to be misled by the enthusiasm of our journalists and media for this latest buzzword. Solzhenitsyn pointed out that:

> the journalists have bowed to the spirit of Helsinki. I know for a fact that western journalists in Moscow who have been given the right of freer movement in return for this and because of the spirit of Helsinki, no longer accept information about new persecutions of dissidents in the Soviet Union. What does the spirit of Helsinki and the spirit of détente mean for us within the Soviet Union? The strengthening of totalitarianism.

If we wish to understand *glasnost* we must learn from history that *glasnost* may, like détente, prove to be no more than a temporary tactical expedient in the service of the same old Soviet strategy. And if we consider how the word is actually being used—devoid of historical or contemporary context—the only change may be that a French buzzword has been replaced by a Russian one. If this is true, Solzhenitsyn's analysis of détente exposes prophetically the meaning of *glasnost*:

It is an imaginary respite; it is a respite before destruction. . . .
You [Americans] recall the tension of the Fifties, but despite that
tension you conceded nothing. But today you don't have to be a
strategist to understand why Angola is being taken. What for? This
is . . . a wonderful position in the Atlantic. . . . Now it is the Soviet
Union that has the navy, control of the seas, bases. You may call
this détente if you like, but after Angola I just can't understand
how one's tongue can utter this word.

And were Solzhenitsyn rewriting his words today, I have no
doubt he would add, "And you don't have to be a strategist to
understand why the Soviet Union, even if it withdraws its troops,
will continue to actively support a communist government in
Afghanistan, or why the Sandinistas and Cuba receive Soviet
support." Solzhenitsyn would surely have pointed out the
strategic value of Afghanistan's borders with Iran and Pakistan,
of Cuba's submarine base at Cienfuegos, and of the naval base
on the Pacific now under construction at San Juan del Sur in
Nicaragua.

In the search for a real as opposed to an illusory peace, we
must wait for the evidence before concluding that Soviet intentions have changed. Up until now the Soviet Union has over the
years clearly demonstrated its commitment to the continuation
of czarist imperialism—renamed the World Marxist Revolution—and following World War II has been a continuing threat
to peace, self-determination, and freedom in every part of the
globe.

But the Soviet Union has also gradually come to understand
public relations. It now has a leader who is a masterful practi-
tioner of that art. Simply on the basis of Mr. Gorbachev's way
with the media and his ability to invoke the siren song of peace,
many are willing to believe that the Soviet Union is no longer a
threat and does not have to be countered by force. Lemmings
have even drawn bold conclusions about the peaceful intentions
of the Soviet Union from the fact that Madame Gorbacheva is
slim and buys her clothes in Paris. But this is nothing new.
Lemmings were reassured by unsubstantiated reports of Yuri
Andropov's fondness for jazz and scotch whisky.

In the spring of 1989 there were encouraging signs out of the
Soviet Union. In the country's first contested elections since 1917,

Communist Party stalwarts were defeated for election to the new Congress of People's Deputies by candidates who openly supported forcing the pace of reform set by Mr. Gorbachev. It remained unclear to what extent if any this Congress would have impact on the way the Soviet Union is run, but an essential first step in democratization had been taken.

A month before the election, the last Soviet soldier left Afghanistan, and observers of the Kabul puppet regime differed primarily as to how soon it would fall.

A week after the election, TASS reported that a mass grave in the Ukraine containing 300,000 bodies, long officially ascribed to German atrocities, was in fact evidence of Stalin's demonic 1930s campaign against the Ukraine. And a joint Soviet-Polish commission was reviewing the Katyn Forest massacre of thousands of Polish officers, still officially blamed in the USSR on the Germans, but now in Poland openly blamed on the Soviets. The commission is expected to confirm the Polish view, which has long been shared by all non-Soviet observers. Now that atrocities once passed off as typically Nazi are officially laid at the door of the Soviet government of the 1930s and 1940s, it is only a short step to the conclusion that at its worst communism is as criminal a system as National Socialism. That the Soviet news media are providing the evidence for such conclusions suggests that *glasnost* is more than a buzzword. At the present rate, it will soon hardly matter whether the situation reflects Gorbachev's intentions or has gone out of his control. It will take a series of regimes as tyrannical as Stalin's to have any hope of obscuring the record now revealed.

But nothing could be more dangerous than for us to act on the untested assumption that *glasnost* and *perestroika,* if successful, will turn the Soviet Union into a peace-loving state. A Soviet Union with a higher standard of living and a less disaffected population might well be a more serious threat. We should judge that threat not on Soviet domestic policy but on Soviet international behavior. Nothing could be more foolish than to affirm the good intentions of the Soviets on the basis of an *a priori* assumption. Nothing could be more sensible than to put the Soviet Union to a series of empirical tests.

If the Soviet Union is serious in its avowal of peaceful intent, let it move seriously toward the equalization of conventional forces in Europe. Mikhail Gorbachev's announcement that the Soviet Union will reduce some of its forces in Europe has attracted wide praise, but it is meaningless unless we know, for example, which tanks are to be destroyed. The Soviets can destroy 10,000—the number announced—of its oldest tanks and still retain crushing superiority in front-line units. Let us see the destruction of many thousands of the latest Soviet tanks in Eastern Europe, where Warsaw Pact forces presently outnumber NATO in main battle tanks 53,000 to 22,000. This is readily verifiable if the Soviets are serious. Another test of Soviet intent would be the removal of the Berlin Wall. That too is easily verified. This proposal will be dismissed as utterly utopian. But why should the restoration of the four-power agreement on Berlin, which the Soviets unilaterally abrogated, be seen as utopian? Only because no one believes the Soviets can tolerate free emigration from even one country in their empire.

Without such demonstrations of Soviet intentions, we are left only with wishful thinking—with the seductive illusion that every human being and every nation wants peace, and that peace is easy to achieve.

This is the flattering song the Siren always sings to those who have enjoyed the fruits of peace, freedom, and prosperity: that these are theirs for the asking, theirs by right, and need not be defended. The American journalist Walter Lippmann described how this siren song came to be heard in the United States before World War II:

> [An] unearned security . . . had the effect upon our national habits of mind which the lazy enjoyment of unearned income so often has upon the descendants of a hard-working grandfather. It caused us to forget that man has to earn his security and his liberty as he has to earn his living. We came to think that our privileged position was a natural right, and then to believe that our unearned security was the reward of our moral superiority. Finally we came to argue, like the idle rich who regard work as something for menials, that a concern with the foundations of national security, with arms, with strategy, and with diplomacy, was beneath our dignity as idealists.

As Lippmann clearly shows, the final stage of idealism is all too often a self-righteous parasitism and a callow ignorance of the realities of life. When World War II brought these realities home, Americans met the challenge. President Truman could proudly and rightly say, "There is one thing that Americans value even more than peace. It is freedom." Nothing in postwar history, however, justifies his statement.

Looking at the INF Treaty signed in Washington on December 8, 1987, it is difficult to avoid the conclusion that the lemmings are running again.

Once again, an American administration anxious to recover its domestic image has negotiated an arms control treaty with the Soviet Union. In the 1984 presidential election, the Democrats widely charged President Reagan with being "the first president since John Kennedy not to conclude an arms control treaty with the Soviet Union." This was meant as a mark of opprobrium, but considering the Soviet presence in Cuba and Nicaragua, and the extent to which the Soviets have violated the ABM Treaty and SALT, President Reagan might well have worn it as a badge of honor. With the signing of the INF Treaty on December 8, President Reagan escaped both the opprobrium and the honor.

It is difficult to understand why arms control has become a cow so sacred that even Ronald Reagan appeared to think that he could secure his place in history only through signing a treaty with the Soviets. We have reviewed how the search for peace by means of arms control negotiations in the 1920s and 1930s led to a great war. Under existing arms control treaties which we have entered into in the pursuit of peace, the Soviets have been able to deploy a formidable new family of intercontinental missiles. They have also made substantial progress on strategic defense systems, which the U.S. believes are clearly prohibited by the ABM treaty. In short, the history of arms control, long- and short-term, suggests that instead of signing new treaties, we ought to reconsider those we have already signed.

The first thing to be made clear about the INF Treaty is that it eliminates only a small subclass of weapons, a fact that must be seen in a larger context: Even with the elimination of intermediate-range nuclear weapons, the Soviet Union will not lose its capability for nuclear blackmail. The Soviet Union will still be capable of delivering nuclear warheads wherever they want to. This is because, as Eugene Rostow pointed out in a January 5, 1988, article in the *New York Times*, every target reachable by intermediate-range missiles can also be reached by longer-range ground or sea-based missiles.

Within this framework, the object of the INF Treaty is in itself sound: The minuscule flight times of Soviet SS-20s and NATO Pershing IIs allow for so-called decapitation strikes. Together with cruise missiles, they could destroy foreign capitals and governments before retaliation could be ordered. The ominous threat presented by the Soviet SS-20s justified NATO's riposte with the Pershings and the cruise missiles. If the INF Treaty would in fact have removed intermediate-range missiles from the face of the earth, it would have deserved ratification.

However, it is far from clear that the INF Treaty will achieve the end for which it is intended. First, there is the problem of verification. Under this treaty, U.S. observers are permitted to be present as workers cut SS-20s into scrap metal. But a serious problem remains: How many SS-20s now exist? We must rely on the Soviets for the true number. Without that we cannot know whether all SS-20s have been destroyed.

When George Shultz was asked about the problem of verification, he said, "Well, you have to have some trust." If we examine this statement logically, we find that it is a demonstrable absurdity. If we can trust the Soviet Union, we do not need verification. If we need verification, we cannot trust the Soviet Union. In fact, it is because we cannot trust the Soviet Union that we must have verification.

If we need any further proof that the Soviet Union is not to be trusted, we may recall the last-minute reinterpretations of the treaty raised by Major General Vladimir Medvedev, the top Soviet INF negotiator. As the Senate was in the final stages of ratifying the treaty, U.S. inspectors learned to their surprise that they would not have the right to examine small crates that might contain individual stages of the SS-20, but that Soviet inspectors would have the right to examine packages as small as the smallest stage of the Pershing II. The INF Treaty contained no such unequal provisions, but the Soviets insisted on this interpretation. Major General Medvedev also insisted that U.S. inspectors could not examine all buildings where SS-20s were once deployed, manufactured, or assembled—only some of them. Not only was this proviso not a part of the INF Treaty, it directly contradicted language in the treaty specifying that inspectors could look anywhere within certain boundaries. By insisting on these unsupportable interpretations, the Soviets were asking the United States for a license to cheat.

Altogether there were some ten verification issues that arose as the Soviet Union, for all the world like children seeking to ensure that the game can only go their way, attempted to change the rules at the last minute. This was how the Soviets interpreted verification before the treaty was ratified on June 1, 1988. We may expect worse after ratification.

In order to realize fully the extent to which the INF treaty is cosmetic rather than substantive, we need only note that the SS-20 is identical to the first stage of the SS-25. In effect, even after all existing SS-20s have been destroyed, SS-20s will continue to be manufactured by the Soviet Union as the first stage of the SS-25, and the factory producing the SS-25 is excluded from verification. If Bluebeard had invited villagers concerned about the disappearance of his wives into his castle and allowed them to inspect every room except three, and the villagers had gone away reassured that Bluebeard was a model of domesticity, their naïveté would have matched that of the United States. All that is needed to resume the manufacture of the SS-20 is to omit the second stage of the SS-25. Before we could react to such a violation, the Soviets could produce and deploy a new generation of intermediate-range missiles.

Even if verification could be assured, geography and the differing natures of the U.S. and Soviet missile forces pose a second problem. Once the Pershings and cruise missiles are destroyed, they cannot be replaced except by the slow process that put them there in the first place: manufacture, transportation, and deployment. The Soviets, on the other hand, do not need to manufacture a replacement for the SS-20. They already have it in the form of the SS-25. It can be fired from mobile platforms that can be rushed from the Soviet Union westward in a few hours. It would therefore be relatively easy for the Soviet Union to denounce the INF Treaty and present NATO with the *fait accompli* of a revived Soviet INF force. It would take years for NATO to respond.

The INF Treaty does not provide symmetrical advantages and disadvantages to the two parties. It endangers the free world.

The Senate, which ratified the treaty on April 14, 1988, should have been willing to perfect the INF Treaty if possible and to reject it if not. Perfecting the treaty would have called for the inclusion of language requiring Soviet compliance beyond any doubt with all existing arms treaties. Recent polls show that 65 percent of the American people think that the Soviets are cheating on existing arms agreements, and 52 percent believe that they ought to be brought into compliance before signing any new ones. Why should members of the Senate, even better informed than the general public about the extent of Soviet violations, be any less skeptical than the general public?

Indeed, President Reagan's place in history will be secured by the INF Treaty. But we can only know what that place will be when we know the consequences of the INF Treaty. Neville Chamberlain was convinced that he had secured his place in history through the Munich Agreement. And so he had.

President Reagan may now go down in history as the man who undermined the NATO alliance and weakened beyond repair the bonds tying the Federal Republic of Germany to the West. Although the aftermath of World War II proved a continuing disaster for the peoples overrun by the Red Army, for that part of Germany occupied by the Western allies the postwar era began promisingly. Only those convicted of specific deeds bore specific war guilt; any thirst for revenge against the German people as a whole had been slaked by the destruction wreaked upon them by Allied bombers. Instead of demanding reparations, the United States offered the Marshall Plan.

Led by a consummate Westerner, Chancellor Konrad Adenauer, a former Lord Mayor of Cologne, the Federal Republic rapidly took its place as a part of reconstructed Europe, allied with its liberators against the new threat from the East, where Stalin, who had taken Hitler's mantle to himself, was constructing a New Order in the countries of Central Europe. Germany in its western part for the first time in history turned its back on its traditional allies—Russia, Austria, and Hungary—

and entered an alliance with the Western powers—France, England, Belgium, the Netherlands, and the United States.

Adenauer's efforts to ally West Germany with NATO did not go unopposed. The Social Democratic Party (SPD) under its leader Erich Ollenhauer strongly opposed entry into NATO and urged instead the Finlandization of West Germany. Later, other leaders of the SPD, Egon Bahr and Willy Brandt, advanced as their *Ost-Politik* the attenuation of West German ties with NATO and the West in order to win concessions from the Soviet Union that might lead to German reunification. To these views, Adenauer and his Christian Democratic Party (CDU) together with Bavaria's Christian Social Union (CSU), led by Franz-Josef Strauss, were adamantly opposed. Freedom, Adenauer insisted, took priority over all other concerns. And since the only guarantee of West Germany's freedom was the strength of the NATO alliance, he argued that the Federal Republic should never abandon NATO as a condition of German reunification.

Adenauer's policy became an orthodox position in the Federal Republic and was supported not only by his successors in the CDU, but also by Chancellor Helmut Schmidt of the SPD, who for the period of his chancellorship succeeded in winning wide support of his own party for the NATO alliance and in minimizing the influence of Willy Brandt and supporters of his *Ost-Politik*. Schmidt's ascension to power required, however, his formation of a coalition government with the Free Democratic Party (FDP), an event that introduced Hans Dietrich Genscher as foreign minister, a man whose views were more closely allied to the *Ost-Politik* of Brandt and Bahr than to Helmut Schmidt's views on the subject. When Schmidt was succeeded by Helmut Kohl, the CDU/CSU could gain power only by entering a coalition with the FDP, and thus the influence of Genscher persisted.

Genscher's position was for the most part successfully checked by both Chancellors Schmidt and Kohl until the vagaries of American foreign policy reduced the credibility of the NATO alliance and gave new life to the idea of German reunification through the abandonment of NATO. President Reagan's apparent commitment at Reykjavik to the abandonment of all nuclear missiles and his enthusiastic pursuit and conclusion of the INF Treaty accelerated in Germany the view that the United

States is no longer firmly committed to the NATO alliance and that, in case of an attack on Germany, the United States might not risk war to come to Europe's defense. The basis for German doubts turns in part on their recognition that the INF Treaty, seriously inadequate on the issue of verification, continues the major advantage of the Soviet Union in intermediate-range missiles without providing major offsetting Soviet concessions in conventional weapons and without Soviet withdrawal from Nicaragua, Angola, and elsewhere.

In the last year, Genscher's influence has risen dramatically while the influence of Chancellor Kohl has been maintained only by his conforming his own views to those long held by Genscher. No one can know how long it will be before a chancellor of the Federal Republic of Germany revives the Ollenhauer position and agrees to the abandonment of the NATO alliance and the Finlandization of Germany as a condition of German reunification.

Thus the INF Treaty and the diplomatic negotiations that led up to it have posed a greater threat to the NATO alliance than any we have witnessed since it was first established. The legacy of Reagan's foreign policy, unless checked by his successor, may be the reversal of the greatest foreign policy triumph in modern American history: turning West Germany toward the West. Increasingly, the citizens of the Federal Republic of Germany are looking eastward in search of security. The songs of *Mitteleuropa* and *perestroika* are heard in the land and Lemmings for Peace are on the march.

There can be little doubt, on the basis of several polls, that the INF is proving popular among the American and German people. Part of this popularity is almost certainly because of a perception that Mikhail Gorbachev is very different from the traditional Soviet leaders and that the Soviet Union under his leadership may be undergoing a significant and humanizing transformation.

No Soviet leader following Stalin found it difficult to appear benign. But Gorbachev has the distinct advantage of looking lively, flexible, and engaging in comparison with his robotlike predecessors Brezhnev, Andropov, and Chernenko. We should be exceedingly cautious, however, before assuming that

Gorbachev's smiling exterior covers a smiling interior. If he turns out to be precisely what he appears, we can only rejoice. But if he turns out to be what Chaucer called a smiler with a knife beneath his cloak, the potential for disaster is immense. Perhaps he is genuine, but prudence and a minimal interest in our survival demand that we wait for the evidence.

Gorbachev's success in strengthening the Soviet Union will rest to a significant degree on his ability to charm Westerners into expanding their generous policy of financing their enemies. An increase in loans to the Soviet bloc was a major item on Gorbachev's agenda in Washington. The success of his economic program can be assured if Western banks and businesses augment the already large flow of cash from west to east.

While many are aware of the extent to which the Soviet Union and its foreign policy are subsidized by the West, few seem to perceive the shocking implications of this fact. Moscow's indebtedness to the West rose to $42 billion in 1987—an increase of more than 90 percent over the last three years. The hard-currency debt of the Eastern bloc nations now stands at $132 billion, a leap of 61 percent from 1984.

Very little of this money is spent on improving the lives of the citizens of the Soviet bloc. Once the money is loaned, it can be spent as the Soviets please—on military projects and the extension of Soviet hegemony throughout the world. In 1987, the Soviet Union earned only $31 billion in hard currency, demonstrating the Soviet Union's insignificance as an economic power. And yet, poor as it is, the Soviet Union spent more than $16 billion propping up its surrogates and puppets in Cuba, Nicaragua, Vietnam, Angola, Ethiopia, and Afghanistan.

As former Secretary of the Treasury William E. Simon pointed out, the trucks that carried Soviet weapons and troops into Afghanistan came from a factory financed by the United States and other nations of the free world—a factory built by American, German, British, and Italian firms.[1] The Soviet economy, as Simon demonstrates, is in shambles. Food is still rationed in many areas, 40 percent of light industrial machinery is obsolete, 50 percent of all new tractors must be cannibalized for spare parts for tractors already broken down. With military expenditures officially at 19 percent of the Soviet GNP, and said by some Soviet economists to be as high as 40 percent—in contrast to U.S. military expenditures at only 5.9 percent of the GNP—the quality of Soviet life often approaches the unbearable. The Soviet Union is the first industrialized nation in peacetime to suffer a significant drop in male life expectancy, from 68 to 65 years, in contrast with 71 in the United States.

Glasnost and *perestroika*—without massive economic aid to the USSR from prosperous democracies—can do nothing to improve the economy of the Soviet Union or to improve the lives of its citizens unless the Soviets reduce their commitment to the building of massive military forces on land, sea, air, in space, and underground. The military buildup executed under the Reagan administration has vastly improved the security of the West, but that buildup has not remotely approached the massive military advances of the Soviet Union. Those who speak of an arms race speak nonsense, for the United States did not run. While the Soviets have increased already massive military commitments, the United States has committed less than one-third of its federal budget to defense. It is sobering to remember that John F. Kennedy committed 49 percent of the federal budget to defense.

Without adequate consideration of the foreign policy implications involved, the West has become a major source of capital for the Soviet Union. Loans to the Soviet bloc are an indirect subsidy of Soviet foreign policy. They are also bad business. Western banks have already written off their share of Poland's foreign debt. Cuba and North Korea are in default on Western loans. The productive capacity of the Eastern bloc cannot generate revenue necessary to service their foreign debts. And yet First National Bank of Chicago, Manufacturers Hanover, and Security Pacific, among others, provide low-interest, unsecured loans to the Soviet Union and the Eastern bloc nations.

Simon notes that the terms of our loans to the Soviet Union and the Soviet bloc nations are often more favorable than those available to an American farmer, and that the banks are more forgiving to Soviet bloc clients than to an American farmer when the terms are not met. When Hungary threatened to default on a $210 million loan, the American banks simply deferred payment deadlines for four years. They shall have to defer them again and again until ultimate default. We have forgotten the old adage: "If you owe the bank a little money, the bank owns you. But if you owe the bank a great deal of money, you own the bank."

It is interesting that the Congress with its passion for sunshine laws has not seen fit to demand public disclosure of interest rates of loans by U.S. banks to the Soviet Union. They would discover, if they pursued this issue, that in 1988 loans were being made to the Soviet Union at one-eighth of a percent above LIBOR, the London interbank rate. American businesses and universities can rarely, if ever, borrow money at this rate despite the fact that their assets are available for repossession should they default.

Unless the American banks have ready access to the Red Army and the KGB, it is inconceivable that they claim security for any of their loans to the Eastern bloc except as that security is guaranteed through government loans secured by the U.S. taxpayers. That is sometimes the case. But the primary reason why American banks lend money to the Eastern bloc is because it is the policy of the government of the United States, in particular, the State Department, to urge the making of such loans.

Thus, American foreign policy—in effect if not in intent— seeks simultaneously to ensure both Gorbachev's success in continuing to build his military and his attempt to bring some improvement to the daily life of Soviet citizens. That is, our policy ensures that Gorbachev's programs of *glasnost* and *perestroika* need be nothing more than a public relations campaign by which to disarm the West.

Realism dictates that we oppose Gorbachev's efforts to secure financing from the World Bank, the IMF, and the prosperous democracies. But so far, Western democracies seem much more inclined to appease Gorbachev and the Soviet Union than to assess realistically and to pursue their own interests.

West Germany, for instance, has become increasingly dependent on the Soviet Union for the supply of fuel essential to its economy. By lending money to the Soviet Union or by bartering goods, machinery, and engineering services for natural gas and oil, West Germany further increases that dependency. The Soviets' success in boring hundreds of miles of deep tunnels to secure continuation of command and control and even the continuation of industrial production in case of war depends upon tunneling equipment received from West Germany.

But this is only the good news. Chancellor Helmut Kohl recently paid tribute to the Soviet Union by his visit to Moscow with $1.9 billion in credit. President François Mitterrand announced his intention to visit Moscow with more than $2 billion in credit lines. The Italians have extended huge subsidized loans in violation of NATO policy, and Italian firms, along with French and German firms, are initiating cooperative projects with the Soviets. And hard as it is to believe, British banks, with the approval of Prime Minister Margaret Thatcher, are negotiating massive lines of credit.

How can we explain the willingness of the Western democracies to finance the development and expansion of the Soviet economy while the Soviets themselves continue to devote most of their resources to the support of their military forces and to imperialistic adventurism in all parts of the world?

If Western credit were denied, the Soviets would have to face the disturbing consequences of their priorities and change them. This change would almost certainly be beneficial to the West. How then do we explain this phenomenon—the Western democracies fulfilling a promise attributed to Lenin that "the Capitalists will sell the rope on which they are hanged and their banks will lend the money"?

The answer is plain to see. European democracies and the State Department of the United States have allowed the wish for peace to obscure the reality of the Soviet threat. As far as the European powers are concerned, the cause may be even more harrowing. It may be that fear of and the desire to appease the Soviets is their motive. For many years, English kings extracted a tax from their people to pay Dane-geld on the promise that the Danes would no longer send marauding bands to prey on English villages. The Western democracies have once again revived this practice. They would be well advised, however, to remember the chilling lines of Rudyard Kipling: "Once you have paid him the Dane-geld, you never get rid of the Dane."

By supplying the Soviet bloc with massive economic and industrial aid, in total disregard for their survival, the democracies are denying themselves essential leverage. All aid to the Soviet bloc should be prohibited until the Soviet Union has passed the empirical tests that I have outlined.

We must not be beguiled by the illusions of peace. But this does not mean that we must abandon the search for genuine peace. To pursue genuine peace, we must understand the realistic conditions on which it depends. Our ability to prevent conventional war depends first on the clear perception by all possible enemies of our capacity to prevail in a conventional war should it come and, second, on our determination to fight if necessary. Our ability to deter chemical warfare—for which the Soviets are exceptionally well-prepared both offensively and defensively— depends upon our capacity to effectively counter their possible use of chemical weapons. Our ability to deter nuclear war depends on our capacity and willingness to inflict unacceptable damage on any enemy who would consider nuclear war. This means that no further consideration should be given to strategic arms reduction prior to the achievement of a reasonable balance of conventional forces and chemical weapons in Europe. It also requires a freeze on loans to the Soviet bloc until the Soviet Union and its satellites have passed that series of tests by which the sincerity of their peaceful intent can be assured.

Peace secured on this basis is no illusion. On any other basis— on the promise of *glasnost* and *perestroika*, on offers of trade financed on credit, on the promise of disengagement, disarmament, or nuclear freeze—peace is only an illusion. Far from being benign, it is a dangerous illusion that can lead only to war or to the gradual Finlandization of the democracies—that is, to a *Pax Sovietica* in which the free world will have become an illusion.

Conclusion

In this book I have tried to hold a mirror up to our times and ourselves to help us see more clearly the direction in which we as individuals and as a society have gone. Although it is not a pretty picture, neither is it an occasion for despair.

I have argued throughout this book that the primary threat to our freedom does not lie beyond our shores—in the Soviet Union or elsewhere. The greatest threat lies within our own borders and within each of us.

We bear the unmistakable traces of self-indulgence. The habits developed through years of ease and plenty have left us, if not at our worst, very far from our best. We seem incapable of making those decisions that, though imperative for our own well-being and that of our children, require unwelcome self-restraint and self-denial. This failure in self-mastery is apparent not only in individual lives but in every aspect of our society. Through self-indulgence and seductive advertising we have turned our luxuries, even our whims, into needs.

We appear to lack the common sense or the self-control to live within our means by deciding which of our expenses are necessary and which are merely desirable. Too often we choose mere consumption over investments in the infrastructure, industry, and research on which our well-being depends. We handicap ourselves in foreign trade by a tax code that creates advantages for our foreign competitors while subjecting individual taxpayers to unnecessary complexities that serve no one but tax accountants and lawyers. Our stock market, established as an exchange for sound investment and profit, is beginning to resemble a casino driven by computer-assisted program trading and junk bond takeovers for the benefit of insiders. We acquiesce in the rapacity of those who carry off the riches of corporations they have impoverished and rendered less productive.

These are consequences of our forty-year experiment with luxury, a luxury unprecedented in degree, in duration, and in distribution. Sunk in luxury, we accept passively the threats posed and losses inflicted by those who prey upon us: drunk drivers who maim and kill tens of thousands each year; callous drug lords who aggressively and intentionally maim and kill; respectable citizens who earn honest livings but pour billions of dollars into the vast international criminal empire that caters to their recreational or addictive drug habits.

We passively accept those who profit from the violence and perversity that television imposes on ourselves and our children as it coarsens our sensibility, pidgins our English, and encourages many of us to waste years of our lives in aimless watching. We have so accustomed ourselves to narcotics—whether chemical or electronic—that we either cannot or will not direct our attention and our energies to those tasks on which our survival as a free people depend.

Our failure as a society is seen nowhere so clearly as in our inability to reform our public schools. While we stood by passively, teachers' unions, which began with the goals of raising professional quality and salaries, transformed our teachers from respected professionals into wage earners, too often more concerned for tenure and limited hours than for the education of the children entrusted to them.

It is only through education that the child is transformed into a civilized adult. An ever-increasing number of our young roam our streets and parks playing out in criminal acts brutal impulses untamed and undirected by the moral heritage of enlightened people. We are beset by barbarians who have emerged within the walls of our own society, the "vertical" barbarians described more than sixty years ago by Ortega y Gasset.

The problem has been exacerbated by social scientists and philosophers who interpret human conduct in ways that exclude all moral considerations. Criminal acts are explained merely as manifestations of social neglect or disease rather than as free decisions of human beings who may be in fact either ignorant or wicked. The idea that there are genuinely cruel and wicked people who act with immoral disregard for the rights of others is rejected out of hand, not on the basis of empirical observation, but on the basis of ideological preconceptions.

Over the past forty years we have cast aside, as merely traditional, arbitrary, irrational, or even inhumane, ancient duties and prohibitions that were developed over thousands of years to improve the chances for fulfillment of individuals and the survival and prosperity of communities. We find these duties increasingly frustrating and unpleasant. They interfere with what we have come to claim as the right of each individual: To pursue a life of pleasure, a life of immediate gratification. This attitude was often explained as a repudiation of Puritan and Victorian moral standards; but in fact these had long ceased to be dominant influences in our lives.

The right to do as one pleased so long as it gave pleasure was accompanied by a corollary "right" to repudiate all unpleasant obligations and commitments. Sincerity, a virtue achievable at an instant, replaced the more difficult virtue of integrity, which involves commitment to relationships and to principles over a sustained period of time. Commitment itself became a dirty word for those whose pleasure-seeking led to the repudiation of unpleasant commitments to parents, children, wives, and husbands, community and country.

The folly of the new morality can be seen in its consequences: The gratuitous misery consequent upon drunken driving, the misuse of drugs, the trivialization of sex, the bitter hardship of children raised without homes, the squalor of those driven from mental hospitals and onto the streets by ideologues who proclaimed the right of the mentally ill to live as they please.

In the midst of this disarray in our institutions, in a society and in a time as confused and as disturbing as our own, are there any grounds for optimism or hope?

I believe there are.

Inexorably, as the shallowness, emptiness, bitterness, and cruelty of the no-fault life become increasingly obvious, the foundations of morality—forgotten or rejected over the past forty years of prosperity—are re-emerging to be re-learned. The moral prohibition of promiscuity, for example, is not animated by a sour puritanical concern to deny pleasure to the carelessly promiscuous. Rather, this moral law, quite apart from its role in the fulfillment of the individual, has as its purpose the protection of the rights of children to proper nurture and a fair chance of personal fulfillment. Thus, paradoxically, our abandonment of traditional moral values and practices has created a situation of brutal hardship and misery that demonstrates the validity of those values and traditions.

By examining the consequences of the way we live now, we are recovering a respect for traditional morality—a respect not grounded on religious faith or on mere social custom, but on rational authority—on our observation that certain moral rules are conducive to human happiness and fulfillment. We are again discovering that without adherence to moral laws there is no possibility of a good society in which the rights of individuals are nurtured and their well-being protected.

We are rediscovering the basic truth that the fulfillment of each individual requires that everyone be willing, and, if necessary, legally required, to accept responsibility for the consequences of free acts. Those who bring children into the world must provide adequately for their physical and intellectual nurture or have them taken from them. Those who drink and drive must no longer be allowed to kill with impunity, but must be treated as the criminals they are. Those teachers who lack either knowledge or the ability to teach must themselves be educated up to standard or removed.

We are the first nation put to a true test of spirit not by adversity but by its absence. Unlike our ancestors, we have not been coerced by poverty, tyranny, disease, and calamity to find solace in spiritual values. Ironically, it is through our very luxury that we are beginning to discern collectively what wise individuals in every generation have known.

I am confident that we are on the threshold of a moral awakening in which we as a people will regain that insight of which de Tocqueville spoke: the importance of a transcendent

Revise?

goal that gives meaning, purpose, and direction to the life of a nation no less than to the lives of individuals.

My optimism for the future of our country rests on the growing dissatisfaction among our people with hedonism and materialism as a way of life. I see this in the growing awareness of and unease about our problems: the homeless, the underclass, crime, drugs, the budget deficit, our apparent inability to compete in world markets, our uncertain and inconsistent foreign policy. I even find a ray of hope in the clumsy excursions of Congress into the ethical reform of its membership.

But I find the most convincing evidence that reform is on the way in the changes I have observed in the young people whom I know best: the thousands of students I have talked with at Boston University and on scores of other campuses where I have taught or visited.

Students have changed radically over the past two decades. In the eighties, faced with the stark reality—borne in upon them by such reality therapy as AIDS, the effects of the OPEC oil shock, the sharp decline of the American economy, and all its attendant political uncertainty—that their future may be less full, more threatening than the future to which their parents could look forward, students have gradually begun to recognize the 'insufficiency of affluence,' to feel a growing boredom with material things and a greater concern for matters of the spirit.

We of the older generation can accelerate the process of necessary reform if we will move at once to the reform of the public schools. Now the seedbed of our barbarism, with reform they can become the seedbed of our civilization. And the growing awareness of the deficiency of our schools and the growing demand of concerned parents, educators, and businessmen for their reform, are further justification for optimism.

If we discipline ourselves to the immediate reform of the public schools, we shall educate a new generation to the moral, no less than the political and economic, requirements of a life of fulfillment and happiness. By regaining our spiritual and moral foundations, we will be able to enjoy the fruits of plenty without being enslaved by them. Once determined to change, we can and we shall change.

I am deeply optimistic. I believe that America may have

passed through its adolescence and lost its innocence, but that it is still a young nation of intelligent, vigorous people. It is a nation continually revitalized by wave on wave of new immigrants who still find in America the land of opportunity where achievement and prosperity are possible with hard work and self-discipline. America is too young to step down, to retire into the second order of nations. We have the ability to sustain a strong economy, a strong national defense, and the means to solve the problems internal to our society. With the determination to be a responsible nation of responsible individuals, we can solve every social problem or reduce it to that minimum established by the intractability of human nature.

Pessimism is just another luxury that we cannot afford. This is a time for hope—as long as Americans have the faith and the determination to ensure their own future.

When we as individuals determine to govern ourselves individually, we shall at the same time regain the power to govern ourselves collectively and politically.

There are problems in America.

And we can fix them.

Notes

Teachers in a Troubled Society

1. Ruth Bell, *Changing Bodies, Changing Lives* (New York: Random House, 1980).

Of Mermaids and Magnificence

1. His father, Maury Maverick, once mayor of San Antonio, coined the term "gobbledygook." His grandfather's habit of putting his brand on any stray calf gave rise to the term "maverick" on the theory that if it were not Maverick's yet, it soon would be, and from this developed the meaning that a maverick is a person who wears no man's brand, or follows no particular political party line.

Poisoning the Wells of Academe

1. Herbert Marcuse, "Repressive Tolerance," in *A Critique of Pure Tolerance*, with Barrington Moore, Jr., and Robert Paul Wolff, p. 109 (Boston: Beacon Press, 1969).
2. Noam Chomsky, *Ethics*, October 1968, pp. 2–3.
3. Noam Chomsky, *American Power and the New Mandarins*, p. 268 (New York: Pantheon Books, 1961).
4. D. F. Fleming, *The Cold War and Its Origins*, Vol. I, p. 436 (Garden City, New York: Doubleday, 1961).
5. *Commentary*, October, December 1969; February, March, May, June 1970.
6. Harry Truman, speech given at Baylor University, March 6, 1947, *New York Times*, March 7, 1947.
7. Howard Zinn, *Phoenix*, Boston, April 12, 1972.
8. See H. J. Eysenck, "The Dangers of the New Zealots," pp. 79–81; and

"Hazards of the Academic Life" (on the case of Richard Herrnstein), pp. 84–85, *Encounter*, December 1972 (both articles).
9. *Chronicle of Higher Education*, December 3, 1973.
10. Noam Chomsky, *Ramparts*, July 1972, pp. 24–25.

The Dean as Educator

1. Neil Megaw, "To the Student," *1969–71 Catalog of the College of Arts and Sciences*, The University of Texas.
2. Translated by William Arrowsmith.

America and the Underclass

1. *The American Millstone*, by the staff of the *Chicago Tribune* (New York: Contemporary Books, Inc., 1986).

The Litigious Society

1. For instance, Bayless Manning, in a 1977 article, "Hyperlexis: Our National Disease" (71 *Northwestern University Law Review*), invents the term "hyperlexis" and calls for causal studies on the subject. The term serves as a starting point for numerous studies, among them Anthony J. Kline's "Law Reform and the Courts; More Power to the People or to the Profession?" (53 *California State Bar Journal*, Jan./Feb. 1978, no. 1), Derek Bok's 1981–82 Harvard *Report*, and studies by Wayne McIntosh ("A Long-Range View of Litigators and Their Demands," paper prepared for the 1982 meeting of the American Political Science Association; also by the same author, "Private Disputes and Environmental Change: An Aggregate Analysis of Litigation Activity in State Trial Court," prepared for delivery at the 1982 meetings of the Law and Society Association, Toronto); William J. McGill ("Litigation-Prone Society: Protection of Professional Life," 78 *New York State Journal of Medicine*, March 1978, no. 2); and others. Meanwhile, in the 1980s, other scholars were reacting against the hyperlexis theme: Ralph Cavanaugh and Austin Sarat in "Thinking About Courts: Toward and Beyond a Jurisprudence of Judicial Competence" (14 *Law & Society Review*, 1980, no. 2, Winter); Lawrence Friedman, in "Litigation and Rights Competence in Modern America" (39 *Maryland Law Review*, 1980, no. 4); and Jethro K. Lieberman, in his book *The Litigious Society* (New York: Basic Books, 1981), who offered varying interpretations, based on statistics and recent history, questioning the notion that Americans were hyperlectic. This led to studies of how various grievances and disputes arise, and these studies and the previous ones were gathered into a study by Marc Galanter of the University of Wisconsin called "Reading the Landscape of Disputes: What We Know and Don't Know (And Think We Know) About Our Allegedly Contentious and Litigious Society" (31 *U.C.L.A. Law Review* 4, 1983). After a masterful

review of the literature, Galanter asks, "What does it tell us?" His answer includes the observations that "knowledge about disputes is the product of interpretive acts, informed by the values and preconceptions of the observer," and that "the information base [is] thin and spotty. . . . If the profession's claim to expertise in such matters as disputes and litigation is to be taken seriously, it will need to adopt ground rules to require more respectful touching of the data base." In other words, we still cannot be sure that hyperlexis exists—and therefore, presumably, it is premature to think about correcting it.

2. Quoted in *The New Republic*, March 4, 1985, p. 8.

3. John Wettergreen, "The Regulatory Revolution," paper delivered at the Chamberlain Symposium, University of Wyoming (1982), p. 3. A revised version of this paper was published as "The Regulatory Revolution and the New Bureaucratic State" (Washington, D.C.: Heritage Foundation, 1988).

4. Ibid., p. 8.

5. Annual Report of the Director of the Administrative Office of the U.S. Courts, 1975 and 1983 (Washington, D.C.: U.S. Government Printing Office).

6. *United States* v. *International Business Machines Corporation*, Docket number 69 Civ. (DNE) Southern District of New York.

7. *Telex Corp.* v. *IBM*, cert. dismissed, 423 U.S. 802 (1975); *Calcom* v. *IBM*, 613 F. 2d 727 (9th Cir. 1979); *Memorex* v. *IBM*, 636 F. 2d (9th Cir. 1980); and others.

8. Charles Dickens, *Bleak House, passim.*

9. *Nut Products: Definitions and Standards of Identity—Peanut Butter*, Dkt. No. FDC-76.

10. NLRB, Case No. 1-RC-13564 (1974); *Boston University* v. *National Labor Relations Board*, 575 F. 2d 301 (1978).

11. NLRB, Case No. 1-CA-11061 (1984).

12. Cong. W. Henson Moore, "The Federal Government's Perspective on Professional Liability," *American College of Surgeons Bulletin*, Vol. 70, no. 3, p. 4.

13. *Bigbee* v. *Pacific Telephone and Telegraph et al.*, 665 P. 2d 947 (Cal. 1983).

14. Council on Wage and Price Stability, *Report* (Washington, D.C.: U.S. Government Printing Office, 1977).

15. Murray Weidenbaum, quoted in Wettergreen, "The Regulatory Revolution," p. 12.

16. Kalikak and Ross, *Costs of the Civil Justice System*, p. 110 (Santa Monica: RAND Corporation, 1983).

17. David Trubek, Austin Sarat, William Felstiner, Herbert Kritzer, Joel Grossman, and the Civil Litigation Research Project, "The Economic Costs of Ordinary Litigation," paper prepared for the National Conference on the Lawyer's Role in Resolving Disputes (Cambridge, Mass.: Harvard Law School, 1982).

18. England, *Rules of the Supreme Court*, Order 62, rule 3.
19. "Note: State Attorney Fee Shifting Statutes: Are We Quietly Repealing the American Rule?" *Law and Contemporary Problems*, Winter 1984, p. 321; "Federal Attorney Fee Shifting Statutes," *Attorney Fee Awards Reporter*, April 1982, p. 2.
20. 434 U.S. 412 (1978).
21. Civil Rights Act of 1964, Title VII, section 706(k).
22. 376 F. Supp. 1067 (WD Va).
23. *Newman* v. *Piggie Park Enterprises*, 390 U.S. 400 at 402.
24. 434 U.S. at 422–424 (1978).
25. *Federal Rules of Civil Procedure*, No. 68; Committee on Rules of Practice and Procedure of the Judicial Conference of the United States, "Proposed Federal Rule of Procedure 68," 98 F.R.D. 337 (1983).

The Kennedy Doctrine

1. *The Report of the President's National Bipartisan Commission on Central America*, p. 69 (New York: Macmillan, 1984).
2. Ibid., pp. 115, 116, 121.
3. Ibid., p. 107.

The Illusion of Peace

1. William Simon, "Should We Bail Out Gorbachev?" *Reader's Digest*, September 1988, pp. 65–70.

Index

Hispanics *(continued)*
  as victims of crime, 210
  see also Minorities
Hitler, Adolf, 56, 76, 77, 80, 296
  appeasement of, 286–289
Hobbes, Thomas, 63, 232
Hoder (Norse god), 53
Hoffmann, Peter, 287
Hollomon, J. Herbert, 123
Holmes, Justice Oliver Wendell, Jr.: on
    free marketplace of ideas, 87, 99,
    100
Homeless, 308
Homer
  The Iliad, 48–49, 256
  The Odyssey, 55
Homicide: abortion as, 193–194
Homosexuality: and moral teaching, 23
Honduras: insurgency movements in,
    265, 272, 275
Hong Kong: human capital investment
    in, 179
Hoover, Herbert, 70 71
House committee staffs, 216
Houston, Sam, 41–42, 56, 58
Hughes, Charles Evans, 285
Human capital
  education as investment in, 179, 182,
    197, 205, 208–209
  need to invest in, 179, 197–198, 209,
    304
Human goals, knowledge of, 00
Human interdependence, *see* Social
    interdependence
Humboldt, Wilhelm von, 64 65
Hungary, 273, 296, 300
Hutchins, Robert, 129

IBM case, 219–221, 237
ICBMs, 287
Ideological license, 98–99
Ideology
  contrasted with truth, 76–77
  leftist in the academy, 109
  and moral equivalence, 76
  refuting and exposing of, 76
Ignorance: and ethics, 250
Iliad, The (Homer): heroic values in, 48–
    49, 256
Illiteracy
  functional, xi
  and television watching, 70
IMF, 301
Imitation: learning by, 68
Immigrants: and bilingual education, 24–
    31
Imperfection: living with, 11–12

Income Contingent Loan program, 180
Independent universities, 158–170
  closings, 166
  cost efficiency of, 160–164
  deficit avoidance at, 162–163
  economic contributions to community
    by, 167
  equal opportunity offered by, 159
  loan defaulting at, 173
  minorities at, 159–160
  need for state support, 165–170, 171–
    182
  number and range of degrees awarded
    by, 160
  public nature of, 158–159
  tremble factor at, 163–164, 169
  Tuition Advance Fund for, 174–182,
    210
  tuition costs at, 160–163, 171–172
  tuition vouchers for, 168–170
India: linguistic identity in, 26
Individual development
  as democratic goal, 37
  and democratic heroes, 37–62
Individual fulfillment, *see* Personal
    fulfillment, right to
Individuality
  denial of: as evasion of social
    responsibility, 57, 207–208
  in mass society, xiii
Indoctrination: vs. controversy, 98–99
Inequality: as fact of life, 186–187
Inequality (Jencks), 115
INF Treaty, 293–298
Infanticide: abortion as, 193–194
Inflation: as moral issue, 192
Instant gratification: and television
    watching, 69–70
Intellectual capital: investment in, 179,
    182, 197, 205, 208–209, 210
Intentions, good
  failures of, 189
  moral law and, 196
Internal Revenue Service: role in Tuition
    Advance Fund program, 174–175
IQ testing: and racism, 114–115
Iran, 290
IRBMs: in Cuba, 263, 266
Isaacs, Charles, 114
Isaiah, 284–285
Italy
  economic aid to Soviets, 299, 302
  peace movements in, 286
Ivanhoe (Scott), 47

Jackson, Andrew, 43
Jackson, T. J. (Stonewall), 260